new
Scenic
café

new Scenic café

the cookbook

Scott Graden

with Arlene Anderson

New Scenic Café, Inc.
5461 North Shore Drive
Duluth, MN 55804
USA

www.newsceniccafe.com

Developmental Editor, Designer, and Writer: Eric Sturtz
Executive Editor, Technical Reviewer, and Writer: Barb Olsen

Drawings by Scott Graden
Photography by Scott Graden, except the following photos:
page 9 (right), 22, 383 (top), 385 (top), 386 (top) by Eric Sturtz
page 11 (top & bottom), 383 (bottom) by Jennifer Berges
page 30 by Stacie Whaley
page 36 by Jenny Keto
page 208, 221 by Brit Erenler
page 294 by Katie Cannon Photography
page 384 (left & right), 385 (bottom) by Rick Sturtz
page 386 by Rus Hurt / Hartwell Etc.
page 400 (1st row, 3rd photo; 2nd row, 1st photo; 3rd row, 3rd photo; 4th row, 1st photo) by Meg Jager Photography
page 401 (2nd row, 3rd photo; 3rd row, 1st photo; 4th row, 2nd photo) by Meg Jager Photography

Cataloging-in-Publication Data is available from the Library of Congress.

ISBN 978 0 615 97529 0

First printing, 2014
Printed in the USA

10 9 8 7 6 5 4 3 2 1

The New Scenic Café has been a personal favorite of mine for years. It has become one of the most consistently popular restaurants on the North Shore of Lake Superior—classy yet casual, upscale but welcoming. Scott Graden is an artist extraordinaire, both with his imaginative cuisine and his camera, as you will see from his photographs and artwork in this book. Dining at the New Scenic Café is definitely worth the beautiful 10-minute drive I take up the lakeshore from Duluth… just as it would be worth a journey across the globe!

Beatrice Ojakangas
cookbook author & food writer

Contents

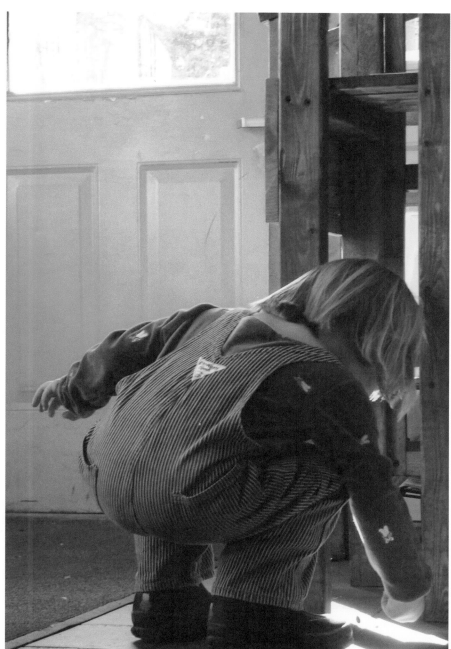

The New Scenic Café

Foreword

The evolution of the Scenic Café, with its hamburgers and onion rings, into the New Scenic Café, home of seared sea scallops and beet salad and grilled prosciutto-wrapped black mission figs, is a progression most of us make in our lives.

When you're 16, you can eat like a farmhand and knock off three helpings of pot roast and mountains of potatoes and have room for dessert, but as you mature your body tells you to pay attention, and that is when the idea of black mission figs wrapped in prosciutto and grilled over a fire becomes very appealing. A burst of pleasure in the mouth, and you don't have to eat 36 of them. Or the lamb meatballs with tiny carrots. Or the fabulous salad of radishes, baby beets, heirloom carrots, blueberries, peas, golden raisins, and broccolini.

There is nothing fussy or pretentious about food that is enjoyable and surprising. We are not sumo wrestlers, and mealtime should be light-hearted as it is at Scott Graden's New Scenic Café on the North Shore of Lake Superior.

I once turned turtle in a sailboat on Superior and was dumped into its frigid waters and crawled up on the hull and lay waiting for rescue, and had I known about grilled black mission figs wrapped in prosciutto at the time, the thought of them would've fortified my will to live.

Garrison Keillor
author, adventurer, & host of A Prairie Home Companion

The New Scenic Café

The True Story
of the New Scenic Café

Long before there was a Scenic Cafe, let alone a New Scenic Café, many, many years ago, before high-speed internet, or television, or even radio, in the days when people traveled the North Shore, by canoe or dogsled, on the very spot where the Café is today, there was a couple who lived in a hollowed-out white pine tree. They were named Haugsrud, I think, or Maki, Mr. and Mrs. They were very old, so old and bent over that their long noses almost touched the ground. They had been there a long time alone and were conversant with the moon, the devil, and the west wind. And they knew how to cook. They knew the herbs and the mushrooms in the woods. They knew what to do with a moose or a duck, or even muskrat… but I won't go into that. They lived a very long time, and Scott was just a tow-headed little boy when he learned from them how to cook using the produce of the forest and the lake. Scott always dreamed of opening a restaurant, and after many years at sea and many adventures in faraway lands, in India and Slovenia and the Solomon Islands, Scott returned to Northern Minnesota and purchased the Scenic Café. He finally began to realize his lifetime dream employing the knowledge he had gained during his travels and the basics he had learned from the Straumsvågs or the Soderlinds… whoever they were….

Scott's New Scenic has since become legendary. People come from all over the world to have the fishcakes or the seared duck breast. Scott himself has become a legend, and some people maintain that there is no Scott Graden really, that there is only an incredible collective of cooks and wait staff, that "Scott Graden" is a made-up figure like Paul Bunyan. But I have met Scott Graden, actually shaken his hand, and he's OK.

Louis Jenkins
a poet who sometimes lives in Duluth

The New Scenic Café

Blue Birds

One morning of Easter weekend, 2004, I set foot outside and entered a surreal scene. I had lived for many years in Duluth, Minnesota, and was accustomed to the extreme weather fluctuations that can occur in early spring. But this day epitomized the volatility of the season. It was as if in the hours since the prior evening, Mother Nature had unleashed all her powers at our town; wind, rain, and cold had all spewed forth at once, and by the following morning the world had been transformed, now purged of nature's force. It was quiet, shining, and ice-covered.

A serene, glittering city had replaced the lawn of green of the day before. Every footstep crunched resoundingly in the silence, shattering the brittle stalks of grass and defrosting from silver to deep forest green the leaves that had been surprised by the cold snap. My family and I carved paths through the pristine grass as we surveyed the trees, which had been shellacked with thick layers of ice. It was early morning, the sun still at a low angle and peeking through for our pleasure. The sunlight warmed the frosty grass and transitioned the atmosphere to a soft gold, prompting a dazzling display of rainbows that arched and radiated throughout the thick, refracting needles of the pine trees. The sky, looking much like the grass, was an uninterrupted sheet of silvery fog, save for the haloed disk of the sun.

It was cold, but these unexpected bursts of frosty spring weather hit the body differently from the biting cold we withstand during winters in the north. Winter presents us with a cold that is numbing, while the snaps that interrupt our slow and muddy defrost are invigorating. Wearing only a light jacket, I played outdoors for hours, shooting arrows into a hay bale that crackled with every successful hit, before going inside to warm up.

Later that day, I returned to the outdoors, where I witnessed a sight that would top even the icy wonder I had so far beheld. Along the sheltered walkway spanning from our garage to the porch, stood a large, dead birch tree. Its branches hung half-broken and at odd angles, gnarled like so many arthritic fingers. I could see the tree through the glass of the window in our front door, as I prepared to walk outside. The long-barren tree was now covered in some sort of foliage, the "leaves" an incongruous deep indigo blue that stood out strikingly against the pale background of the frosted yard. As I started to exit the sheltered entryway to investigate, the low, pale golden light of the late afternoon shone much as before, reflected in a beam from the window across to the trellised wall of our garage. The light panned from one side of the garage to the other, and as it did so, dozens of blue jays were startled from their rest. They sprang from the tree all at once, and the ice that had remained undisturbed by their gentle, individual landings came crashing down in a resounding, crystalline cascade. I could only stand there and watch as it happened, looking on in astonishment and listening afterward to the silence, before going inside to tell my family what I, alone, had seen.

Never since have I witnessed anything so refreshing, so inspiring as that wild and unexpected departure of the blue birds. Every sense felt awakened by its briskness, winter nudged aside by its beauty, and it will forever stand in my memory as the definitive Duluth spring moment.

Nicholas Cleary
New Scenic Café cook

The New Scenic Café

The Scenic Cafe
1960-1999

It was the 1960's, and a small seasonal drive-up cafe located at 1623 London Road in Duluth, Minnesota had become an enormously popular hangout for local teenagers. The London Inn introduced the California Burger to the area and created a passionate following for its famed onion rings. Hilbert Johnson, owner of The London Inn, eventually moved it a few miles up the North Shore of Lake Superior to the location where the New Scenic Café stands today.

In 1972, Art and Esther Turnquist bought the restaurant, and it became the Scenic Drive Inn, featuring indoor seating and window service. Bob and Jan Fox purchased the business in June of 1980 and changed its name to the Scenic Cafe. It had six stools at a counter near the entrance and six tables in the dining room. Many locals tell stories about working their way through college back in those days by serving as wait staff and cooks at the Scenic.

Bob and Jan Fox's daughter, Polly, and her husband, Charlie Merhar, became the next owners in 1989. Just 25 years old at the time, they ran the restaurant during the summer and switched to life on the ski hills during their winter months off. Over the years, the Cafe began to leave its fast food roots behind and offered more homemade foods and vegetarian meals. Polly and Charlie added wine and beer to the menu, along with picnic lunches that people could buy and take with them as they traveled up the shore. Finally, in 1990 the Scenic Cafe braved the winter winds and for the first time remained open the entire year. The patio blew down in the 1990s, making way for the construction of a front entryway, dining room, and bathrooms.

It was on April 1 of 1999 that Scott Graden and his aunt, "Rita B," bought the restaurant and renamed it the New Scenic Café. And that, of course, is where their story begins. And where it continues to be told to this day, along the shores of the scenic Lake Superior.

The New Scenic Café

A Conversation with Scott

Outside the windows of the New Scenic Café, along the clear blue waters of Lake Superior just north of Duluth, Minnesota, the season is ever-changing. Lively summer days are evolving into the brilliant colors of autumn.

Proprietor and chef of the Scenic, Scott Graden, pokes his head around the corner and says with a harried smile, "Two more minutes—I'll be right there!" He connects momentarily with a staff member about an item on the Café's new menu and heads back into the kitchen, on what is yet another busy evening in the Café.

I'm sitting at one of the restaurant's hand-crafted wooden tables, surrounded by the Scenic's diverse mix of diners. At the next table, a young couple looks like they are on a first date, dressed to impress. In the corner, a group of friends seems to be catching up on each other's lives. Outside in the parking lot, an older couple gets out of a convertible and walks toward the front door, looking into the restaurant's expansive windows with anticipation. A family of three, all sporting dreadlocks, climbs back into a VW bus to continue their journey along the adjacent North Shore Highway 61. Since opening in 1999, the New Scenic Café has always drawn a wide range of clientele.

It's the type of evening and the sort of experience that brings people back to the Scenic time after time. Outside, the lake is a north woods ocean, with brisk breezes and the sounds of the waves. Inside, one feels sheltered and warm. Decorative birch branches extend from the floor to the ceiling, with knotty pine walls furthering the sense of being enveloped in a natural setting. The wooden tables and playfully mismatched lamp shades remind one of stopping at a friend's cabin, where you're welcomed with open arms and no pretenses. "Come as you are," the Scenic seems to say. "We've got a lovely meal waiting for you."

Scott draws up a chair, takes off his apron with one quick movement, and flashes a smile. "Sometimes when I look around the Café, I think to myself, 'Be careful what you wish for!'"

The bustling New Scenic Café has grown every year it has been open. In the cuisine, the environment, and the invisible yet essential underlying philosophy, Scott's uniquely creative touch is evident.

ROOTS

"I considered being an emergency room doctor," Scott replies when I ask how he chose this work. "It seemed every day and every patient would be unique." He has always been drawn to pursuits that are fast paced and offer frequent, unpredictable challenges, he explains. "I also thought about being a lawyer because I like the analytical aspect of legal work, orchestrating how each unique case gets put together."

Fortunately for his epicurean fans, however, the groundwork for Scott's culinary path was laid early on.

"The kitchen in my parents' home was always a comfortable place," he continues. "It was the heart of our family life. We'd all gather there–my siblings, cousins, parents, and grandparents."

Even at the early age of four, Scott demonstrated a sense for food—and for a gourmet's honesty. During a visit with his grandmother, Vi, he was offered one of her freshly-baked cinnamon rolls. He ate one and then accepted a second. But when he was offered a third, Scott replied, "Grandma, they weren't *that* good!"

Scott credits his mother, Mimi, for making sure children felt welcome in the kitchen. "It was also a solution for her," Scott explains. "If she needed to watch us kids and make dinner, she made it a collaborative undertaking, sometimes even using family projects in the kitchen to teach us shapes and math."

"When I was five, my aunt and uncle, Julie and Eric, gave us a Betty Crocker children's cookbook," Scott reminisces. "My mom would bring out the book, and my sister, Karen, and I would pick out something to make. I still keep that cookbook in my office. And Mom would also allow us kids to choose the vegetable for dinner. It sounds like a little thing, but it gave us the sense of being involved, of having our food opinions matter."

PROVIDENCE

Following in his older brother Craig's footsteps, Scott left his hometown of Duluth to study chemistry at a college in Montana. His brother was working as a cook at a restaurant there called Carrito's Mexican Fiesta and asked Scott to cover his shifts while he went on vacation. After a crash cooking course from Craig, Scott found himself on his own.

"I remember the owner well," Scott tells me. "Caroline was from Mexico City. I was supposed to make fried rice, and it ended up like Asian rice, white and fluffy. Caroline had to quickly school me in proper Mexican rice making."

Throughout his time in Montana, Scott worked his way up at the restaurant, until he was a shift manager. But, he says, he still didn't take working with food very seriously.

When he eventually returned to Duluth, Scott considered employment at several local restaurants while he continued his studies in chemistry. Augustino's, an Italian restaurant located in Duluth's historic Fitger's Brewery complex, was one of them. "My job-search approach was a bit unusual," Scott explains. "I went in to Augustino's, asked to speak to the manager, and offered to come in and serve. 'If at any time you'd like me to leave, just tap me on the shoulder and I'll go,' I told him. 'But, if you like my work, we can talk about employment. Consider it a live audition.'"

An hour later, Scott's phone rang. The manager asked if Scott knew how to cook, and somewhat reluctantly Scott admitted he did. "I knew cooks typically worked hard but didn't necessarily make much money," Scott explains. But he took the offered job.

There was a lot to learn—about cooking and about life. "The chef decided to start me out on the grill. He also showed me how to fillet fish. Since I had been fishing many times in Northern Minnesota's Boundary Waters Canoe Area, I showed off my own filleting techniques. The unfortunate result was that I was assigned to clean every fish that came in the restaurant door!"

When his boss left, at the age of 20 Scott was promoted to the head chef position. He worked full time, while still attending college. "I remember propping flash cards for my chemistry classes up in the restaurant's kitchen so I could study while I cooked," Scott recalls, laughing. "The cards were always getting covered with marinara sauce. But, as a study technique, it worked."

RESOLVE

By the time he was 21, Scott had created his first full menu—and the challenge and excitement of the experience helped convince him to leave school and focus on the culinary world.

He worked several head chef jobs and did menu development for other businesses, both generating and testing concepts. By 1997, however, Scott was 27 years old and feeling frustrated. "I felt at a dead end. I knew I either had to figure out how to take on the restaurant business for myself or simply make food a hobby."

As he wrestled with this choice, Scott says, it was his family's love for good food that once more helped him see the way.

"My stepfather, Ken, traveled the world and brought a lot of culturally-influenced food into our home—Greek food, Japanese food, global influences. He also taught me a lot about entrepreneurship. He said, 'Figure out where you want to be, and then figure out how to be there.'"

It was 1998, and Scott often took his girlfriend for rides on his motorcycle up along the North Shore of Lake Superior. Inevitably, they would stop for hamburgers and malts at the Scenic Cafe, located just eight miles north of Duluth on Highway 61. "The Scenic was a very small restaurant back then," Scott recalls. "It had a simple

menu with good road food, and you could get a picnic lunch to take with you." In those days, Scott remembers with a smile, the restaurant had a pay phone booth out front.

Scott and his Aunt Rita had been talking about starting a restaurant together but so far had not found the right location. Then one day, his friend, Chris Maras, called to say the Scenic Cafe was for sale. "I think our dream is about to come true," Scott told his aunt. Nine months later, the restaurant was theirs.

Their first night in business was April 1, 1999, and the newly renamed "New Scenic Café" was packed. Scott and Rita were ecstatic. "It was like fireworks on a first date!" Scott says.

In those early days, Scott lived in a garage on the restaurant property, determined to do whatever was needed to make the Scenic a success. "During our first three years in business, we took only one week off," Scott recalls. "On the days the Scenic was closed, Rita and I would sink into the old lawn chairs we kept behind the restaurant and dream of even greater days for the Scenic."

As chef, Scott designed the Scenic's menus, filling them with creations like "rainbow trout veronique with red grapes, bell pepper and asparagus," still one of the Scenic's featured specials. And there were "tandoori chicken with chana," "pork chops with cranberry apple sauce," and "curly carrot salad with citrus vinaigrette"— epicurean delights not found elsewhere in the region. Rita's passion was baking from scratch, and her pies, cakes, and breads inevitably lured diners back. The Scenic had begun the tradition that holds to this day: drawing people who love good food.

"Rita is also an artist," Scott explains, "so she was our liaison to the local art community. Our plan had always been to create an eclectic atmosphere in the restaurant by bringing in the works of local artists, and Rita made that happen." Local artists Ann Jenkins and Adu Gindy were house staples from the beginning, and the Scenic has continued to bring in work by artists Kate Whittaker, Wendy Rouse, Dick and Debbie Cooter, Lou Pignolet, Diane Daniels, Cecilia Ramon, and Louis Jenkins. And Scott believes in giving the very young their chance as well. The work of a 9-year-old artist named Ruby has become a favorite at the Scenic, as has the art of students from the nearby North Shore Elementary School.

The Scenic's growth in those early years was exponential, and it soon became common for guests to wait more than two hours for a table. It was time to expand. "We created the front garden in 2000," Scott says, "so guests could meander outdoors and enjoy the Lake Superior view while they waited." Scott brought in walk-in coolers and a freezer. He increased storage and service space.

"During restaurant hours, I wore an apron," Scott recalls. "And when the doors closed, I switched to a tool belt." By mid-2001, he had led the building of another dining room, and the New Scenic Café could now seat diners more quickly and host wedding parties and other large group events.

In those early years, another Scenic tradition was born: the diner's journal. "When I was a kid, my parents kept a journal for our guests at the family cabin," Scott says, "and that gave me an idea. I wanted to give our diners a way to tell us about their dining experiences at the Scenic and also express themselves." Today, diners still fill those journals with stories of romantic anniversary dinners, kids' pictures, menu likes and dislikes, and loves lost. "The journals create a shared experience between the guests."

The years moved on, and the seven-year commitment Rita had made to the venture was over. In 2005, Rita retired, and Scott bought Rita's share of the business. He has been the sole proprietor ever since.

Scott returned to college, taking classes while operating the Café. I ask how he managed it, with a restaurant to run. "It took me many years to finish that undergraduate degree," Scott says, "but I did it." He went on to earn a Master of Arts in Management and continues to work on a Master of Business Administration. Amidst his busy life at the Scenic, today Scott also teaches as an adjunct faculty for the Department of Business and Technology at The College of St. Scholastica in Duluth.

LEARNING

"If one of your guests is allergic to gluten, what on our menu will you suggest?" Scott might ask at one of the Scenic Café's lively staff meetings, which are sometimes run like classroom pop-quiz sessions.

The New Scenic's menus do not include descriptions. Instead, Scott simply lists each menu item's main ingredients. It's his way of intentionally prompting wait staff and customers to have real conversations about the dishes, their ingredients, and how they're prepared. "To make this work, I have to be sure my wait staff is well versed in the details of every dish," Scott says, "so they'll be able to recommend the best choices."

Scott creates distinctive food combinations that have an international flair, allowing people to try individual foods and dishes they wouldn't experience in any other way or at any other restaurant. And his menus give diners a chance to try a small taste of something without having to invest too deeply in an unfamiliar choice. "My goal is to give our customers an enjoyable culinary experience while exposing them to something new," Scott explains. "For example, back when we first started no one else in this area was using goat cheese. People would ask, 'What's this?' Now we use goat cheese extensively, and it has become a common ingredient."

"Creating food is more a process than a moment. It's like being a conductor. My job is to pull it all together to create an efficient way to build many menu items without duplicating. For example, you don't want all the dishes to have the same sauce." After all these years, Scott explains, this process feels as if it comes about naturally.

"As a chef, there's an optimal combination of the ability to work with precision and a spiritual, Zen-like approach. When I'm braising meat, for instance, there's an ideal point in time and temperature. If you go beyond that point, the meat will still soften, but it will begin to break down and lose flavor. It's a science. On the Zen side, I think of how I put the food on the plate or garnish the dish. When I position the food, I do it so it looks natural, not stiff or architectural. And I don't place the garnish; I let it fall."

I ask Scott how he creates the inimitable combinations on his ever-changing menus. "I look for what's seasonal, novel, new, unique. I also consider what's not being used by anyone else. Availability is huge, too. You have to be able to acquire the products." Then, Scott says, he starts putting the ingredients together.

"I want the best, and to get the best I buy ingredients from a large variety of vendors—the best doesn't usually come on one truck. I have relationships with many local farmers."

Then Scott's challenge is to find a way to assure his guests that the distinctive and unique menu items he's offering are worth ordering.

"The best approach is to make sure the staff is excited and knowledgeable about the new dishes," Scott explains. Before offering any new menu item to the public, Scott holds a series of staff meetings, at which he talks through the details of dishes, answers questions, and allows everyone the opportunity to taste them. Scott credits the Scenic's employees with being a key part of this creative process. "There's no way this would work without the staff. The best staff members are the ones who truly believe in us."

One of his early mentors, Andy Andrews, told Scott he should feel free to make all the mistakes he needed to make but that there was a price for that freedom. "Andy told me I had to own up to my mistakes and explain to him exactly what I learned from every one of them. It was a strategy that really encouraged me to learn." When he selects and trains staff, Scott continues that strategy. "The emphasis at the Scenic is on understanding rather than memorization so that employees can apply the concepts they learn to different situations."

The Scenic Café's staff has gone beyond the call of duty over and over, Scott adds. "Early on, I had a server who knew our breakfast cook was leaving when we still had two months of the intense summer breakfast season to go. He offered to learn the job and do it until the season ended, to help out. Others stay late, run errands for the Café on their way to work, step in when other staff members need help. I know that quality among employees isn't found everywhere, and I'm aware of what a huge part staff members play in making the Scenic a success. And in those moments when I'm thinking only of how much is yet to be done, I'm grateful for those times when staff members remind me of how far we've come."

SATISFACTION

Scott says he's often asked where he received his formal culinary training. "I say I got it though experience, in the kitchen that is life," Scott explains. And Scott values that kind of experience in others. "Culinary school has its place, but it's no substitute for hands-on restaurant experience. Some people have a hard time when I tell them I didn't attend culinary school. But I believe the ability is in each of us, and while that might not be a popular view, it's how I see it. You just have to go out and do it."

"I never thought the Café would fail," Scott goes on. "But I also didn't see it growing to the level it has. At first, we averaged 20 guests a day. Now, we average 300. Our peak was over 400 guests in one day."

The New Scenic Café isn't situated in a main population hub, but in Scott's estimation its location facing the shores of Lake Superior is one of the Cafe's greatest assets. When something is really good, he says, people will make the effort to get there.

"The journey along the lakeshore is part of the experience," he says. "The restful views of the lake, the sunrises and sunsets, the trees, the winding road—it adds to the anticipation and brings value. But you have to pull through with the quality dining experience, too."

Scott's father, Bruce, once told him, "It's not the equipment that makes the athlete, it's the athlete that makes the equipment." In the same way, Scott explains, location can be a benefit but should not be the sole driver of success. "You also need to offer an excellent product and deliver it with style—great service, a warm welcome, an alluring atmosphere. I think we've been able to do that."

"The food we offer appeals to 'foodies' because they appreciate the subtleties. It appeals to 'non-foodies' because it's just good cooking. It appeals to 'locavores' because I buy top-quality, locally-produced foods. And it appeals to kids because we put a significant amount of thought and care into food for them, which is something commonly overlooked in restaurants. It's great to watch a 3-year-old loving our classic 'dirt and worms' dish!"

So, I ask Scott, what's the core satisfaction he gets from putting so much of his life into his craft?

"Some of the simplest times are the most rewarding," Scott replies. "I love it when I try hard and I can see my efforts are panning out. I love it when a new dish I've created draws a smile of appreciation. I love it when I read a guest's entry in one of our journals that says they return to the Scenic year after year to share each anniversary with their wife or husband. It just doesn't get any better than that."

Outside the Scenic Café's windows, the sunlight is dwindling, turning the landscape into silhouettes. Inside, the dining room is beginning to grow quiet. Most of the tables are still filled with guests, but the diners are nearing the ends of their meals; anticipation giving way to satisfaction. Servers are making their rounds, still moving quickly but without the urgency of the earlier evening. Through an opening into the kitchen, I see the cooks joking, now with enough time on their hands to relax just a bit.

And as I look at Scott, I see a man who appears a little weary after a busy night but whose face shows the pride of the craftsman in his craft and the satisfaction of a job well done. He's set a standard here at the New Scenic Café and created a tradition that has touched countless lives. I realize he's right: It just doesn't get any better.

Arlene Anderson

The New Scenic Café

A Letter to the Readers

Dear Readers,

The New Scenic Café is a restaurant built and run on passion—for excellent food, great ingredients, good people, and a splendid setting. It's where I've been able to live out my belief that if people work with passion, their cups will overflow. I hope you've had a chance to visit us here at the Café. But even if you've never joined us for a meal, cooking from the recipes in this book will be your step into the creativity, entrepreneurship, and risk-taking that we take such pride in here in this restaurant on the shores of Lake Superior.

This book is written for people who enjoy creating good food and who appreciate the processes involved. The recipes will give you a foundation in the textures, flavors, colors, and presentations of the dishes I've created and served to diners over the years. I hope you'll enjoy trying them.

This cookbook is not meant to be an inflexible tour but instead an illuminating and friendly guide to the possibilities. It is a framework to inspire comfort in the kitchen, learn about various ingredients and approaches, and experience the unique cultural influences behind the foods. The recipes might push you into unfamiliar territory at times, but none of them require a great amount of experience in order to assemble the dishes successfully. I encourage you to use this book with flexibility. If you are at home and don't have a specific ingredient, modify the recipe to use what you have. If you are shopping and can't find an ingredient, search for something similar. The goal is not so much to duplicate each recipe but to be creative and to prepare good, honest food.

One of my greatest hopes is that this cookbook will be a vehicle for you and others to share experiences with one another. Perhaps you would like to send the book to a friend whom you have told about the New Scenic Café, to share and extend your personal Café experiences. Maybe you will invite friends to your home and cook for them—or cook with them—using the cookbook as a starting point for a tasty and rewarding social event. Or you might simply take time for yourself to create and enjoy good food, not once but over and over as you try the many recipes on these pages. I have constructed this cookbook to be more than an index of recipes. It is a book that is meant to be shared and, ideally, worn out. I would consider it a high compliment to hear someday from readers who have used this book so much it is falling apart!

I encourage you to take notes and write in the book as you use it. Capture the memories of who prepared a recipe and how it turned out. Make notes about adjustments you made or important lessons you learned along the way. This is what my mom did for my family. And just like my family, in a year or two or twenty, you will be able to look back and remember those times together. You might even consider using the book like a photo album or journal, storing shared memories and imagery to bring back experiences you have had, even sharing them with a new person in your life, just like walking them down the hall at your grandmother's house to look at family photos.

More than anything, the New Scenic Café is a community and a family, of which you are an integral part. People come to the Café for dinner and easily find themselves talking to the diners at the table next to them, broadening everyone's experience. In that same spirit, you are invited to step closer into the fold of the New Scenic Café community as you use this book. Please take a photograph of your creation, and share it with us. Tell us about your experience. Send a photo of your dinner party, and write a story about the event. Or send us a picture of the marked-up pages in your copy of this cookbook, with your notes about the recipes. (See our website at www.newsceniccafe.com for email information.) Together, we can make this a living document.

Above all, enjoy! Enjoy the ingredients, the learning, the sharing, the cooking, and the dining. I thank you for your company along this road of enjoyment.

Scott Graden
proprietor & chef, The New Scenic Café

The New Scenic Café

Using this Book

Whether you are preparing food in a restaurant or at home, being organized helps make the job easier—and more fun. So, please be sure to read through all parts of the recipe you are using before you begin cooking, along with any sub-recipes that are included. (The sub-recipes are the core recipes, such as for sauces or toppings, that are used as a part of many of the recipes in this book.)

We have written the recipes with care and precision, and you will be able to cook most of them without having to look to other sources. But the recipes do not always contain detailed instructions on every process involved. Be prepared to look to outside sources for information on basic cooking skills that you might not be familiar with already, such as how to toast nuts and spices or sauté vegetables.

You need not feel you have to create exact duplicates of the food as presented in these recipes, although many home cooks do enjoy following instructions to the letter and knowing the results will turn out precisely as planned. If you are one of those cooks, following these instructions will deliver the distinctive flavors and textures almost exactly as diners enjoy them at the New Scenic Café. But if you like, you might enjoy using the recipes as reliable guides instead, while being flexible, bringing in your good judgment and intuition, and putting your creative focus on simply making delicious food. Please keep in mind, also, that any variations in the ingredients and tools you use, as well as the quantities you are preparing, can give you slightly different results from what we create at the Café. But over time, cooks develop a sense of the results they can expect and learn to adapt to changing circumstances.

Good-quality ingredients are important. You'll get the results you want if you do your best to get the finest quality in food that you can find wherever you are shopping, whether at a grocery store, gourmet shop, farmer's market, local producer, or roadside stand. When you cannot find a particular ingredient for one of these recipes, or if the quality of what you find is poor, don't be discouraged. See if you can find a substitute that will work, and enjoy trying the recipe anyway!

Here is some other information we hope you will find helpful as you use this cookbook, regarding standards used, additional information you can find in other sections, and the measurement abbreviations the book employs.

Unless specified otherwise, throughout the book we use the following standards:

- Butter is salted.
- Salt is kosher salt.
- Pepper is cracked black pepper.
- Olive oil is pure but not virgin or extra virgin.
- Temperatures are measured in degrees Fahrenheit.
- Cooking times are for guidance only and are based on using a convection oven. You might need to adjust the cooking time slightly for a standard oven.

These are the measurement abbreviations used in this cookbook:

Abbreviation		What it means
C	-	cup(s)
T	-	tablespoon(s)
t	-	teaspoon(s)
pinch	-	1/16 teaspoon
lb	-	pound(s)
oz	-	ounce(s)
fl oz	-	fluid ounce(s)
g	-	gram(s)

You will find additional information about what supplies you will find useful, what the cooking terms used mean, and how to acquire some ingredients by checking these other sections:

- Pantry (page 40)
- Tools (page 41)
- Glossary (page 372)
- Sources of Specialty Ingredients & Equipment (page 376)

Pantry

There's nothing like a well-stocked pantry to make you feel you're ready to dive into any recipe. So please take a few moments to look through these lists of useful pantry items.

You'll find having these seasonings, oils, vinegars, and other general ingredients on hand will serve you well. They're the ingredients used repeatedly in this cookbook and the ones we make sure to keep within reach in the kitchen at the New Scenic Café. Most of them are products you can keep for long periods of time, and they are great staples to have available as well when you want to experiment with making your own creations.

The recipes in this book also use some less-common ingredients or specialized foods made by small producers and not available on every grocery store shelf. You'll find helpful information about where to find those in the "Sources of Specialty Ingredients & Equipment" section (page 376). In addition, the recipes themselves also include suggestions for acquiring some ingredients.

Seasonings

Stock your pantry with these seasonings, and you will be ready to go:

bay leaves
black peppercorns
cayenne pepper
Chinese Five Spice
cloves (whole)
coarse sea salt
crushed red pepper flakes
cumin seeds
curry powder
dill weed
dried chives
dried oregano
dried tarragon
dried thyme
ground cinnamon
ground clove
ground cumin
ground nutmeg
kosher salt
Mexican oregano
parsley flakes
rubbed sage
saffron threads
star anise
Thai red curry powder
white pepper

Oils

Many delicious oils are available; these are the ones you will use most often for the recipes in this book:

black truffle oil
butter (salted)
canola oil
extra virgin olive oil
olive oil
pan release
sesame oil
walnut oil
white truffle oil

Vinegars

This variety of vinegars will offer you a flavorful range for your cooking ventures:

apple cider vinegar
balsamic vinegar
champagne vinegar
red wine vinegar
rice vinegar
sherry vinegar
white wine vinegar

General Ingredients

Some of these other general ingredients are pantry basics, and some are less standard. They'll all be useful as you work your way through the recipes:

all-purpose flour
amarena cherries in syrup
canned chipotle peppers (in adobo)
chicken base
cornstarch
corn masa harina
cream sherry
crystallized ginger
Dijon mustard
gelatin (silver grade sheets)
granulated sugar
orange blossom water
orange oil
panko bread crumbs
powdered sugar
soy sauce
Sriracha hot sauce
vanilla beans
vanilla extract
vegetable base

Tools

Having the kitchen tools you need will make it easier and more fun to dive into the recipes in this cookbook. And using the best-quality tools you can will make your experience in the kitchen even better. Here, you'll find a list of the appliances, measuring tools, pots and pans, knives, and other tools and supplies that are most useful for making the dishes described in this cookbook—and for cooking in general. We use them over and over again at the New Scenic Café, and you might find you already have many of them in your own kitchen. You need not feel, though, that you must have all of these tools to cook the dishes in this book. As you look through the recipes, you'll get a good idea of which tools will be most essential for the recipes you want to use. And collecting kitchen tools over time can be fun. Many of these tools can be found in department stores, specialty food stores, second-hand shops, Asian markets, or kitchen supply stores. Check the "Sources of Specialty Ingredients & Equipment" section in this book (page 376) as well for more information about where we buy many of our tools and supplies for the Café.

Appliances
blender
food processor
grill (charcoal preferred)
oven/range (gas preferred)
spice grinder (or coffee grinder)
stand mixer (with paddle, whisk,
*   dough hook, and pasta roller)*

Measuring Tools
eyedropper
glass measuring cups (1 and 2 cup)
kitchen scale (11-pound capacity,
*   with 1-gram increments)*
measuring cups
*   (1/4, 1/3, 1/2, and 1 cup)*
measuring pitcher (1 quart)
measuring spoons
*   (1/4, 1/2, and 1 teaspoon*
*   plus 1/2 and 1 tablespoon)*

Pots/Pans
baking pan (9" x 13")
bread loaf pan (8 1/2" x 4 1/2")
bundt pan (10")
cake pans (10" or 12")
cast-iron skillet (10" or 12")
fry pans (8", 10", and 12")

muffin tin (12 cup)
pie pan (9")
roasting pan (16")
saucepans (2, 3, and 4 quart)
sheet pan extender (9" x 13" x 4")
sheet pans (9" x 13" and 13" x 18")
springform pan (9")
stock pot (12 or 16 quart)
tart pans (4")

Knives
chef's or Santoku knife (8")
paring or petty knife (4")
slicing knife (10" or 12")

Utensils/Tools
bamboo skewers (assorted sizes)
bamboo steamer basket (10")
bench knife
brulée torch
cutting board
fine mesh strainer (chinois)
flan ring molds (3")
food mill or potato ricer
instant-read digital thermometer
*   (range 32°F to 450°F)*
kitchen towels
mandoline slicer (with julienne blade)

meat grinder
metal kitchen tongs
microplane grater/zester
mixing bowls
*   (heatproof, assorted sizes)*
offset spatula (small, thin, metal)
palette knife
pastry bag and tips
pastry brush
pepper mill
ring molds (assorted sizes)
rolling pin
rubber spatulas (heatproof)
silicone baking mat (11 1/2" x 16 1/2")
squeeze bottles (small, fine-tipped)
spider skimmer
wire cooling racks
wire whisk

Other
acetate film sheets
aluminum foil
cheesecloth
parchment paper
plastic wrap
ziplock bags (quart and gallon size)

Garden

The Garden at the New Scenic Café

Each year in spring, along the front of the New Scenic Café, hundreds of brightly-colored tulips sway in the cool Lake Superior breeze. They are a centerpiece of the Scenic Café's garden, which was planted to greet diners and offer a haven of quiet rest.

Some guests arrive early to sit in the garden's Adirondack chairs and relax with a glass of wine before dinner. Others wander through the garden, admiring the flowers and the plants and watching the hummingbirds and butterflies mingle among the blossoms. And when their dinner reservations are called, guests meander back through the garden, passing rows of well-tended hanging flower baskets and window boxes as they enter the Café's front door.

From within the dining room, the Scenic's garden provides a vibrant foreground for the expansive views of Lake Superior. Guests often linger for a while even after dinner is finished, enjoying the colors and fragrances before turning for home.

The passion to create a garden at the New Scenic Café originated with Scott's Aunt Rita, his original business partner. Years ago, she began by drawing extensive sketches and plans, in collaboration with a team of garden experts.

Most of the garden's plants come from another aunt figure, "Aunt Rosie," the aunt of long-term Café manager Crystal Carlson. Rosie is the owner of a one-woman greenhouse operation in the town of Lakewood, located seven miles from the Café. The abundant garden at the New Scenic Café is the result of years of collaborative experimentation with Aunt Rosie to determine which plants could thrive amidst the lake winds.

The New Scenic Café's garden calls to mind the ever-changing phases of life, the continual cycles of growth and renewal. And each season appears with its own gifts.

A variety of herbs, such as fresh chives, join the tulips to signal the arrival of spring. Summer flowers include cheerful rhodochitons, a purple bell-shaped flower that is planted in the hanging baskets just outside the dining room's windows. The window boxes below contain scaevola and delicate anagillis, which are blue star-shaped flowers that have yellow centers. The newest addition is the tomato plants that grow on the Café's roof in the summer season.

As summer meanders into fall, the ornamental cabbage and kale in the garden grow brighter. A local farmer delivers corn husks and stalks, mums, and straw bales for the autumn garden, along with a colorful assortment of squash and pumpkins. The scaevola remain lovely even as they dry and begin to resemble vines.

With the coming of winter, each year the staff carries on the tradition of putting lights on the beloved but humorously forlorn "Charlie Brown tree" that graces the front of the Scenic. They hang pine bows on the front door for a festive touch. And in this snowy season, the Café keeps a nearby yurt warm and cozy with a toasty fire and comfortable chairs, to welcome those hearty souls who want to enjoy the outdoors and the lovely views even in the colder months.

The New Scenic Café's hosts and managers are the primary weeders, waterers and caretakers for the garden. The entire staff knows and enjoys the garden, though, and any of them can answer most questions about the garden that guests ask. One question the staff cannot answer is the mystery of why the local deer, so challenging for most other gardens in the area, leave the New Scenic garden intact.

As is true of the food served at the New Scenic Café, a creative force is obviously at play. The garden is tended, but it is not overly manicured. Careful craftsmanship combines with the elements that fall naturally into place.

New growth awaits in the garden. Welcome to the New Scenic Café.

Arlene Anderson

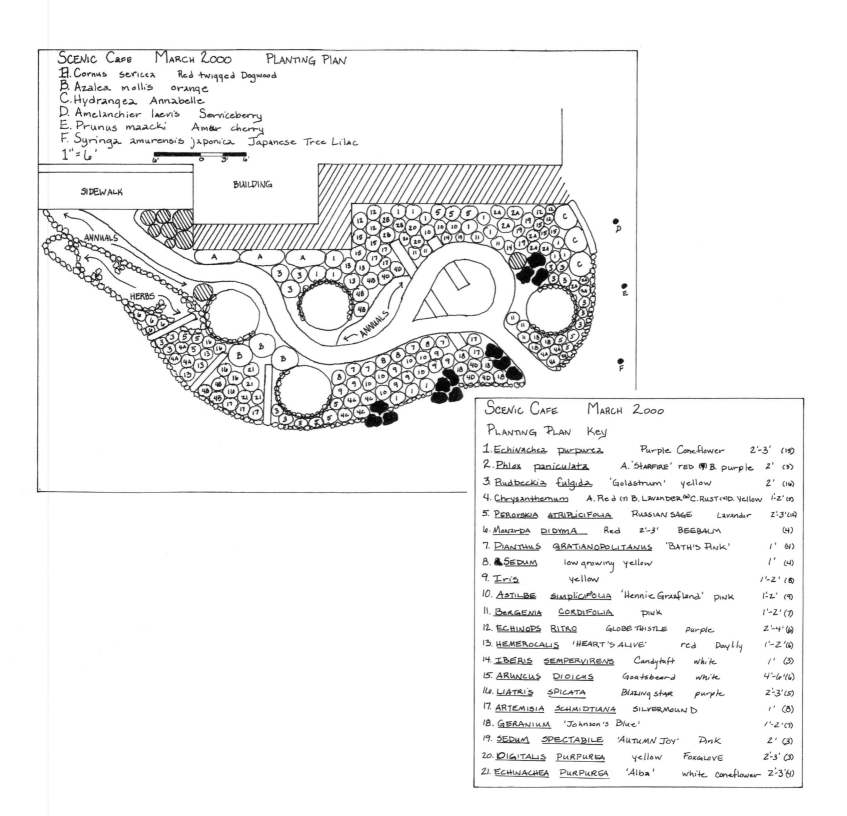

SCENIC CAFE   MARCH 2000   PLANTING PLAN

A. Cornus sericea   Red twigged Dogwood
B. Azalea mollis   orange
C. Hydrangea Annabelle
D. Amelanchier laevis   Serviceberry
E. Prunus maacki   Amur cherry
F. Syringa amurensis japonica   Japanese Tree Lilac

1" = 6'

SIDEWALK

BUILDING

ANNUALS

HERBS

ANNUALS

SCENIC CAFE   MARCH 2000

PLANTING PLAN   Key

1. Echinachea purpurea   Purple Coneflower   2'-3' (15)
2. Phlox paniculata   A. 'Starfire' red (9) B. purple   2' (3)
3. Rudbeckia fulgida   'Goldstrum' yellow   2' (16)
4. Chrysanthemum   A. Red (7) B. Lavander (10) C. Rust (4) D. Yellow   1'-2' (5)
5. Perovskia atriplicifolia   Russian Sage   Lavander   2'-3' (17)
6. Monarda didyma   Red   2'-3'   Beebalm   (4)
7. Dianthus gratianopolitanus   'Bath's Pink'   1' (4)
8. Sedum   low growing yellow   1' (4)
9. Iris   yellow   1'-2' (8)
10. Astilbe simplicifolia   'Hennie Graafland' pink   1'-2' (9)
11. Bergenia cordifolia   pink   1'-2' (7)
12. Echinops ritro   Globe Thistle   purple   2'-4' (6)
13. Hemerocalis   'Heart's Alive'   red   Daylily   1'-2' (6)
14. Iberis sempervirens   Candytuft   white   1' (3)
15. Aruncus dioicus   Goatsbeard   white   4'-6' (6)
16. Liatris spicata   Blazing star   purple   2'-3' (5)
17. Artemisia schmidtiana   Silvermound   1' (8)
18. Geranium   'Johnson's Blue'   1'-2' (7)
19. Sedum spectabile   'Autumn Joy'   Pink   2' (3)
20. Digitalis purpurea   yellow   Foxglove   2'-3' (3)
21. Echinachea purpurea   'Alba'   white coneflower   2'-3' (4)

The New Scenic Café

Garden

The New Scenic Café

50   *The New Scenic Café*

Garden

52

The New Scenic Café

Garden

The New Scenic Café

Garden

Canapés

The New Scenic Café

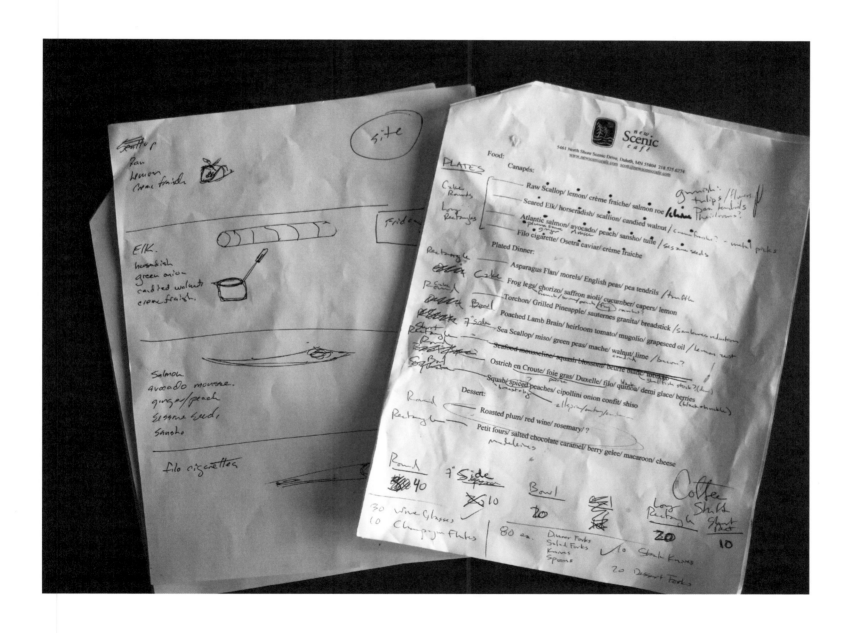

salmon tartare

yield: 12 pieces

Good-quality salmon, like a lot of seafood, is at its best when it is raw, and salmon tartare offers an excellent vehicle to show off that flavor. When I first looked for ways to serve salmon tartare, I took an approach similar to one used by chef and restaurateur Thomas Keller, with a rolled sesame tuile shaped like a cone. But I wanted something that had a shape more like a spoon—something with a long handle and a cavity that would carry the food to the mouth. The first elongated, triangle-shaped tuiles I created were fragile and, when picked up, simply broke. Over time, I found the right combination of flour and butter, to create a tuile that, when it bakes, curls up at the sides, giving it added rigidity and texture. Then, I use primarily sockeye salmon because of its high, rich fat content (although ivory salmon or king salmon work beautifully as well). I place a small amount of tartare in the tuile and finish with a touch of avocado mousse and a few sesame seeds. This is a light canapé, appropriate for summer.

Ingredients:

Curly Tuile:

5	T	all-purpose flour
4	t	sugar
1	t	kosher salt
2	each	egg whites (cold)
1/4 +	C	all-purpose flour
8	T	soft butter

Salmon Tartare:

2	oz	fresh salmon
1	t	olive oil
1/2	t	sesame oil
1/2	t	white truffle oil
1	t	minced shallot
1/2	t	minced garlic
1	pinch	dried thyme
1	t	chopped chives
1/2	t	kosher salt
1/4	t	cracked black pepper

Other:

1/4	C	avocado mousse (p. 362)
1	T	toasted sesame seeds

Method:

Curly Tuile:

Make the tuiles in advance, and keep them in an airtight container. You will need to find or make a stencil that you can use to shape the tuiles. A clean sheet of thin cardboard works for a one-time use; plastic works great if you want to reuse the form. (I simply cut my stencil out of a semi-rigid lid from a plastic box.) To make your stencil, cut out as many long, thin triangle shapes as will fit on your sheet.

Preheat the oven to 300 degrees.

Using a paddle attachment on an electric mixer, blend the 5T flour with the sugar and salt. Add the egg whites one at a time, and blend until smooth.

Slowly add the remaining flour until thick elastic bands form. You might need to use a bit less or more flour, depending on the size of your egg whites. Add the softened butter to the mixture in small amounts, and blend thoroughly.

Place a silicone baking mat on a sheet pan, and place your stencil on top of the mat. Using a flexible, thin spatula, spread the batter into the stencil shapes and pull the stencil away. Bake just a few minutes, until the tuiles are light golden brown and the edges have curled down.

Take the pan out of the oven immediately, remove the tuiles from the silicone mat, and set them on a counter. Allow them to cool completely before handling further.

(continued on page 65)

(continued from page 64)

Salmon Tartare:

Dice the salmon finely by hand. (Or, as a time-saving alternative, you can put the salmon in the freezer until it is semi-frozen and then pulse it in a food processor to mince it.)

Combine the salmon, oils, shallot, garlic, herbs, salt, and pepper in a small mixing bowl, and stir it together gently.

Assembly:

Lay the tuiles on a platter "upside-down" from the way they were baked, with the outer edges curled up, creating a bowl shape to hold the tartare.

Use a spoon to place a bite-size amount of tartare on the wide end of each tuile.

Cut about 1/8-inch from one corner of the bag of avocado mousse, and pipe a little "kiss" on top of each bite of tartare. Finish the canapés by sprinkling a few toasted sesame seeds on the top of each one.

Canapés

The New Scenic Café

grilled adobo shrimp

yield: 12 pieces

Shrimp are a popular appetizer at parties, but as a finger food they can be hard to eat, especially when you're wearing your best clothes and attempting to show your best manners. To address that issue, I spear shrimp on bamboo skewers, flattening them on the skewers so they can be nibbled with ease. Using skewers also allows the cook to turn them on the grill easily. I coat the shrimp while I grill it with a red chile adobo, which is a sauce that offers a deep, complex flavor one might compare with a barbecue sauce. I like to finish this dish with cilantro, but fresh cilantro leaves wilt in a moment. Instead, I make a cilantro beurre monte by pureeing butter and cilantro; it's similar to a pesto but uses butter instead of oil. I dip the top end of each grilled shrimp in the beurre monte so the cilantro flavor is there on the first bite and covers the palate. When I serve these shrimp at weddings, my wait staff says they can hardly get through the entry door before guests flock to them!

Method:

Use long (9- or 10-inch) bamboo skewers. Soak the skewers in water in the refrigerator for at least 24 hours prior, to prevent them from burning on the grill.

If the shrimp has not yet been peeled and de-veined, peel and de-vein it, leaving the tails attached.

Hold each shrimp down on a work surface, and straighten it with one hand. With your other hand, insert a skewer, starting at the tail and pushing it straight through to the "head" of the shrimp.

After you have skewered all the shrimp, place them on a hot grill, with the ends of the skewers hanging off the side.

While it cooks, brush the shrimp on all sides with the adobo, using the skewer's end to move the shrimp as you coat it. The sauce will form a glaze on the outside of the shrimp.

When they are cooked all the way through, remove the shrimp from the grill and dip the "head" end of each one in the cilantro beurre monte. Arrange the shrimp on a serving dish, and serve hot.

Ingredients:

12	each	raw shrimp (16/20 count, tails on)
1/4	C	red chile adobo (p. 369)
1/4	C	cilantro beurre monté (p. 364)

filo cigarettes

yield: 12 pieces

The osetra caviar used in this smoothly intense bite is Russian sturgeon roe. It comes in a range of colors, but here I use a variety that is intensely dark brown, essentially black. A classic way to serve caviar is on blinis with crème fraîche. For our version, I cut filo dough into strips, roll the strips into "cigarette"-shaped cones, and bake them until crisp. Then I fill the cooled cones with crème fraîche and add a dollop of black caviar on the end, to look like the "ash," for a nice nuttiness mixed with the flavor of the fish oil. The crème fraîche offers creaminess and mellows out the caviar.

Ingredients:

12	each	filo dough strips (2" x 8")
1/4	C	melted butter
1/2	C	crème fraîche (p. 365)
1	oz	osetra caviar

Method:

Note that this recipe uses crème fraîche, which requires 2 to 3 days of preparation time, so you will want to plan ahead.

Preheat the oven to 300 degrees.

Brush each strip of filo dough lightly with melted butter. Roll the filo from one end to the other to create a small, narrow cone that is slightly tapered. The narrow end should be almost closed, and the wide end should have an opening of about 1/2 inch.

Lay the cones on a baking sheet, and bake them until they are lightly golden and crisp, about 5 minutes. Remove the sheet from the oven, and allow the cones to cool.

Whip the crème fraîche with an electric mixer until stiff peaks form. Put it into a small ziplock bag, and cut about 1/8 inch from one of the bag's corners. Squeeze the crème fraîche into the open end of each one of the filo rolls, filling them up until just before the end.

Carefully spoon a bit of caviar onto the end of each cone so that the caviar fills the hole and covers the crème fraîche.

Line the "cigarettes" up on a platter, and scatter a few microgreens or flowers over the top to brighten the plate.

Canapés

The New Scenic Café

sashimi scallop

This glistening, colorful canapé uses thinly-sliced raw scallops. When you buy scallops, be sure they are fresh and have no tears or cracks. Good-quality sea scallops taste best when raw, but a raw scallop is difficult to offer as a canapé, so to carry the scallop to the mouth I use a thin lemon slice. The lemon offers a beautiful vehicle and transfers a subtle citrus flavor to the scallop itself. To lift the flat food up a bit, I tie it with a chive to create a folded shape and then fill the center of the scallop with a small amount of whipped crème fraîche and salmon roe. You can eat the lemon slice for a palate cleanse to finish.

Method:

Note that this recipe uses crème fraîche, which requires 2 to 3 days of preparation time, so you will want to plan ahead.

Slice the lemons into rings—as thinly as you can so they are almost translucent yet do not fall apart—and arrange them on a platter.

Heat a small pot of water to a boil. Dip the chives into the boiling water, and then quickly plunge them into ice water. Blot the excess water from the chives with a paper towel, and carefully lay one full chive across the center of each lemon slice. (Note: The chives have a tendency to break, so you will want to blanch a few extra.)

Using a sharp knife, carefully cut the scallops into thin, disc-shaped slices. (You should get approximately four slices from each scallop). Lay one scallop slice on top of the chive on each slice of lemon.

Whip the crème fraîche with an electric mixer until stiff peaks form. Put it into a small ziplock bag, and cut about 1/8 inch from one of the bag's corners. Squeeze about 1 tablespoon of the crème fraîche in a line across the center of each scallop slice, perpendicular to the chive.

Carefully lift both ends of each chive to pull the scallop into a folded "taco" shape. Enlisting a second pair of hands to hold up the scallop makes this gentle tying process easier.

Tie the chive into a knot, holding the whole bundle together as you do. Place about a teaspoon of salmon roe across the top of each canapé and serve.

Ingredients:

4	each	sea scallops (size U10)
2	each	lemons
1	C	crème fraîche (p. 365)
2	oz	salmon roe
16+	each	fresh chives

prosciutto-wrapped rabbit tenderloin

yield: 24 pieces

This idea came about because I was buying whole rabbits to create an entrée but primarily using only the legs, so I wanted to find something useful and innovative to do with the tenderloin. I found that wrapping the tenderloin into a "cigar" with a bit of prosciutto, cooking it in a sauté pan, and then slicing it produced a wonderful accompaniment to the rabbit entrée (page 159), bringing together the sweetness of the tenderloin with the saltiness of the prosciutto. It wasn't until later that I considered turning it into a canapé, and it has been a hit ever since. If you cannot get rabbit tenderloins, you'll find this combination works quite well with chicken.

Ingredients:

6	each	rabbit tenderloins
12	slices	prosciutto
3 - 4	T	fennel & coriander honey glaze (p. 366)
2 - 3	T	olive oil

Method:

Lay two slices of prosciutto on a cutting board side by side, so that the edges overlap about 1/2 inch. Tear off a 12-inch-wide piece of plastic wrap that is 10 to12 inches long, and lay it flat on the counter, to the side.

Rabbit tenderloins are usually about 8 to10 inches long and taper from about 1 inch in diameter down to almost nothing. Cut a tenderloin into two 4- or 5-inch pieces, and lay the pieces together side-to-side on the prosciutto, at a bit of an angle near one end.

Roll it all up tightly, like a "cigar," working slowly and carefully because the prosciutto can tear easily. Pick up the roll, and place it along one edge of the plastic wrap.

Roll the "cigar" tightly and evenly in the plastic wrap. Then pinch the air out of both ends, and twist them like the ends of a candy wrapper. Keep twisting until the plastic wrap is tight and firm and the roll is nice and evenly cylindrical. Fold the ends of the plastic wrap under so that they stick to each other and will keep the roll from unraveling.

Repeat this process with the remaining 5 tenderloins, and refrigerate them for at least 2 hours—or overnight. When you are ready to cook them, take the rolls out of the refrigerator and carefully peel off the plastic wrap.

Pour the olive oil into a large sauté pan, and heat it over high heat. Add the rolls. Sear them on all sides, until the prosciutto is nicely brown and crisp, and the rabbit is cooked through.

With a knife, nip off the ends of the rolls, and then cut each roll into 4 equal cylindrical pieces. Stand the pieces on end on a platter, and insert a bamboo pick in each one at an angle--they will end up looking like small corncob pipes. Drizzle a dab of fennel & coriander honey glaze on each piece.

grilled asparagus & prosciutto

yield: 12 pieces

This summery canapé is easy to make and can also serve as an accompaniment to a main dish or as a side dish for a barbecue. Cut the tips off the asparagus, wrap small bundles of the asparagus tips in thin slices of prosciutto, and grill them. To enhance the "mouthfeel," serve with a little mustard aioli.

Method:

Mustard Aioli:
Place the egg yolks, minced garlic, cayenne pepper, kosher salt, lemon juice, mustard seed mix, and Dijon mustard in a food processor and pulse the mixture for about 15 seconds.

With the processor running on low speed, pour the oil in slowly, in a steady, thin stream. The aioli will be very thick at this point. Add water in increments of 1 tablespoon, until the aioli reaches a consistency that can be poured from a spoon. Use the mustard aioli immediately, or store it in the refrigerator.

Assembly:
Use only the tips of the asparagus—about the top 3 inches. If they are particularly thin, you will not need to blanch or shock the asparagus, but if they are thicker than a pencil, you will. (You can use the remaining asparagus stems elsewhere. Try "sea bass & asparagus flan" on page 157.)

Lay the slices of prosciutto on a cutting board, and cut each into 3 long strips. Lay 3 asparagus tips on each strip of prosciutto, and roll it around the asparagus like a bandage.

When it is nearly time to serve, grill the wrapped asparagus for a just a few minutes, until the prosciutto is browned and the asparagus shows a bit of char, which adds a nice flavor. If a grill is not available, you can bake them briefly in an oven or cook them in a skillet.

Arrange the asparagus on a dish, and top with a little mustard aioli. The sweet asparagus combined with the salty prosciutto create a simple yet elegant canapé.

Ingredients:

Mustard Aioli:

2	each	egg yolks
1/2	T	minced garlic
1	pinch	cayenne pepper
1/2	T	kosher salt
1	T	lemon juice
2	T	mustard seed mix (p. 368)
1	T	Dijon mustard
2	C	canola oil
		water

Other:

36	spears	small, young asparagus (pencil-thin)
4	slices	prosciutto

togarashi lobster

yield: 12 pieces

I was looking for a way to bring out the sweet flavor of a shellfish, and pairing it with the unique spiciness of the Japanese spice blend, togarashi, was my answer. This canapé combines the sweetness of lobster with the spiciness of the sansho powder, sesame seeds, nori (seaweed), dried orange peel, and other ingredients in togarashi, which is a dusting-type seasoning that can be put on just about anything. Sansho powder is a Japanese spice made from the ground berries of the prickly ash tree. It has a lemon-pepper flavor and a spicy heat that lingers on the tongue. You can find sansho powder online or in many Asian grocery stores (however, freshly ground black pepper will work as an acceptable substitute). I butter-poach the lobster, which gives the butter itself a lot of lobster flavor, and then toss the lobster chunks in togarashi, put them on picks, and place them on pieces of toasted brioche to add body to the canapé. For the final presentation, I simply pour the butter over everything. The brioche and lobster together create rich, sweet bites, in a canapé that also offers a nice citrus and spice combination.

Ingredients:

Togarashi:

3	t	sansho powder (or freshly ground black pepper)
1	t	nori flakes
5	t	dried orange peel
3	t	crushed red pepper flakes
1	t	black sesame seeds
1	t	golden sesame seeds
1	t	poppy seeds
2	t	granulated garlic
1	t	ground ginger

Other:

6 - 8	oz	lobster tail
2	C	butter
4	oz	brioche (p. 281)

Method:

Togarashi:
  Mix all of the ingredients together evenly in a small bowl, until they are combined evenly.

Assembly:
  Preheat the oven to 300 degrees.

  Melt the butter in a small pot, and heat it to 160 degrees. It is important to use an accurate thermometer to avoid overcooking the lobster.

  Add the lobster tail to the butter. The addition of the lobster will cause the temperature to drop, so you will need to bring the heat back up, keeping it as close to 160 degrees as you can (and being sure not to let it exceed 190 degrees). A single lobster tail will take 5 to 10 minutes to cook all the way through and will reach an internal temperature of 140 degrees when it is done.

  Remove the lobster tail from the butter, and set the butter aside. Cut the lobster into 12 equal pieces, and toss it in a small bowl with about 2 tablespoons of togarashi.

  Carefully cut any crust from the brioche and discard. Cut the brioche into 12 1-inch cubes, and toast them in the oven for just a few minutes, until they are a bit crisp on the outside but still soft on the inside.

  Using small bamboo picks, skewer each piece of lobster, and stick the picks upright into the brioche cubes so that they stand up. Arrange the pieces on a serving dish, and spoon the warm lobster-flavored butter over each of them so that the butter soaks into the brioche. Serve immediately.

The New Scenic Café

grilled flank steak brochette

yield: 12 pieces

Flank steak is a bit of a "hidden treasure," especially in a combination such as this rich and colorful canapé, so summery in its appearance and flavors. Although many people gravitate toward a cut of beef like filet mignon, considering it "the best" because of its lean and tender texture, for this recipe I wanted the deeper flavor and greater "bite" of flank steak. I marinate the steak, grill it, and cut it into 3/4-inch cubes, enjoying the flank's savory and almost Mediterranean "umami" flavor and aroma as I work. I cut the cucumber and feta cheese as well and skewer them, along with the meat, tomatoes, and kalamata olives. This canapé offers a rich mix of colors, with the deep blacks, bright whites, brilliant reds or oranges, the pink of the meat, and the crisp cucumber green.

Method:

Marinate the flank steak in your favorite beef marinade for about 2 hours. Or you can keep it simple and rub the steak with olive oil and season it with salt and pepper. Then grill it to the temperature you like (although I find cooking it beyond medium tends to reduce the steak's flavor).

After the steak has cooled, cut it into 12 cubes, each 3/4-inch on all sides. Cut the feta and cucumber into similar size cubes.

Using medium-length bamboo skewers, skewer a tomato, an olive, and then a cube of cucumber. Skewer the feta next, doing it slowly so it remains intact. Finish with a cube of flank steak, and lay each finished skewer on a serving platter.

Ingredients:

8	oz	flank steak
1	small	cucumber
8	oz	block feta cheese
12	each	kalamata olives
12	each	small tomatoes (grape, pear, sungold)

crab louie

yield: 24 pieces

I enjoy being creative with food, coming up with original recipes or with my own renditions of standard dishes. But I also appreciate working with classic flavor combinations that stand on their own and can scarcely be improved upon. One such classic is the Crab Louie salad, which usually combines crab meat, iceberg lettuce, tomatoes, asparagus, avocado, and a creamy salad dressing similar to a Thousand Island or Green Goddess dressing. For a tasty twist on that classic, I created a canapé version, substituting Belgian endive leaves for the iceberg lettuce and using a single endive leaf as a small, edible bowl to serve a bite-size portion of lump crab meat, avocado mousse, and diced heirloom tomatoes. (If heirloom tomatoes are not available, other good-quality tomatoes will work well.) I also substitute a Sun-Dried Tomato Vinaigrette in place of the creamy dressings that are typically used, to add more tomato flavor and make the canapé a bit lighter. This recipe could be adapted easily to a full-size salad by using larger pieces of tomato, chopping the avocado rather than making avocado mousse, and adding fresh asparagus spears. Or the ingredients could be layered in a small dish and served as a dip, along with freshly fried or baked tortilla chips.

Ingredients:

Sun-dried Tomato Vinaigrette:

1/2	T	cream sherry
1	C	red wine vinegar
3	each	raspberries (fresh or frozen)
2	T	shallots (minced)
1	t	garlic (minced)
1	pinch	dill
1	pinch	kosher salt
1	pinch	cracked black pepper
1/4	C	sun-dried tomatoes (in oil)
1/3	C	olive oil

Other:

4	heads	Belgian endive
3/4	C	heirloom tomatoes (diced)
1 1/2	C	lump crab meat
1	C	avocado mousse (p. 362)
1/2	C	microgreens

Method:

Sun-dried Tomato Vinaigrette:

Combine all of the ingredients in a blender, purée them on high speed until the mixture is smooth, and then allow the vinaigrette to rest for about 10 minutes, until any remaining air bubbles have risen to the top. Use the vinaigrette immediately, or pour it into a container and store it in the refrigerator.

Assembly:

Pull off any outer leaves that are brown or damaged on the heads of Belgian endive, and wipe off the remaining outer leaves with a damp cloth. (It is not necessary to wash the leaves, since endive is grown in sand, not soil.) Then cut off the root end of each head of endive, and peel away 6 nice-looking, medium-size leaves from each head, for a total of 24 leaves. (We refrigerate the remaining small heads of endive to use later in a salad.) Arrange the 24 endive leaves on a serving platter, with their bowl sides facing up.

In a small mixing bowl, combine the diced tomatoes with 2 tablespoons of the Sun-Dried Tomato Vinaigrette. Use a spoon to toss the tomatoes gently and coat them with the vinaigrette.

Drain any excess moisture from the lump crab meat, taking care to keep the pieces intact and avoid crumbling or shredding the crab.

Cut one corner off a small ziplock bag, fill it with the avocado mousse, and pipe about 2 teaspoons of avocado mousse in the center of each endive leaf. Set 2 or 3 pieces of crab meat (totaling about 1 tablespoon) on top of each portion of avocado mousse. Then use a spoon to place 1/2 tablespoon of diced tomato over the top of the crab meat on each canapé.

Garnish each portion with 3 individual sprigs of the microgreen, and finish the canapés by dusting their tops lightly with kosher salt and fresh cracked black pepper.

cucumber & smoked salmon mousse

yield: 12 pieces

This is a simple canapé to prepare, yet it delivers a deliciously light and summery flavor. I cut the English cucumber on a mandoline slicer to create a long ribbon, roll the ribbon into a coil, fill it with salmon mousse, draw a pick through it, and then top it off with salmon roe. The cool, refreshing cucumber combined with the smoky salmon and bright bursts of roe is quite refreshing. I have also topped this canapé with fresh herring roe or tobikko roe.

Ingredients:

Smoked Salmon Mousse:

5	oz	Boursin soft cheese
3 1/2	oz	cream cheese
1/2	t	dried thyme
1/2	t	white truffle oil
1	t	granulated sugar
3	oz	smoked salmon

Other:

1	each	large English cucumber
1	oz	salmon roe

Method:

Smoked Salmon Mousse:
Allow the Boursin soft cheese and the cream cheese to soften at room temperature for about 20 minutes. Combine the cheeses, dried thyme, white truffle oil, and granulated sugar in the bowl of an electric mixer. Using a paddle attachment, whip the mixture on high speed for 5 minutes.

Turn off the mixer, crumble in the smoked salmon, and whip the mixture on medium speed for about 30 seconds, until the salmon is broken apart but is still in small, visible pieces.

Assembly:
Cut the English cucumber 1/8 inch thick, lengthwise, on a mandolin slicer. If the cucumber is long enough, you can cut each ribbon in half to create two sections, each 5 to 6 inches long.

Roll each cucumber ribbon into a coil, and draw a bamboo skewer through it to hold it together—it will it look a bit like a corn-cob pipe.

Put the salmon mousse in a small ziplock bag. If the mousse is cold and firm, squeeze the bag in your hands to warm and soften it.

Cut about ½ inch from one of the bag's corners. Using the ziplock like a pastry bag, fill each cucumber coil with about 1 tablespoon of mouse.

Place the coils on a serving platter, and spoon a few pieces of salmon roe on top of each piece. Serve immediately.

asiago nests

yield: 12 pieces

If you've ever used shredded parmesan cheese to create a baked crisp or bowl, you'll find this a tasty enhancement to that method. It uses asiago cheese, which has a bit more flavor and body and doesn't "oil out" as fast as parmesan. Asiago also allows you to bend it before it cools. I sprinkle circles of asiago on a silicone mat, bake them, and press them into the cups in a mini muffin tin—you could also use an egg carton or small cups. After they're cool, the "nests" maintain their shape. I fill them with an herbed goat cheese mousse and sprinkle them with a few fresh herbs such as chive and parsley. (You can fill these nests with many other ingredients, being mindful, of course, that there are holes in them. They are, after all, "nests" and not bowls!) These canapés are light, fresh, and wonderful with champagne.

Method:

Preheat the oven to 425 degrees. If available, a convection oven works particularly well.

Place a silicone mat on a sheet pan. (There is no substitute for a non-stick silicone baking mat for this process. You can find one at most specialty kitchen stores or online.)

Sprinkle about 1 tablespoon of shredded asiago cheese in a 3-inch circle on the mat, using a round, hollow form—like a ring mold or a round cookie cutter—to help guide the shape as you sprinkle. Repeat until you have 6 circles of cheese.

The strands of cheese in the circles can overlap, but there should also be some blank space so you do not have a solid layer of cheese. Also be sure to sprinkle the cheese thinly enough so it will cook evenly and get crisp.

Place the sheet pan in the oven, and watch it carefully. After a few minutes, the cheese will begin to bubble and change color. As soon as it turns a light gold, remove the pan from the oven. Using a thin metal spatula, remove a cheese circle, pressing it quickly into the mini-muffin tin or your cup-size mold of choice. I find the mini-muffin tin works well, since it creates a bite size that is easy to handle.

Repeat this process with the remaining circles. The cheese will cool and harden rapidly, so it is important to press the cheese circles into the molds as fast as possible.

After the sheet pan and silicone mat have cooled for a few minutes, repeat this process to create another 6 asiago nests for a total of 12. (You might want to make a few extra nests in case any of them break).

Put the goat cheese mousse into a small ziplock bag, and cut about 1/2-inch from one of the bag's corners. Using it like a pastry bag, pipe about 1 tablespoon of mousse into each of the asiago nests. Carefully remove the filled nests from the muffin tin, arrange them on a platter, and sprinkle each with a few bits of fresh chive and parsley. Serve immediately.

Ingredients:

1	C	shredded asiago
1	C	herbed goat cheese mousse (p. 366)
1	T	chopped fresh chive
1	T	chopped fresh parsley

prosciutto-wrapped black mission figs

yield: 12 pieces

This canapé is a simple one, and yet its combination of sweet and smoky flavors is the true essence of culinary synergy. A fig is sweet and meaty. Wrapped in prosciutto, skewered, and grilled, it delivers a taste that our senses often crave: salty and sweet combined. If you find that you are eating a fair number of sweets, your palate will soon tell you that you now need salt, or vice versa. And with this canapé, you get both! You can substitute smoky bacon for the prosciutto and achieve the same delicious effect.

Ingredients:

12	each	*fresh black mission figs*
4	slices	*prosciutto*

Method:

Note that you will need to soak a dozen bamboo skewers in water in the refrigerator overnight, to prevent them from burning on the grill, prior to preparing this recipe.

Lay the prosciutto on a cutting board, and cut each slice into 3 long strips.

Wrap one strip of prosciutto around each fig, and stick a bamboo skewer through so that it penetrates the prosciutto on both sides, to help keep the prosciutto in place.

When you are nearly ready to serve, grill the figs for just a few minutes, rotating them so that the prosciutto is cooked on all sides and the figs are warmed through.

The New Scenic Café

seared duck breast

yield: 12 pieces

Duck breast by itself has a splendid flavor. Duck paired with cherries is a natural marriage of flavors, and adding fingerling sweet potatoes to the mix creates a tasty and alluring canapé. I added the potato because I wanted a base that would be delicious yet would not conflict with the other flavors. A small fingerling potato that has been roasted in advance and then sliced into small barrels works well, and for an autumn rendition I use fingerling sweet potatoes. Their bright orange color and additional sweetness bring a welcome change of flavor and appearance. I cook the duck to medium or medium rare. Meat on the medium side is a bit easier to eat, I find, while medium-rare is a little more chewy. The amarena cherry is a dark, sour Italian variety of cherry, bottled in sweet syrup. Amarena Fabbri is the most common brand that we use, but there are other brands available as well. I skewer the cherries, the cubes of duck breast, and the fingerling sweet potatoes on bamboo skewers, bringing together the beautiful combination of purplish-red cherry, the pink of the duck, and the bright orange potato.

Method:

Duck Breast:

This canapé is best served at room temperature, so you will want to cook the duck breast first so it has time to cool.

Put the olive oil in a small sauté pan on medium heat. Season both sides of the duck breast with kosher salt, and sprinkle the garam masala only on the side of the duck that has no skin.

Place the duck breast, skin side down, in the sauté pan, and sear it, allowing the fat to render out of the skin. After the skin is nicely brown and crisp, flip the duck breast over, and cook it to medium-rare or medium. (For more detailed information about searing duck breasts, see page 181.)

Remove the duck from the pan, and either allow it to cool to room temperature or place it in the refrigerator. Cut the duck breast into 12 equal cube-shaped pieces.

Sweet Potatoes:
Preheat the oven to 250 degrees.

In a small bowl, toss the potatoes with the olive oil, salt, and pepper, and then lay the potatoes on a baking sheet. Place the sheet in the oven, and roast the potatoes until a knife tip can be inserted easily into their middle.

Remove the potatoes from the oven, allow them to cool, and then cut them into thick, round slices that are roughly the same size as the cubes of duck.

Assembly:
Drain the syrup from the cherries. Using short bamboo skewers, on each skewer spear a cherry, a piece of duck, and then a piece of potato. Stand the skewers on end on a platter, and serve.

Ingredients:

Duck Breast:

1	each	duck breast (skin on)
2	t	kosher salt
1/2	t	garam masala (p. 366)
1	T	olive oil

Sweet Potatoes:

4	each	fingerling sweet potatoes
1	T	olive oil
1/2	t	kosher salt
1/4	t	cracked black pepper

Other:

12	each	candied amarena cherries

spanikopita

yield: 24 pieces

A good friend of mine is Greek, and when he helped me cater an event years ago we asked his mother to make the Greek classic, spanikopita. It was a delicious, buttery treat, and ever since then I've looked for ways to bring spanikopita into my menus. Traditionally, it is prepared in a large pan and then cut, using layers of filo dough filled with butter, feta cheese, lemon, and a bit of spinach. I wanted to turn it into a canapé, so I laid out the strips of filo, put a dab of filling on each, and folded them into triangles. That shape allowed me to create individual portions that baked evenly and didn't fall apart. For the filling, I used wilted, chopped spinach that I'd mixed with a touch of garlic, shallot, lemon zest, and crumbled feta cheese. Then I looked for a way to finish the dish by giving it a bit of butter flavor without a lot of oil. I discovered that by adding a light dusting of nutritional yeast at the end, along with a brushing of butter, the spanikopita took on a lovely, light buttery taste and an attractive crackle texture.

Ingredients:

Filling:

8	oz	baby spinach leaves
1	T	olive oil
1	T	minced shallot
1/2	T	minced garlic
6	oz	feta cheese (crumbled)
2	t	lemon zest
1	t	kosher salt
1	t	cracked black pepper

Other:

48	strips	filo dough (2" x 10 - 12")
1/4	C	melted butter
2	T	nutritional yeast flakes

Method:

Filling:

Make the filling ahead of time. If needed, it can rest in the refrigerator for a few hours.

Put the spinach leaves in a medium sauce pot, and heat it over low heat until the spinach wilts and releases most of its moisture. Wrap the spinach in a clean towel or cloth napkin, and over the sink squeeze out as much liquid as possible. Chop the spinach finely, and put it in a mixing bowl.

Heat the olive oil in a sauté pan, add the shallots and garlic, and "sweat" them until they are translucent. Add the shallots and garlic mixture, feta cheese, lemon zest, salt, and pepper to the chopped spinach, and mix thoroughly, breaking up any spinach clumps with your fingers.

Assembly:

Preheat the oven to 350 degrees.

On a clean work surface, lay 2 strips of filo dough on top of each other. (Using 2 layers helps prevent tearing.) Brush the top strip lightly with melted butter, and set about 2 teaspoons of filling on one end.

Starting at the end with the filling, fold one corner of the filo dough over the top, on an angle, creating a triangle shape. Continue folding the dough in this fashion, as if you were folding a flag, until the entire strip of filo dough is folded into a triangular pouch.

Repeat this process with the rest of the dough and filling, and lay the pieces on a baking sheet pan. Brush the tops lightly with melted butter. Then dust them with salt, pepper, and nutritional yeast flakes, and bake them until they are light golden brown, crisp, and plump from the warm filling—about 10 minutes. Arrange the spanikopita on a platter, garnish them with a scatter of microgreens, and serve warm.

Canapés

The New Scenic Café

elk tenderloin

yield: 12 to 24 pieces

Diners seem to be opening up to the idea of eating more wild game, leading the way for creative options beyond the ubiquitous beef, pork, and chicken. Elk is appealing, easy to eat, and elegant—perfect for a canapé. Like many canapés I have created, this one I first served as a full entrée and then condensed it into one or two flavorful bites. I grill the elk and cut it into small cubes. Then I mound the elk with whipped crème fraîche, shave fresh horseradish over the top, and sprinkle it with finely chopped candied walnuts. The result is a savory combination of the clean and meaty flavor of the elk, the smooth texture of the crème fraîche, the sharp tang of the horseradish, and the sweetness of the candied nuts. This combination also works well with beef tenderloin, ribeye, and flank steak.

Method:

Note that this recipe uses crème fraîche, which requires 2 to 3 days of preparation time, so you will want to plan ahead.

Candied Walnuts:
Preheat the oven to 350 degrees. Spread the walnuts on a sheet pan, and toast them for about 5 minutes. Set them aside to cool.

Put the granulated sugar in a small sauce pot over medium heat. As the sugar begins to melt, stir it gently with a wooden spoon. Continue cooking the sugar for about 2 minutes, stirring it frequently, until the sugar caramelizes to a medium-brown color.

Add the toasted walnuts to the pan, and stir them immediately to coat them with the caramelized sugar. Pour the sugar-coated walnuts onto a sheet pan that you have lined with either a silicone baking mat or parchment paper, spreading them out so they are separated from one another. Sprinkle the candied walnuts with a pinch of kosher salt, and allow them to cool.

Assembly:
Rub the elk tenderloin with olive oil, and season it with salt and pepper. Grill the elk to your desired temperature. (Medium rare delivers the best flavor and is the easiest to eat.) Cut the meat into 3/4-inch cubes.

Using small bamboo skewers, spear 1 or 2 cubes of elk onto each skewer, and place them on a serving platter.

Whip the crème fraîche with an electric mixer until it is thick, like whipped cream. Put the whipped crème fraîche into a small ziplock bag, and cut about 1/8 inch from one of the bag's corners. Squeeze about 2 teaspoons of crème fraîche onto each cube of skewered elk. Using a microplane grater, shave as much fresh horseradish as you prefer over the top of each one.

Shave or finely chop the candied walnuts with a knife, and sprinkle about 1/2 teaspoon of the nuts onto each canapé. To finish, scatter a few chopped fresh chives over the top of the canapés, and serve.

Ingredients:

Candied Walnuts:

1 1/2	C	raw walnuts
1/2	C	granulated sugar
1	pinch	kosher salt

Other:

16	oz	elk tenderloin
2 - 3	T	olive oil
1/2	C	crème fraîche (p. 365)
1	each	small horseradish root
2	T	chopped fresh chive

lamb meatball

yield: 24 pieces

I began making ground lamb meatloaf as an entrée and decided to adapt the same recipe to a canapé. I settled on creating small meatballs from the meatloaf ingredients and then looked for the most attractive and appetizing accompaniment, selecting the Parisian carrot. These short, wonderfully shaped, and vividly bright orange carrots are also quite sweet, which complements the mild game flavor of the lamb nicely. Instead of finishing the canapé with salt, I use a bit of tangy apple cider gastrique. The cider offers a bright "pop" as it pulls all of the flavors together. This canapé has a classic autumn flavor and appearance, but I find it appealing to the palate and the eye any time of year.

Ingredients:

24	each	Parisian carrots
24	oz	lamb meatloaf mix (p. 367)
2 - 3	T	olive oil
1/4	C	apple cider gastrique (p. 362)

Method:

Parisian carrots are also sometimes called "Thumbelina carrots." They are short and fat, like a small beet or a radish. If you can't find Parisian carrots, you can also cut regular carrots into a similar size and shape.

Heat a medium-sized pot of water to a boil, and add the carrots. Boil them for a few minutes, until they are cooked through and a knife tip penetrates to their middle with relative ease.

Remove the carrots from the water. If they are small, use one whole carrot for each canapé. If they are a bit larger, you can cut them in half or into quarters.

Scoop the meatloaf mixture into 3/4-ounce portions, and roll each one in your hands to shape them into spheres.

Heat 2 to 3 tablespoons of olive oil in a large sauté pan, and add the meatballs, rolling them around the pan until they are browned on all sides and cooked through. Or, you can place the meatballs on a baking sheet lined with parchment paper and bake them at 450 degrees for about 8 minutes.

Using small bamboo skewers, spear one carrot and one meatball. Arrange the skewers on a platter, and pour a bit of cider gastrique over each one. If left on, the green ends of the carrots add another bright touch to this tasty and colorful canapé.

medjool date-filled sfogliatelle

yield: 24 pieces

Sfogliatelle are coiled Italian pastries that look a bit like seashells and are traditionally filled with dessert fillings such as pastry cream, marzipan, or a sweet ricotta mixture. The word "sfogliatelle" means "many leaves," which describes the formation of the pastry. I stretch the dough until it is thin, brush it with butter and shortening, roll it tightly into a log, and then cut the dough into discs, each with many tightly-coiled layers. I shape the discs into cones, fill them, and bake them until the dough is crisp and golden brown. Sfogliatelle are usually the size of a scone or small muffin. I wanted to do something different, though, so I made them quite a bit smaller and filled them with a rich Medjool date mixture made with spicy Thai chile peppers. I originally created this version of the sfogliatelle pastry to be served with a beef tenderloin entrée (page 201), but they were greeted with such enthusiasm I began offering them as a canapé to be enjoyed on their own.

Ingredients:

Dough:

2	T	olive oil
1/2	C	water
12	oz	all-purpose flour
1	t	kosher salt
1/4	C	butter (softened)
1/4	C	vegetable shortening

Filling:

4	oz	Medjool dates (pitted)
2	T	white wine
1	each	Thai red chile pepper
1	t	kosher salt
1	t	vegetable base
1	T	cilantro (chopped)
1	t	cumin seeds (toasted & ground)
1	t	garlic (minced)
1/4	C	white onion (small-diced)
1/4	C	water

Method:

Note that this recipe requires 1 day of prior preparation to chill the sfogliatelle dough overnight.

Dough:

Combine the olive oil and water in an electric mixer bowl. In a separate dish, sift the all-purpose flour and kosher salt together. Then add them to the bowl. Mix the ingredients with a dough hook until a stiff, uniform ball forms. Remove the dough from the bowl, wrap it tightly in plastic wrap, and refrigerate it.

Using the mixer, whip the softened butter and vegetable shortening together until they are smooth and mixed evenly. Allow the mixture to rest at room temperature.

Remove the dough from the refrigerator, and use a pasta roller to roll it as thinly as possible into one long sheet. As needed, dust the dough lightly with flour to keep it from sticking.

Lay the sheet of dough on a counter, and use a spatula to brush a very thin layer of the butter and shortening mixture over the top. Roll the sheet of dough up tightly, from one end to the other, creating a coiled log that is 1 1/2 to 2 inches in diameter. Cover the log of dough, and chill it in the refrigerator overnight.

Filling:

Combine all of the ingredients in a small pot. Cover it with a lid, and simmer the mixture over low heat, stirring occasionally, until most of the liquid is absorbed and the dates are soft.

Spread the mixture on a sheet pan to cool. Then transfer it to a food processor, and pulse it a few times (taking care not to puree it) to chop the dates lightly. Put the date mixture in a ziplock bag, and store it in the refrigerator.

(continued on page 94)

The New Scenic Café

(continued from page 92)

Assembly:

Slice the chilled log of dough into 1/2-inch discs, and return them to the refrigerator. Preheat the oven to 400 degrees.

The next step requires practice and patience: Work with one disc at a time, keeping the others in the refrigerator so the dough stays firm. Gently tease the layers of the disc slightly apart, pushing the center of the disc out and slowly working your way outward so you end up with a spiral cone shape that is about 2 1/2 to 3 inches long.

Cut off about 3/8 inch of a corner of the ziplock bag that holds the date filling, and squeeze 1 to 2 tablespoons of filling into the center of the cone. Pinch the open end of the cone shut, pressing it firmly so the dough ends seal together. Then set the filled pastry on a sheet pan lined with parchment paper. Repeat this process with the remaining dough and filling.

(If you want to preserve the sfogliatelle to use later, wrap the sheet pan tightly with plastic wrap, and place it in the freezer, being sure to thaw the frozen sfogliatelle first when you are ready to bake them.)

Bake the sfogliatelle until they are golden brown and crisp, about 10 minutes.

seared sea scallop

yield: 24 pieces

This canapé, with its wonderful flavor combinations and textures, is perhaps my most popular. Good-quality, fresh sea scallops are amazing to eat raw and require little enhancement to create an impressive dish. But if the scallops are not going to be served completely raw, I have yet to find a better way to prepare them than by quickly searing the outside to a caramelized, crisp texture. To sear properly, the scallops must be as fresh as possible, so it's best to find out from your seafood supplier when their product arrives and plan your purchase accordingly. Look for dry-pack scallops. They receive a minimum of handling and are simply shucked, packed fresh, and shipped on ice. They contain no additives or preservatives and have not been soaked in a brine solution, which tends to give less desirable results in the cooking process. Because these seared sea scallops are only partially cooked, they offer a way to bring the world of sushi to the beginner, in a beautifully appealing concentric style.

Method:

Use a circular shape, such as a biscuit cutter or a round cookie cutter, to cut the wontons into circles, about 2½ inches in diameter.

In a small pot, heat 2 to 3 cups of canola oil to 325 degrees, and fry the wonton rounds to a light golden color. They will look like round, crisp crackers.

Season the scallops lightly on both sides with salt and pepper. In a large sauté pan, heat 2 to 3 tablespoons of oil and begin searing the scallops a few at a time, making sure there is sufficient space around each scallop so they sear properly.

After the scallops are a medium brown color on the first side, flip them over and sear the second side. Remove them from the pan, and repeat this process with the remaining scallops, adding more oil as needed.

Slice each scallop across the middle so you have 2 round pieces, each with one seared side.

Place a small dab of wasabi in the center of each wonton round, and then put one piece of scallop, seared side up, on top of each wasabi dab to "glue" the scallops to the wontons.

Arrange them on a platter, and pour a few drops of sesame soy sauce on each one. Finish by softening each wonton-scallop round with a bit of microgreens on top. Micro cilantro or cross-cut chives work great.

Ingredients:

12	each	sea scallops (10/20 count)
24	each	wonton wrappers
1/4	C	sesame soy sauce (p. 370)
2	T	wasabi paste
2 - 3	C	canola oil (for wontons)
2 - 3	T	canola oil (for scallops)

Starters

The New Scenic Café

miso-marinated sea bass

yield: 4 servings

This small, simple-looking dish brings together a delicious collection of complex flavors. It began as an entrée (page 168), and the flavor of the miso marinade worked so well I decided to create this smaller dish to give people another option for trying it. Sea bass is sweet, smooth, and rich and pairs well with the bright acidity of the pickled vegetables.

Method:

Note that you can easily prepare the pickled carrot and pickled daikon for this recipe while the sea bass is marinating.

Cut the sea bass into 4 equal, cube-shaped portions. The cubes need not be perfect in shape, but try to avoid cutting thin pieces, since they tend to overcook quickly and become dry.

Roll the pieces of fish around in the miso marinade so they are well coated, and then let them sit in the marinade in the refrigerator for 1 to 2 hours—but no longer. Because the pieces are relatively small, if they sit in the marinade too long they will actually start to "cook" from the acidity.

Preheat the oven to 450 degrees. Lightly spray a sheet pan with pan release or line it with parchment paper, and place the sea bass on the pan. Roast the fish in the oven for 8 to 10 minutes, until it is just cooked through and the marinade has begun to caramelize and darken on the edges.

Set each piece of sea bass in the center of a small plate, and top it with 1/2 ounce of pickled daikon, 1/2 ounce of pickled carrot, and a small pinch of micro cilantro (or a few leaves of regular cilantro). The bass will cool quickly, so serve it immediately.

Ingredients:

8	oz	fresh sea bass (skinned)
1/4	C	miso marinade (p. 368)
2	oz	pickled carrot (p. 368)
2	oz	pickled daikon (p. 368)
		fresh cilantro

fettuccine alla carbonara
yield: 1 serving

One of my first professional culinary experiences was as the chef at Augustino's, an Italian restaurant in the historic Fitger's building in Duluth, Minnesota, where we served authentic northern Italian food with a bit of southern Italian influence. I fell in love with the artistry and the heritage of that cuisine, and although these days I rarely include pastas on my menus, fettuccine alla carbonara remains one of my favorites. I make it as a smaller appetizer portion, using fresh homemade pasta, but if you use a good-quality dried pasta you'll find it also produces great results in this recipe. I turn a fresh egg into the cooked pasta and the prosciutto, add diced tomato and peas, and place a nest of shaved Pecorino Romano on top with a quail egg yolk in the center. This beautiful presentation of an authentic carbonara honors the classic Italian cuisine I grew to love.

Ingredients:

1	t	olive oil
1/2	t	minced garlic
1	t	minced shallot
1	slice	prosciutto (cooked & torn into small pieces)
4	oz	cooked fettuccine
1	each	egg
1	T	tomato (finely diced)
2	T	green peas
1/4	C	Pecorino Romano "snow"
1	each	quail egg
1	sprig	fresh basil

Method:

You can prepare several servings of this dish all at once using a large sauté pan or pot, but making one small serving at a time yields better results. It can be more challenging to prepare the individual servings if you need to make a number of them to serve as one course for a group. But I find that if I get all the ingredients ready in advance, I can prepare multiple servings one after another pretty quickly.

Start by preparing the romano "snow." Using a fine microplane grater, shave a piece of hard Pecorino Romano, place the shavings in an airtight container, and store the container in a cool place.

Heat the olive oil in a large sauté pan over medium heat. Add the garlic and shallots, sweat them in the pan for a few seconds, and then add the torn pieces of prosciutto, stirring until the prosciutto is hot. Add the cooked fettuccine pasta.

If you are using fresh pasta, time its cooking so you can take it directly out of the boiling water and add it to the sauté pan. If you are using dried pasta, you can either take it straight out of the water and put it in the sauté pan or cook and drain the pasta, toss it with a bit of olive oil so it won't stick together, and set it aside in a warm place until it is needed.

(continued on page 103)

(continued from page 102)

Stir the pasta together with the garlic, shallots, and prosciutto, and then remove the pan from the heat. Add about a tablespoon of the leftover pasta water to the pan, and then crack the egg into it.

Quickly stir the egg into the other ingredients, coating the noodles while the residual heat of the pan cooks the egg gently into a creamy sauce. As you stir, move the pan on and off the heat briefly, as necessary, to control the temperature. Too much heat will scramble the egg, and too little heat will leave it raw.

Add the diced tomato and green peas, stir until they are warm, and season the pasta with salt and black pepper. Use tongs to transfer the pasta into a serving bowl, twirling the noodles as you set them down so they pile up nicely.

Place the romano snow in a mound on top of the pasta, and then use a spoon (or your fingertip if you prefer!) to create a small "well" in the mound.

Open the quail egg, and gently separate the yolk, setting the egg white and shell aside. Put the yolk in the well in the romano snow. Garnish the bowl with a small sprig of fresh basil.

The New Scenic Café

seared sea scallops
yield: 4 servings

No matter what the season, the distinctive citrus-chile sauce used in this dish seems to bring with it the aroma of summer. Each serving includes just two scallops, but they are large. And because only one side is seared, the scallops get just the right amount of caramelizing and texture on the outside while remaining rare inside. For the sauce, I use the Japanese chile paste red yuzu kosho and the pungent Japanese yuzu juice, mixed with a bit of orange juice and a few seasonings to create a bright summer flavor. I originally served this dish solely with citrus supremes, but over the years I've added mango, avocado, and a touch of cilantro to bring more body and breadth to the plate. It can be challenging to find a wine pairing that handles both the pungent flavors of the chile paste and yuzu and the acidity of the orange juice, but I find the crisp fruitiness of a Prosecco wine nicely complementary.

Method:

Red Yuzu Kosho Sauce:
  Combine the red yuzu kosho paste, yuzu juice, orange juice concentrate, salt, and brown sugar in a blender. Purée the mixture well, and then let it sit for 5 to 10 minutes to allow the air to work its way out. Stir before using.

Assembly:
  To make the citrus supremes, cut off both ends of the citrus fruits, set each fruit on one of its cut ends, and slice off all of the peel, exposing the fruit. Carefully slice directly alongside the membrane that separates the sections of each fruit. You can then remove perfect wedges of citrus, with no skin or pith attached. Cut the mango and avocado into wedges of similar size.

  Season the scallops with salt and pepper. Add the olive oil to a sauté pan, and heat the pan until it just begins to smoke.

  Carefully place the scallops in the hot pan. They will stick at first, but don't try to pull them off or they will tear. The scallops will release themselves from the pan when they are seared sufficiently.

  Sear the scallops only on one side, until they are medium-brown and crisp. Take the pan off the heat, and flip the scallops over, letting them sit in the pan for a few seconds to warm the bottoms. Remove the scallops from the pan, and set 2 of them on each serving plate.

  Spoon about 1 tablespoon of red yuzo kosho sauce over the top of each pair of scallops, and then add 2 pieces each of orange, blood orange, lime, mango, and avocado. Finish with sprigs of fresh cilantro, and serve.

Ingredients:

Red Yuzu Kosho Sauce:

1	T	red yuzu kosho paste
3/4	C	yuzu juice
4	t	orange juice concentrate
1/2	t	kosher salt
2	t	brown sugar

Other:

24	pieces	citrus supremes (orange, blood orange, & lime)
1	each	mango
1	each	avocado
8	each	sea scallops (U10 size)
2 - 3	T	olive oil
4	sprigs	cilantro

sashimi tuna tacos

yield: 8 tacos (2 servings)

The idea in creating this dish was not so much to grab onto the popularity of tacos as to get sashimi into the hands of guests who might not otherwise have tried it. I sear the tuna so that it is not technically raw, even though it essentially still is. To make the idea of eating such lightly-cooked tuna more palatable to the uninitiated, I include avocado and sesame soy sauce in the dish, which seems to do the trick. I join the tacos with a Thai peanut coleslaw for added body and serve it with sides of pickled ginger and spicy wasabi to deliver a full spectrum of flavors. People come from long distances to enjoy a plate of these tuna tacos and will often call in advance to make sure we have them. I have even gone so far as to put an ad in the local newspapers that says simply, "We've got tacos!"

Ingredients:

Wonton Shells:

| 3 - 4 | C | canola oil |
| 8 | each | wonton wrappers |

Tuna:

| 6 | oz | sashimi grade ahi tuna |

Thai Peanut Slaw:

1	C	red cabbage (shredded)
2	C	green cabbage (shredded)
1	C	napa cabbage (shredded)
1/2	C	carrot (shredded)
1/2	C	cilantro (chopped coarsely)
1/2	C	Thai peanut slaw dressing (p. 371)

Other:

1	each	ripe avocado
8	sprigs	fresh cilantro
2	T	sesame soy sauce (p. 370)
2	T	pickled ginger
2	t	wasabi paste

Method:

Wonton Shells:
You can find baskets specifically made for frying taco shells, but to use them requires a large pot of oil, so they're best for large commercial fryers. At home, fry the shells one at a time in a small pot, and then form them over an object that will hold their shape. A clean wooden dowel or metal rod about 1 inch in diameter works well.

In a small pot, heat the canola oil to 325 degrees. Carefully lay one wonton flat on the surface of the oil, let it fry for a few seconds, and then use a pair of metal tongs to flip it over for another few seconds, until it is very light brown. Pull the wonton out after a total of 8 or 9 seconds.

Quickly lay the wonton at an angle on the dowel or rod, and push the corners down while it is still hot and supple, to form an upside-down triangular taco shape. After it has cooled, it will be crisp, and you can remove it from the rod. Repeat this process with the remaining shells, being sure to check the temperature of the oil before you fry each wonton.

Tuna:
A seasoned, oiled cast-iron pan works great for the tuna, or you can coat a small sauté pan with about a teaspoon of canola oil. Heat the pan to smoking hot, lay the tuna in the pan, and sear it for 10 seconds. Flip it, and sear the other side for another 10 seconds. Remove the tuna from the pan, and use a very sharp knife to slice the tuna as thinly as you can, across the grain.

Thai Peanut Slaw:
Combine the cabbage, carrot, cilantro, and Thai slaw dressing in a bowl, and mix evenly.

Assembly:
Split the avocado in half, remove the pit, scoop out the flesh, and slice it thinly. Divide the tuna and avocado slices evenly among the shells, and line up four filled tacos on each of two serving plates.

Place the slaw in a mound alongside the tacos, and garnish the slaw with sprigs of fresh cilantro. Pour a bit of sesame soy sauce over each taco, and serve the dish with sides of pickled ginger and wasabi paste.

sashimi tuna

yield: 4 servings

This starter shares some similarities in flavor with our café's signature tuna tacos, but its simple elegance elevates the sashimi tuna a step further. I place mashed avocado in a clean line along the middle of a serving plate and add a crisp sesame tuile to create a "shelf." On top, I place diced raw tuna that has been tossed with wasabi paste and sesame soy sauce, add a layer of citrus supremes, and finish with a few leaves of micro cilantro. The combination of the umami of the avocado, the crunch of the tuile, the brightness of the citrus, and the tangy flavor of the wasabi and soy on the tuna make this a New Scenic Café favorite. The construction is the challenge with this dish, but it is worth the effort for what is another wonderful way to present sashimi tuna.

Ingredients:

Sesame Tuile:

8	oz	butter (softened)
1 1/8	C	all-purpose flour
2	T	granulated sugar
1/2	T	kosher salt
4	each	egg whites
1/4	t	sesame oil
1/2	C	sesame seeds (black & white)

Other:

24	pieces	citrus supremes (orange, grapefruit, & lime)
8	oz	sashimi grade ahi tuna
1	t	wasabi paste
1	T	sesame soy sauce (p. 370)
2	each	avocados
1/4	C	micro cilantro

Method:

Sesame Tuile:

Make the tuiles in advance, and keep them in an airtight container. You will need to make a stencil that you can use to shape the tuiles. A clean sheet of thin cardboard works for a one-time use; plastic works great if you want to reuse the form. (Plastic that is 1 millimeter thick works best. I simply cut my stencil out of a semi-rigid lid from a plastic box.) To make yours, cut out as many long rectangle shapes as will fit on your sheet, each about 1 inch by 5 inches.

Using an electric mixer, whip the butter until its texture is smooth and similar to mayonnaise.

In a separate bowl, combine the flour, sugar, and salt, and then add the egg whites and sesame oil. Beat them together for 1 minute on medium speed, using the electric mixer's paddle attachment. Continue to blend on medium speed while adding the whipped butter into the egg mixture in small amounts. Refrigerate the finished batter until it is firm—about 30 minutes.

Preheat the oven to 300 degrees. Lay the stencil on a baking sheet that has been lined with a silicone baking mat. Using a small, thin offset metal spatula, spread the tuile batter into the cut-outs, scraping it so that it is even and the same thickness as the stencil sheet.

Coat each rectangle with sesame seeds, and peel up the stencil carefully. Put the sheet pan in the oven, and bake the tuiles for about 5 minutes, until they are golden brown. Remove the pan from the oven. Use a spatula to transfer each tuile to a flat surface to cool before handling them further. (You might want to make extra tuiles, in case any break when you assemble the dish.)

Assembly:

To make the citrus supremes, cut off both ends of the citrus fruits, set each fruit on one of its cut ends, and slice off all of the peel, exposing the fruit. Carefully slice directly alongside the membrane that separates the sections of each fruit. You can then remove perfect wedges of citrus, with no skin or pith attached.

(continued on page 109)

The New Scenic Café

(continued from page 108)

Cut the tuna into 1/4-inch cubes. Mix it in a bowl with the wasabi paste and sesame soy sauce.

Cut each avocado in half, remove the pits, and scoop out the flesh. Then chop the avocados into approximately 1/4-inch pieces. Place the avocado chunks in a small bowl, season it with salt and pepper, and mash it lightly with a fork.

In the center of each plate, create a line of mashed avocado about 1 inch wide by 5 inches long by 1 inch tall. Set a sesame tuile, with its sesame seeds facing up, on top of the avocado, and gently press it down to secure and level it, taking care as you work because the tuiles are fragile.

Cover the top of the tuile with enough raw tuna to match the line of avocado, making sure to reserve enough tuna for the other servings. Lay 5 or 6 pieces of citrus across the tuna, and garnish it with fresh cilantro. Repeat this process until you have assembled all four portions, and serve.

two-egg omelet

yield: 4 servings

This beaten-egg omelet brings together the bright red of roasted bell pepper, the savory spiciness of North African lamb Merguez sausage, and the creaminess of goat cheese. For the roasted red peppers, either purchase good-quality canned peppers or roast your own at home (page 370). I cook each omelet in a nonstick pan, folding it over in a classic tri-fold and serving it with a side salad and roasted sweet potatoes. One omelet can make a nice shared starter for two people, but most often I serve the full omelet as a dish for one. The salad with vinaigrette and the starch of the sweet potatoes give this omelet starter a warm, summery feel.

Ingredients:

Sweet Potatoes:

4	each	fingerling sweet potatoes
2	T	olive oil

Omelets:

8	each	eggs
4	T	milk

Other:

4	oz	Merguez sausage (p. 368)
1/2	C	roasted red bell peppers (cut into thin strips, p. 370)
1/2	C	goat cheese (chevre)
2	T	basil pesto (p. 362)
2	C	mixed field greens
1 - 2	T	vinaigrette

Method:

Sweet Potatoes:
Preheat the oven to 225 degrees. Coat the sweet potatoes with 1 tablespoon of olive oil, and season them with salt and pepper. Lay the potatoes on a sheet pan, and roast them for about 20 to 25 minutes, or until you can poke a knife easily through their centers. Allow the sweet potatoes to cool, and then cut each one into 3 to 4 small pieces.

Omelets:
It can be a challenge to make all four omelets and serve them at the same time, but I find that if I prepare all the ingredients in advance, the omelets come together quite easily.

Heat one small pan with the crumbled Merguez sausage and roasted red bell pepper strips side-by-side, leaving them warming on low heat. Heat a non-stick, 8-inch sauté pan over medium-low heat. Spray it lightly with pan release to be sure your eggs will not stick.

Crack 2 eggs into a bowl, add 1 tablespoon of milk, and beat them with a fork or small whisk, counting to 80 strokes to be sure they are mixed thoroughly. Leave the sauté pan sitting flat on the stove, and pour the beaten eggs into the pan slowly so that they do not splash up the sides.

Do not stir the eggs or tilt the pan. When the eggs are just cooked through, remove the pan from the heat, and in a line across the middle of the omelet spread about 1 ounce of Merguez sausage and 5 to 6 slices of red pepper. Crumble a few pieces of goat cheese over the top.

Slide a heat-proof rubber spatula underneath one side of the omelet, carefully fold that side partway over the top, and then gently lift the folded edge and roll it over once more. (Picture folding a letter into thirds.) Slide the omelet out of the pan and onto the center of a plate, with the seam still facing down.

Assembly:
Crumble 1 tablespoon of goat cheese over the omelet, and spoon 1 teaspoon of pesto on top. Heat a small sauté pan with the olive oil, and brown the cut sides of the sweet potatoes. Dress the greens lightly with vinaigrette. Place a handful of greens on one side of each omelet and 3 to 4 pieces of sweet potato (the equivalent of one fingerling) on the other side.

smoked salmon filo cigars

yield: 4 servings

Not to be mistaken for the filo "cigarettes" with osetra caviar (page 68), these are a larger version of filo "cigars" that I fill with creamy mousse made of smoked salmon and soft cheese. Using smoked fish allows me to extend the longevity of that ingredient into the off season. In the "shoulder" seasons of spring and autumn, I like to take advantage of savory smoked fish in dishes such as this, while in the summer I prefer to work with fresh fish. When mixing the mousse, I add potato flakes, which keeps it creamy yet solid enough to remain tidily inside the filo. I roll the "cigars" and fill them with the salmon mousse. Then just before serving, I brush them lightly with butter, dust them with nutritional yeast flakes, and bake them until they are crisp. Over their tops, I put flecks of smoked salmon and salmon roe and then finish the plate with a salad of microgreens and a sprinkle of apple cider gastrique. This dish works wonderfully with an aperitif or as a nice finish to a meal.

Method:

Smoked Salmon Mousse:
Allow the Boursin and cream cheese to soften at room temperature for 15 to 20 minutes before mixing. Combine the cheeses, dried thyme, truffle oil, and sugar in the bowl of an electric mixer. Using a paddle attachment, whip them on high speed for 5 minutes.

Turn off the mixer, crumble in the smoked salmon, and whip the mixture on medium speed for 30 seconds, until the salmon is broken apart but is still in visible pieces. Transfer the salmon mousse to 2 small ziplock bags, and cut off about 1/2 inch from one corner of each bag.

Cigars:
You can prepare the "cigars" a couple of hours ahead of time and refrigerate them. Preparing them too far in advance, though, can cause the filo to become soggy. Be sure to work quickly with the filo, keeping any dough you are not using wrapped tightly so it does not become dry.

Lay 5 individual layers of filo on top of each other on a flat work surface. Using one of the ziplock bags of salmon mousse, squeeze out a generous line of mousse about 5 inches long, across the center of the filo. Roll one edge of the filo dough tightly up over the mousse, and continue to roll it like a cigar, keeping the seam on the bottom when you have finished.

Crimp the ends of the "cigar" with your fingers, pinching them so they look like the ends of candy wrappers. Repeat this process to create a total of 8 "cigars," and lay them on a sheet pan.

Assembly:
Preheat the oven to 350 degrees. Brush the tops of the "cigars" with butter, and sprinkle them with nutritional yeast flakes. Bake them for 7 to 8 minutes, until they are golden brown.

Remove the pan from the oven, and set 2 "cigars" side by side in the centers of 4 plates. Crumble about 1 ounce of salmon over each pair of "cigars," and spoon 10 to 12 pieces of salmon roe on top. Add a small bunch of microgreens to each, finishing with a light drizzle of cider gastrique.

Ingredients:

Smoked Salmon Mousse:

5	oz	Boursin soft cheese
3 1/2	oz	cream cheese
1	T	potato flakes
1/2	t	dried thyme
1/2	t	white truffle oil
1	t	granulated sugar
3	oz	smoked salmon

Cigars:

40	pieces	filo dough (cut 6" by 8")
1/4	C	melted butter
2	T	nutritional yeast flakes

Other:

4	oz	smoked salmon
1	oz	salmon roe
1	C	microgreens
2	T	apple cider gastrique (p. 362)

sweet corn flan

yield: 4 to 6 servings

This starter blends fresh sweet corn with a bit of shallot, yellow bell pepper, cream, egg yolks, and spices, in a dish I first created as one small part of an entrée. Over time, I began serving it on its own, its simple beauty accentuated and the natural sugars in its ingredients giving the flan a beautiful, silky texture. I cover the flan base with fresh chanterelles that I sauté lightly with shallot and garlic and then finish with sweet corn kernels, tomato, Spanish chorizo, and a sprig of fresh cilantro. This is a wonderful late-summer dish, when fresh chanterelles are available and the corn crop is good.

Ingredients:

Sweet Corn Flan:

1/2	t	cumin seeds
2	t	olive oil
1	C	sweet corn kernels
1	T	minced shallot
1	t	minced garlic
1/2	each	yellow bell pepper (diced)
1/4	t	turmeric
1/2	t	brown sugar
1/2	T	kosher salt
1	pinch	white pepper
1/2	t	white truffle oil
1/2	C	heavy cream
3	each	egg yolks

Other:

2	T	butter
2	C	chanterelle mushrooms
2	T	minced shallot
1	T	minced garlic
1	C	sweet corn kernels
1/4	C	tomato (diced)
1/4	C	Spanish chorizo (diced finely)
8	sprigs	fresh cilantro

Method:

Sweet Corn Flan:

You can make the flans just prior to serving them, or you can make them in advance and keep them in the refrigerator. If you make them in advance, be sure to allow the flans to warm to room temperature for 30 minutes before you deliver them to the table.

Place the cumin seeds in a small sauté pan, and heat them over low heat, stirring them frequently, until the seeds are toasted lightly. Take them out of the pan, and allow them to cool.

Heat the olive oil in a large sauté pan over medium heat. Sauté the corn, shallot, garlic, and yellow bell pepper until they are soft and translucent.

Add the ground cumin, turmeric, brown sugar, kosher salt, pepper, and truffle oil to the sauté pan. Then add the heavy cream, and continue to heat the mixture until it just comes to a low boil. Transfer it to a blender, and purée the mixture until it is creamy and smooth.

In a bowl, whisk the egg yolks by hand until they lighten in color and thicken slightly. "Temper" the yolks by pouring the blended hot cream mixture slowly into the beaten yolks, whisking steadily as you pour. Strain the mixture through a fine mesh strainer, and discard the solids.

Preheat the oven to 300 degrees. Spray 4 to 6 small ceramic, oven-safe ramekins with pan release, and then dust them with flour. Pour the flan batter into the ramekins, and place them in a baking pan that is deeper than the height of the ramekins. Pour enough hot water into the larger baking pan to fill halfway up the ramekins' sides.

Cover the baking pan with aluminum foil, and poke small holes throughout the foil to vent the steam. Carefully place the baking pan in the oven, and bake the flans until they are firm and a knife inserted near their center comes out clean. The length of baking time will vary depending on the size of the ramekins and how many you are baking. Check the flans every 10 minutes.

(continued on page 113)

(continued from page 112)

Remove the baking pan from the oven, and remove the flans from the pan, allowing them to cool for at least 15 minutes before handling them.

Assembly:
Using your fingertips, carefully coax the outer edge of each flan away from the side of the ramekin all the way around, and then tip it upside down to release the flan into your hand. The flan should release on its own or when shaken very gently. If needed, you can also run a knife around the outside to help release the flans. Place each flan in the center of a plate.

Heat a sauté pan over medium heat, and add the butter. Add the chanterelles, and sauté them until they soften and begin to brown.

Add the minced shallots and garlic, and sauté them until they are soft. Then add the corn, and cook the mixture, stirring regularly until it is hot. At the end, stir in the tomato and Spanish chorizo.

Spoon this sauté mixture over the top of each flan, and garnish the dish with sprigs of fresh cilantro.

warmed black mission figs

yield: 2 to 4 servings (1 portion)

This simple yet rich and tasty dish is the number one or two most requested appetizer on my menus. I warm fresh black mission figs and toasted walnuts in browned butter maple sauce and then pour that mixture over a wedge of creamy Danish blue cheese, garnishing the plate with fresh sage leaves and serving it with toasted ciabatta bread. This starter is quick to prepare yet offers great depth of flavor.

Method:

Browned Butter Maple Sauce:

Add the butter to a medium sauce pan, and place it over medium heat. Stirring frequently, heat the butter until the milk solids turn a light- to medium-brown color.

Allow the butter to cool for about 5 minutes before adding the maple syrup. Bring the mixture to a boil, and then remove the pot from the heat, but leave it in the pot. As the sauce cools, use a whisk to stir it frequently until it is evenly combined.

You will use only 1/4 cup of the sauce for a single portion of this dish, but the rest can be stored in the refrigerator for later use.

Assembly:

Cut the black mission figs into quarters (or sixths or eighths if they are large). Place them in a cold sauté pan, along with the toasted walnuts and browned butter maple sauce.

Warm the figs gently over medium heat until they are warmed through but not cooked, tossing the figs and nuts gently in the sauce to coat them.

In the center of a small bowl, stand a wedge of Danish blue cheese on end. Carefully spoon the figs and walnuts around the outside of the cheese, and pour the remaining sauce over the top.

Garnish the plate with a couple of fresh sage leaves, and serve it with warm slices of toasted ciabatta bread.

Ingredients:

Browned Butter Maple Sauce:

1	C	butter
1 1/4	C	pure maple syrup

Other:

4 - 6	each	fresh black mission figs
1/4	C	toasted walnuts
2	oz	Danish blue cheese
2	each	fresh sage leaves
4	slices	sourdough ciabatta (p. 285)

corn masa tamale

yield: 8 servings

Ingredients:

Tamales:

2	C	corn masa harina
1	t	kosher salt
1	pinch	ground coriander
1	T	ground cumin
1/2	t	dark chili powder
1/4	t	cayenne pepper
2/3	C	vegetable shortening
2	t	minced garlic
2	T	water
1/4	C	red onion
1	T	cilantro
2	C	corn kernels
1/2	C	brown sugar

Other:

20	each	dried corn husks (soaked overnight)
2	each	bell pepper (mixed colors)
1	each	poblano pepper
1	each	tomato
1	C	chocolate mole (p. 364)
24	each	shrimp (tails on)
2	t	olive oil
1/2	C	cilantro beurre monté (p. 364)
1/2	bunch	cilantro

In my early days as a chef, I fell in love with the cuisine and culture of Mexico's Oaxacan region and the cooking of such masters as Rick Bayless and Diana Kennedy. This tamale starter originated from that love of all things Oaxacan, although I do not take a strictly classic approach to creating it. My goal is to start with the essence of the classic tamale and take it in a different direction. I get a lot of positive feedback about this dish, but I also get a few negative remarks because my version of the tamale is not what some people expect. A traditional tamale is moist and sticky. I make it more like a light and fluffy baked potato, cutting shortening and spices into the mix and adding a little water. After steaming the tamales, I set them on a pool of chocolate mole, which is a chile sauce of Oaxacan origin with nuts, seeds, and bittersweet chocolate. To brighten the dish, I serve it with shrimp that I sauté and coat with bright green cilantro beurre monté. I add a "confetti" of bell and poblano peppers and some cool, ripe tomato pieces and finish the plate with a touch of fresh cilantro.

Method:

Note that the dried corn husks need to be soaked in water overnight to make them soft and easy to work with, so you will want to plan ahead.

Tamales:

Combine the masa harina, salt, coriander, cumin, chili powder, and cayenne pepper in a food processor. In small amounts, and using quick pulses with the processor to combine the ingredients, add the shortening and garlic. (Be sure to keep the shortening as cold as possible while you work.) Add the water, and pulse it a few times again. The mixture should be slightly moist yet light, like the texture of damp sand. It should barely stick together when pressed.

Dice the red onion into small pieces, and chop the cilantro finely. Combine them with the corn kernels and brown sugar, and then mix them by hand into the masa mixture.

Lay one larger size corn husk on a work surface so it curls up like a bowl. If the husks are smaller, overlap 2 or 3 husks so they are large enough to wrap the whole tamale.

Take another, smaller piece of corn husk, and tear it into "strings" about 1/4 inch wide. (You will need a total of 16 strings, but make a few extra in case some break.)

Place 2/3 cup of filling in the center of the husk. Wrap the sides up, and overlap them over the top. Crimp one end of the roll, and tie one of the corn husk "strings" around it to hold it closed.

(continued on page 117)

(continued from page 116)

Lift the tamale and tip it up, so the filling settles toward the end that is already tied. Fold and crimp the second end, taking care not to squeeze the filling. Lay the tamale down, and tie a string around the second end. Repeat this process to prepare the other tamales.

Assembly:
Dice the bell and poblano peppers very finely, and mix them together into a "confetti." Cut the tomato into a small dice.

Place the tamales in the basket of a steamer, and steam them, covered, for about 10 minutes, until they are hot all the way through. I use a simple bamboo steamer over a pot of boiling water.

While the tamales are steaming, put the chocolate mole in a small pot, and begin warming it on low heat. Season the shrimp with salt and pepper, and sauté them in the olive oil. After they are cooked, add the cilantro beurre monté to the warm pan, and toss the shrimp to coat them.

In the center of each plate, spoon about 2 tablespoons of warm chocolate mole. Set one tamale in the center of the mole. Using a knife, cut a slit lengthwise down the center of the tamale, spread it open like a baked potato, and use a fork to "fluff" the tamale's filling.

Arrange 3 shrimp on top of each tamale, and sprinkle some of the pepper "confetti" over the top, scattering a few pieces of tomato around the outside. Finish the dish with a couple sprigs of fresh cilantro.

The New Scenic Café

curried blue mussels

yield: 1 to 2 servings (1 portion)

For this dish, I use a whole pound of blue mussels, which are smaller than some other varieties and an easier introduction to mussels for those who are not accustomed to them. You'll find this recipe works well, though, with whatever kind of mussels you prefer. I originally did the traditional French classic, "mussels marinière," but because one of my goals is to stretch the boundaries of the classics, I decided to depart from the wine and herbs used in that recipe to something a bit more robust and contemporary, and this dish is the result. For the sauce, I use red curry sweetened with apple cider, adding heavy cream to smooth it and give it some viscosity so the sauce will hold to the mussels. The sauce garners rave reviews, although people often tell me they can't say exactly why they love it. Perhaps it's the East Indian flavor of the curry. Or maybe the "X factor" is the apple cider, which softens the sauce and adds a sense of sweetness and perhaps even familiarity to it. I finish the mussels with a touch of cilantro and serve it with thick slices of toasted ciabatta that have been drizzled with olive oil and sprinkled with black pepper. Many of our guests tell me they come to the New Scenic Café just for a plate of our curried blue mussels.

Method:

Put the mussels in a large pot or pan. It's best to use something shallow, like a large sauté pan, so the sauce will reduce faster. (A deeper pot works equally well but requires more time.)

Add a couple tablespoons of water to the pan, put a lid over it, and place it on medium-high heat. Steam the mussels until all of them open. Discard any mussels that do not open or that have broken shells.

Remove the lid, and continue cooking the mussels a few more minutes, allowing some of the moisture to evaporate. When only a couple of tablespoons of liquid remain in the pan, tilt the pan toward you, so that the liquid pools along the edge of the pan directly in front of you.

Add the curry paste, and stir it into the liquid to dissolve it. Add the apple cider and heavy cream, stir to mix all of the ingredients, and return the pan to the heat.

Cook the mussels until the sauce reduces, thickens, and then starts to darken in color. Toss the mussels in the sauce to coat them. Toast the ciabatta, drizzle olive oil over it, and dust it with black pepper.

Pour the mussels and any remaining sauce into a serving bowl. Garnish the mussels with a few sprigs of fresh cilantro, and serve them with the warm slices of toasted ciabatta.

Ingredients:

1	lb	blue mussels
1	t	mild red curry paste
1/2	C	apple cider
1/4	C	heavy cream
2 - 4	slices	sourdough ciabatta (p. 285)
2	T	olive oil
4	sprigs	cilantro

taleggio fondue

yield: serves 2 to 4 (1 portion)

Taleggio is a soft cow's milk cheese from Italy, with a flavor that is unparalleled and an aroma you won't soon forget! It has a vegetable wash on the outside that acts as a brine, and as this cheese goes through the aging process it becomes quite pungent. I would even go so far as to say it stinks. The first time I made Taleggio fondue for guests was for a catering event, where it was a huge hit but somewhat of a shock to the nose and a real topic of conversation. At the New Scenic Café, I offer this fondue in the fall and early winter, and many guests tell me they look forward to its return and come in just to order it. Truth be told, when a guest is enjoying a Taleggio fondue I have even seen people at the next table lean back in their chairs seemingly to investigate whether the guest behind them has a problem with personal hygiene. I have had to explain that it is actually the fondue they smell, which as some people say, "stinks so good." This dish goes great with a fall beer and also pairs well with a wide variety of wines. I often enjoy cooking it for myself at home. After all, what more could one ask for than delicious toasted bread, a glass of wine or beer, and stinky cheese.

Ingredients:

4	oz	Taleggio cheese
1/2	C	heavy cream
2 - 3	C	assorted bread
		(cut into 1-inch cubes)

Method:

Preheat the oven to 400 degrees.

I leave the rind on the Taleggio cheese because it has the most intense flavor. But if you prefer a more mild taste, slice off the rind before you begin. Cut the Taleggio into small pieces, and put them in a cold sauté pan. Add the heavy cream, and place the pan over low heat. Allow the cheese and cream to melt slowly—it will take about 10 minutes—and stir occasionally to ensure the heat is distributed evenly.

At the Café, we make croutons out of the end pieces of all of our loaves of sandwich bread, so we regularly have on hand a mix of cranberry pecan, dark raisin rye, 3-seed sourdough, and ciabatta breads. For your croutons, cut whatever good breads you like best into 1-inch cubes.

Spread the bread cubes on a baking sheet, and toast them in the oven until they just begin to brown but are still soft.

If you have a fondue pot, pour the cheese mixture into it to keep the cheese warm. If not, simply pour the fondue into a bowl, and serve it with the toasted croutons for dipping. (You can use small dinner forks instead of fondue forks if you like—they'll work just fine.). Enjoy the Taleggio fondue quickly while the cheese is creamy and hot!

The New Scenic Café

artichoke slather

yield: 6 to 8 servings

Back in the 1990s, while working in other restaurants I enjoyed creating unique versions of standard dips—out of spinach, shrimp, or artichokes. This artichoke dip is one of my favorites. It focuses on the dominant flavor of young asiago cheese, which works well because it doesn't get oily and stays nice and soft. To the ever-popular artichoke hearts, I add sun-dried tomatoes, herbs, garlic, and a bit of mayonnaise and then pack the mixture into a small baking dish and bake it for about 10 minutes. It comes out steaming hot, the cheese melted and deliciously browned. People love to slather this dip on the crusty, toasted baguette I serve it with—hence, the name "artichoke slather." Over the years, the name has stuck, and my guests have continued to enjoy this flavorful, cheesy dish.

Ingredients:

1/2	C	sun-dried tomatoes
4	oz	shredded asiago cheese
1	t	dried chives
1/2	t	dried thyme leaves
1/4	C	mayonnaise
1	pinch	crushed red pepper
1/4	t	minced garlic
22	oz	canned artichoke hearts (quartered)
1	whole	sliced baguette (p. 274) (or flat bread or crackers)

Method:

Cut the sun-dried tomatoes into thin strips.

Place the sun-dried tomato strips and all of the other ingredients except the artichoke hearts into the bowl of an electric mixer. Using a dough hook or a paddle attachment, mix the ingredients on low speed for about 30 seconds, until they are combined evenly.

Drain any excess liquid out of the artichoke hearts. Add them to the mixing bowl, and mix the ingredients on low speed for another 30 seconds. Turn the mixer off, and use a spatula to stir all the way to the bottom of the bowl to be sure all the ingredients are mixed evenly. Refrigerate the mixture for at least 1 hour.

For small portions, place the artichoke mixture in small ceramic dishes, filling each with about 8 ounces. Or you can put the entire mixture in a ceramic quiche or pie pan to serve a larger group of people. Return it to the refrigerator until you are ready to bake it.

Preheat the oven to 300 degrees, and bake the "slather" for 10 to 15 minutes or until the top is lightly browned and the mixture is hot and melted all the way through (larger portions will require longer baking time). Serve the dip hot, with toasted slices of baguette, flat bread, or crackers.

Salads

The New Scenic Café

The New Scenic Café

raw vegetables

yield: 4 servings

Because most of the food we eat has been transformed from its original state, the simplicity and honesty of raw food can offer a pleasing surprise. It might sound simple to create a dish of raw ingredients. But I find that their unaltered state makes it necessary for each aspect of the dish to be perfect. In this salad, I use several root vegetables and slice them very thin, holding them in ice water to crisp them and stop them from oxidizing. I layer the slices with a bit of acai vinaigrette and add broccolini tops, wild blueberries and fresh English peas pulled from the pods. I also add golden raisins, which work particularly well with the fruity açaí vinaigrette, though any dried fruit combines with it well. I have used sliced cauliflower and broccoli before, but these days I prefer the broccolini. The result is a crunchy salad that brings in both sweetness and acidity. This dish works wonderfully on a summer day and pairs especially well with a sparkling Rosé wine.

Method:

Açaí Vinaigrette:
> Put all the ingredients except the oil, berries, and golden raisins in a blender, and purée them until they are smooth. Then with the blender running on low speed, add the oil slowly to emulsify the mixture.

> Turn off the blender, and add the berries. Pulse the blender a few times to blend the berries in until the ingredients are smooth. Stir in the golden raisins by hand. Store the vinaigrette in the refrigerator.

Assembly:
> Using a mandoline slicer, slice the radishes, beets, and carrots into wafer-thin discs. As you finish slicing each type of vegetable, place the slices in a separate small bowl of ice water. Cut the tops off the broccolini (and save the stems if you like, to use in a soup or other dish). Slice the blueberries in half.

> On 4 plates, begin layering the sliced vegetables, shaking off as much water as you can before placing them on the plate. After you have layered 4 to 5 slices of one vegetable, begin layering another. After every two layers, pour 1 to 2 teaspoons of açaí vinaigrette over the slices.

> Continue layering the vegetables and the vinaigrette until you use all of the vegetable slices, and then top them with the broccolini, blueberries, and English peas. Finish with salt and black pepper, garnishing as you prefer—I like to use micro flowers and fresh garlic scapes when they are available. Serve the salad immediately, while the vegetables are deliciously cold and crisp.

Ingredients:

Açaí Vinaigrette:

1	T	ginger root (peeled & minced)
1	T	garlic (minced)
2	T	shallots (minced)
1	C	champagne vinegar
1	T	orange juice concentrate
1/3	C	brown sugar
1/2	t	dried thyme
1/2	t	dried tarragon
1 1/2	T	cream sherry
3/4	C	açaí juice
1 1/4	C	grapeseed or canola oil
1	C	raspberries & blueberries
1/3	C	golden raisins

Other:

3	each	breakfast radishes
1/2	each	watermelon radish
6	each	baby beets (red, gold, & Chioggia)
3	each	baby heirloom carrots
2	pieces	broccolini
1/2	C	fresh blueberries
1/2	C	English peas

pistachio-crusted goat cheese

yield: 4 servings

Back in 1999, this pistachio-crusted goat cheese salad was the very first item on the New Scenic Café menu. It has never left the menu since, and considering its enduring popularity I do not think it ever will! (At one point, I even considered changing the name of the Scenic to the Pistachio Café.) This is an easy approach to the classic French-style green salad that has not changed much in its lifetime at the Scenic. The only change has been the choice of vinaigrette. I began with a roasted garlic vinaigrette, moved to an elephant garlic vinaigrette, and now use a bright and lively red wine vinaigrette. To build the salad, I first create "coins" out of the goat cheese by letting it soften, scooping out balls, pressing the balls into finely-ground pistachios, and then refrigerating them. Coating the balls allows me to later warm the cheese without completely melting it. And pistachios have a subtle, peppery hue that is attractive and combines beautifully with the creamy goat cheese. I toss the greens with the red wine vinaigrette, put a portion on a serving plate, place two goat cheese coins atop the greens, and finish with sliced grape tomatoes and fresh cracked black pepper. This salad goes wonderfully with fresh, hot slices of baguette.

Ingredients:

12	oz	soft goat cheese (chevre)
1	C	pistachios (finely ground)
10	oz	spring greens
3	oz	red wine vinaigrette (p. 369)
20	each	grape tomatoes
2	T	olive oil

Method:

You'll want to prepare the goat cheese "coins" ahead of time and keep them in the refrigerator for at least 30 minutes, until just before you use them.

To make the coins, allow the goat cheese to soften to room temperature, and then use an ice cream scoop or melon baller to scoop out eight 1 1/2-ounce balls.

Put the ground pistachios on a plate or other flat surface, and press the softened goat cheese balls into the pistachios, coating each one completely. Shape the balls into slightly-flattened coins that are roughly 2 inches wide and 1/2 inch thick. Refrigerate them for at least 30 minutes or until they are cold and firm all the way through.

In a mixing bowl, gently toss the spring greens with just enough red wine vinaigrette to lightly coat the leaves. Place the dressed greens on 4 large plates, mounding them in the center.

Slice the grape tomatoes in half, season them lightly with salt and black pepper, and on each plate scatter the tomatoes around the outside of the greens.

Put a sauté pan on medium-high heat, and add the olive oil. Carefully place the goat cheese coins in the hot oil, making sure the pan is not crowded and the coins are not touching. (You can sauté them in 2 or 3 batches if necessary.)

Sauté the coins for 1 to 2 minutes, until they are golden brown, and then flip them over. Cook them for another minute, and remove them from the pan. Place two coins on top of each dressed salad, and finish with fresh cracked black pepper. Serve the salads immediately, while the goat cheese is hot and creamy.

smoked salmon

yield: 4 servings

This was the second salad I put on the New Scenic Café menu, back when we first opened in 1999. To this day, I offer it as a special, its flavorful combination of soft and creamy Boursin cheese and freshly smoked salmon making it a perennial favorite. And offering it allows me to do something I try to accomplish often: bringing another small business together with the New Scenic Café so we can share with our customers the stories of our food creations. In this case, it's Northern Waters Smokehaus, located in Duluth, whose delicious smoked salmon takes this salad to a whole new level. I toss the mixed baby spring greens with the roasted garlic vinaigrette, mound the greens on serving plates, and scatter sliced grape tomatoes around the greens. Then I crumble the Boursin cheese and smoked salmon over the greens and finish with fresh cracked black pepper. Even if you don't have Northern Waters' smoked salmon on hand, you'll find most any smoked fish will combine beautifully with these ingredients.

Method:

In a large mixing bowl, gently toss the spring greens with the roasted garlic vinaigrette.

Place the greens on 4 large dinner plates, mounding them nicely in the center.

Slice the grape tomatoes in half, season them with a bit of kosher salt and cracked black pepper, and scatter them around the perimeter of the greens.

Divide the Boursin cheese and smoked salmon evenly, and then crumble them over the greens. Finish the salad with a dusting of fresh cracked black pepper.

Ingredients:

10	oz	*mixed baby spring greens*
3	oz	*roasted garlic vinaigrette (p. 370)*
20	each	*grape tomatoes*
5	oz	*Boursin soft cheese*
8	oz	*smoked salmon*

tomato & chorizo

yield: 4 servings

I've created several renditions of this salad over the years, from simple to complex, but this version remains my favorite. Its high acidity awakens the palate. And it is an example of how challenging yet rewarding it can be to offer food that is "simple" yet exhibits culinary artistry and is unique and appetizing. In complex dishes, lesser-quality ingredients, preparation errors, and visual flaws can remain more easily hidden. But in simple dishes, the high-quality ingredients stand out, as does the handling of those ingredients. I always think of this summer salad as having a Spanish "soul," with its Spanish chorizo and Idiazabal cheese, which is a Spanish cheese made from sheep's milk that has a subtle smokiness and blends well with the chorizo.

Over time, I found I needed to cut the spice of the mustard seeds used in this salad, so I added sherry vinaigrette to mellow the favors. And most recently, I added the fresh flavor of cucumber, via a trendy and scientific culinary process called "spherification," which I've looked forward to bringing to the home kitchen. It's easy to identify all the other ingredients in this salad—one can see the tomatoes, the sausage, and the cheese, for instance—but the final touch I add is cucumber in the form of gelatin "pearls" that I create through spherification. I purée the cucumber, season it, add gelatin, and then use an eye dropper to drop the cucumber mixture into a cold bath of olive oil. Small droplets of cucumber liquid form and solidify in the cold oil, creating pearls or "caviar" of cucumber. I strain the cucumber spheres out of the oil and drop them in clusters around the outside of the salad, their bright green contrasting nicely with the red on the plate This dish pairs well with a crisp summer white wine, a rosé wine, or a light pilsner or nut brown beer.

Ingredients:

2 - 3	each	heirloom tomatoes (variety)
12	each	grape tomatoes
4	each	pear tomatoes
2	oz	cream sherry vinaigrette (p. 365)
1	oz	mustard seed mix (p. 368)
2	oz	Spanish chorizo sausage
2	oz	Idiazabal cheese
1/4	C	cucumber pearls (p. 365)
1/4	C	micro cilantro leaves

Method:

This salad has little resting time from preparation to serving, so you'll want to make the cream sherry vinaigrette, mustard seed mix, and cucumber pearls in advance. Also keep all the ingredients chilled until you are ready to use them. And keep your serving plates ready so you can begin assembling the individual salads as you prepare each ingredient.

Cut the heirloom tomatoes into roughly 3/4-inch pieces. Slice the grape and pear tomatoes in half, and place all the tomatoes in a small mixing bowl. Toss the tomatoes in the cream sherry vinaigrette and the mustard seed mix, and then place them in equal portions on 4 plates.

Cut the Spanish chorizo sausage in half lengthwise, and then lay each half on the cut side. Crosscut it at a 45-degree angle, creating thin half-moon shapes. Taking the time to cut the sausage so thinly that it is translucent will produce the best results for the finished dish. On each plate, drop the chorizo pieces lightly over the tomatoes.

Cut the cheese into 1/2-inch by 1/2-inch "French fry-like" sticks. Hold 2 or 3 sticks together in one hand, and pull a vegetable peeler across the ends of the sticks to shave the cheese into square, postage-stamp-sized pieces. Scatter the squares over the tomatoes.

Using a spoon, scoop small quantities of cucumber pearls from the oil, dropping clusters around each salad until you've used all the pearls. To finish, sprinkle micro cilantro leaves over the salads, along with a pinch of salt and ground black pepper, and serve immediately.

The New Scenic Café

king crab

yield: 4 servings

Chefs strive for interesting food combinations and textures, and they also enjoy the challenge of building a dish that includes the element of height. I first presented this salad more than a decade ago, with the goal of "lifting" all the components off the plate. At the New Scenic Café, we call this king crab dish the "cappuccino of salads"—meaning that anytime a guest orders it, the pace of production in our kitchen slows. Despite the extra time and effort, though, my staff enjoys creating this dish and our diners love eating it. This salad represents one of the first culinary logistical efforts I undertook that pushed my staff to take cooking and serving fine food to another level of presentation.

I begin with chopped avocados, king crab meat, and a thick slice of tomato and finish with a bouquet of baby greens–including frisée, lolla rosa, red and green lettuce, spinach, arugula, and dandelion greens. The greens spring up and out like a bouquet of flowers from the lively reds, greens, and whites on the plate. And the curry emulsion acts as the "vinaigrette," creating a ring around the rest of the salad. The combination of primary flavors—the flavorful greens, acidic tomato, sweet crab, and savory avocado plus the buttery curry emulsion—creates a rich dish that pairs well with a viognier or a rosé wine. A chardonnay would also complement the varied umami flavors in this salad.

Method:

Curry Emulsion:

In a medium-size pot, combine all the ingredients except the butter. Bring them to a boil, and then reduce the heat and simmer the mixture for 10 minutes. Remove the pot from the heat, and stir in the butter one spoonful at a time, incorporating each spoonful fully before adding the next one. Pour the mixture into a blender, and purée it on high speed until it is smooth. Until you are ready to use it, you can leave the curry mixture in the pot or pour it into a squeeze bottle.

Assembly:

Cut the avocados in half, and remove the pits. Scoop out the avocado using a spoon, and dice each of the four portions of avocado separately. Season each portion with salt and black pepper.

Cut the tomato into 1/2-inch thick slices, and use the tip of a small knife to remove the core. Place a 3-inch ring mold in the center of a plate. Place one portion of the diced avocado in the bottom of the mold, and press it down with the back of a spoon to create an even layer.

Crumble 3 ounces of king crab meat on top of the avocado. Again, press it down to create an even layer. Place one tomato slice on top of the crab, and season it with salt and pepper.

Poke a clean fingertip down through the hole in the tomato slice to create a cavity inside the crab meat. Cluster a mix of about 15 leaves of baby greens, stems down, in one hand, creating a "bouquet." Push the stems of the bouquet carefully through the hole in the tomato slice, down into the cavity in the crab meat.

Lift the ring mold up about 1/2 inch from the plate. Using a spoon or squeeze bottle, distribute the curry emulsion evenly around the outside of the avocado, creating a ring about 2 inches wide. Remove the ring mold gently, and sprinkle the salad with a few chopped chives.

Ingredients:

Curry Emulsion:

14	oz	coconut milk (canned)
4	oz	red vindaloo curry paste
1/3	C	curry powder
1/2	C	vegetable base
1/2	t	minced garlic
1	pinch	dried oregano
1	pinch	dried thyme
1/2	t	paprika
2/3	C	water
4	t	granulated sugar
4	t	Cointreau liqueur
1 1/3	C	butter (room temperature)

Other:

2	each	avocados
2	each	tomatoes (3-inch diameter)
12	oz	king crab meat
60	leaves	mixed baby greens
2	T	chives (chopped)

red & gold beets

yield: 4 servings

Red and gold beets work beautifully in this salad, although at times I have used a variety of beets, depending on what is available and of good quality. And using baby beets does particularly well. They give this dish a dainty look and more sweetness, as compared with the flavor of larger beets, which is good but can sometimes be diluted. When I first looked for an element of acidity to add, I did not think tomato was the right acid, so I tested different fruits, including blackberries, raspberries, and even kumquats. I eventually found that in this dish blueberries are best. They taste great in combination with the other flavors and look attractive. For the fennel mustard vinaigrette, I toast fennel seeds, pulverize them, and then create an emulsion with a number of elements including olive oil, vinegar, and mustard seed. The fresh Ciliegine mozzarella, which is a round mozzarella ball that is smaller in size than a golf ball, fills out the richness of the salad. I toss all the ingredients together, scatter them on a plate, and garnish them with a mixture of microgreens. This salad also serves well as a small plate—like tapas or an amuse bouche—with a small amount on a side dish alongside a couple slices of toasted baguette. This salad pairs nicely with most white wines, handling both sweetness and acidity equally well.

Ingredients:

3	C	roasted red and gold baby beets (p. 369)
1/4	C	fennel mustard vinaigrette (p. 366)
1/2	C	blueberries
1/2	C	fresh Ciliegine mozzarella
1/2	C	mixed microgreens

Method:

Roast and peel the baby beets ahead of time. Then allow them to cool completely in the refrigerator. If they vary in size, cut the smaller beets in half and the larger ones in quarters so that all the pieces are roughly the same size.

In a mixing bowl, toss the beets with the fennel mustard vinaigrette until the beets are coated evenly. Add the blueberries and fresh Ciliegine mozzarella, and toss the ingredients again to coat them.

Spoon the mixture gently onto four small plates or into shallow bowls. Garnish it with microgreens and fresh cracked black pepper.

peach caprese

yield: 4 servings

The traditional caprese salad uses tomato, which is delicious, but in this salad I instead substitute fresh and juicy peach, delivering an unexpected delight to the palate. I remove the skins from the peaches, which can sometimes be tough, leaving only the tender, succulent flesh. And instead of cow's-milk mozzarella, I layer the peach with buffalo mozzarella. It costs more, but buffalo mozzarella offers added flavor that really stands out in this dish. (If you cannot find the buffalo version, cow's-milk mozzarella will work just fine.) I start at the bottom with a layer of peach, add a layer of mozzarella, and continue the layering until I end at the top with peach. To create a "vinaigrette" for the salad, I pour a bit of sharp balsamic vinegar reduction on the plate and dribble walnut oil over the top. This forms a lovely decoration for the plate and also gives the diner the means to deconstruct the dish by rolling bites of peach and mozzarella around in the reduction. With each bite, one can get a piece of the crispy fried basil leaves as well because they crumble easily to the touch. Frying the basil leaves makes them more rigid and transportable, meaning diners do not have to try to cut fresh basil leaves with a knife. The fried basil's translucent appearance also adds a unique visual flair to this elegant plate.

Ingredients:

Fried Basil Leaves:

12	each	fresh basil leaves
1 - 2	C	canola oil
		kosher salt

Other:

4	each	ripe peaches
12	oz	fresh buffalo mozzarella
2	T	balsamic reduction (p. 362)
4	T	walnut oil
1/4	C	toasted walnuts
		coarse sea salt

Method:

Fried Basil Leaves:

Use the freshest basil leaves you can, to ensure they remain bright green after you fry them. In a large sauté pan, heat the canola oil until it just begins to smoke. Hold the basil leaves in one hand. In the other hand, hold a lid that is large enough to cover the sauté pan.

Drop the leaves in the oil, and immediately set the lid on top. The oil will splatter, so the lid will prevent a mess as well as the risk of getting burned. After a few seconds, the splattering will slow down. Remove the lid, and stir the leaves to be sure they are separated.

Use a strainer or pair of tongs to remove the basil leaves from the oil, and set them on a plate covered with a paper towel. While they are hot, sprinkle the leaves with kosher salt. As the basil leaves cool, they will become crisp and will have a beautiful, translucent green appearance.

Assembly:

Begin heating a large pot of water over high heat, and prepare a large ice-water bath.

On the pointed end of each ripe peach, use the tip of a small knife to make 2 shallow cuts in an X pattern on the skin.

After the water has reached a rapid boil, turn off the heat, and lower the peaches gently into the hot water. Allow them to sit in the water for about 45 seconds, and then remove them using a slotted spoon or skimmer.

Place the peaches immediately into the ice-water bath, and allow them to cool completely (about 2 minutes).

(continued on page 139)

(continued from page 138)

Using the score marks cut into each peach as a starting point, pull or rub the skin off of the peaches gently. If the skin does not come off easily, return the peaches to the hot water for another 45 seconds, chill them in the ice water again, and try peeling them.

After each peach is peeled, return it to the ice water for at least 1 minute to prevent it from turning brown.

You will use one peach per serving. Slice the peach one time, horizontally and directly through the center around the pit. Twist the peach slightly to free it from the pit. Discard the pit, and cut the two peach halves into round, 1/4-inch-thick slices.

Cut the fresh buffalo mozzarella into slices that are the same thickness as the peach slices.

Working on a flat surface, make stacks that alternate from peach to mozzarella, starting at the bottom with a slice of peach and finishing at the top with peach. Throughout the process, season each layer of peach and mozzarella lightly with sea salt and black pepper.

Drizzle balsamic reduction on the 4 serving plates in a random, thin line. Place a stack of peach and buffalo mozzarella slices in the center of each plate, and pour a tablespoon of walnut oil over the top of each. Crush a few roasted walnuts in your hand, and sprinkle them on top. Finish each plate with the fried basil leaves and a dusting of sea salt and black pepper.

Salads

The New Scenic Café

mizuna & arugula

yield: 4 servings

During the winter months in northern Minnesota, the lack of sunlight often leaves northerners yearning for the brightness and foods of the warmer seasons. So, winter is perhaps the perfect time to make and enjoy a mizuna and arugula salad, which to me speaks of spring and healthy eating. A centerpiece in the dish is Meyer lemons, which can often be found in specialty grocery stores and food co-ops between December and May. I was introduced to them years ago and was amazed by their flavor. They are a citrus hybrid of lemon and mandarin orange and are native to China. Using them in this dish creates a sweeter, less acidic lemon vinaigrette. For the greens, I combine arugula and mizuna. Arugula is a small, leafy green that has a distinctly peppery and bitter flavor, and baby arugula is particularly tender. Mizuna is similarly peppery, though more mild, and has a beautiful feathery appearance. I have appreciated using both of them separately in other dishes and thought bringing the two together would work well in this salad, along with shaved fennel and fennel fronds and sliced shallots. I grate the Pecorino Romano cheese finely into a "snow" that I distribute equally over the salad, to create a touch of richness and sharpness amidst the citrus flavors, and then finish with toasted pine nuts and candied pepitas.

Method:

Meyer Lemon Vinaigrette:
Zest the lemons, taking care to grate only the colored peels and not the white pith. Then juice the lemons. In a blender, combine the lemon zest and juice with all the other vinaigrette ingredients, and purée them until the mixture is smooth and emulsified. Store the vinaigrette in the refrigerator.

Assembly:
Use a microplane grater to shave a block of Pecorino Romano cheese into a fine "snow." Set the grated cheese aside in a cool and dry location.

For each salad, place 1 cup of baby arugula and 1 cup of mizuna in a mixing bowl, along with 1/4 cup of thinly-shaved fennel, 2 tablespoons of finely-sliced shallots, and 4 to 5 small sprigs of fennel frond. Dress them with 1 1/2 tablespoons of Meyer lemon vinaigrette, tossing the ingredients lightly by hand to coat them.

In the center of each of the 4 serving plates, place one portion of the dressed salad in a raised mound. Garnish the top of each with 1 tablespoon of toasted pine nuts and 1 tablespoon of chopped candied pepitas (candied pumpkin seeds), 2 tablespoons of Pecorino Romano snow, and a dusting of cracked black pepper.

Ingredients:

Meyer Lemon Vinaigrette:

2	each	Meyer lemons (zest and juice)
1	T	minced shallot
1/2	T	minced garlic
1 1/2	T	fresh thyme leaves
1/4	C	white wine vinegar
3/4	C	olive oil
1/2	t	kosher salt
1/2	t	cracked black pepper
2	T	granulated sugar
1/4	t	xanthan gum or guar gum

Salad:

1/2	C	Pecorino Romano cheese (shaved finely into "snow")
4	C	baby arugula
4	C	mizuna
1	C	shaved fennel
1/2	C	sliced shallots
20	each	small fennel fronds
4	T	toasted pine nuts
4	T	candied pepitas (p. 363)

fennel panna cotta

yield: 6 servings

This salad offers a great way to bring both flavor and texture to a dish. It is reminiscent of a classic Waldorf salad and makes for a wonderful fall plate. The fresh fennel delivers the subtle flavor of anise, and the panna cotta incorporates the inviting creaminess of buttermilk. Using the panna cotta as the main body of the salad allows the other elements to serve as flavorful accompaniments. I use a small amount of greens, a sweet ripe pear, creamy Danish blue cheese, and add pear cider gastrique to capture the pear flavor and unify the dish, brightening it with its acidity. The walnuts bring a savory earthiness, and the petite mache adds a mild, nutty flavor. Panna cotta is not a particularly popular item in northern Minnesota, where forays into foods that are custard-like in texture are often reserved for desserts, such as crème brûlée or crème caramel, so it can be challenging to engender true enthusiasm for a savory panna cotta. But I find that this salad, with its combination of subtle flavors and creamy textures, successfully entices even the most reluctant diner. It pairs well with a lively sparkling Moscato d'Asti or with a buttery Chardonnay.

Ingredients:

Fennel Panna Cotta:

2	each	fennel bulbs (with fronds)
2	each	garlic cloves (cut in half)
2	T	butter
2	C	half & half
1	C	buttermilk
1/4	C	Pernod or Anisette liqueur
2	each	whole star anise pods
1	t	kosher salt
1	T	granulated sugar
1	pinch	cracked black pepper
1	C	italian parsley leaves (loosely packed)
1	T	powdered gelatin

Other:

3	each	Bosc pears
1/2	C	toasted walnuts
1/2	C	Danish blue cheese
1 1/2	C	petite mache
1/2	C	pear cider gastrique (p. 368)

Method:

Fennel Panna Cotta:

These will need to set up in the refrigerator overnight, or for a minimum of 6 hours, so plan accordingly.

Cut the stalks and fronds off of the fennel bulbs, pull off all of their bright green frilly fronds, and discard the thick stalks. Set the fronds aside for now. Roughly chop the fennel bulbs into 1-inch pieces, and place them in a large pot along with the halved garlic cloves and the butter.

Put a lid on the pot, and place it on the stove on low heat. Sweat the ingredients for about 15 minutes, stirring them occasionally (and making sure to replace the lid after each stirring) until the fennel and garlic begin to soften. Do not let the pot get so hot that the vegetables begin to caramelize.

After the fennel is soft and somewhat translucent, add the half and half, buttermilk, liqueur, whole star anise pods, kosher salt, sugar, and cracked black pepper. Bring the mixture to a simmer, replace the lid, and simmer for 30 minutes.

While that mixture is simmering, bring a small pot of salted water to a boil, put the fennel fronds and parsley leaves in the boiling water for 5 seconds to blanch them, and then place the fronds and leaves directly into a bowl of ice water. Let them sit in the ice water for a few seconds, remove them, squeezing out as much excess water as possible, and then chop them.

Put the chopped fennel fronds and parsley leaves in a blender, along with 1 cup of hot liquid from the pot of fennel mixture. Purée those ingredients until the solids break down and the liquid turns a pale green.

(continued on page 143)

(continued from page 142)

Add the green liquid to the pot of fennel mixture, and stir it evenly. Strain the entire mixture through a fine mesh sieve, using a spoon to press as much liquid out of the solids as you can. Discard the solids.

You should have about 2 1/2 cups of liquid. Measure 1/2 cup of the liquid, put it in a wide bowl, and place it in the refrigerator for 10 minutes to cool it. Keep the other 2 cups of liquid warm.

Sprinkle the powdered gelatin over the 1/2 cup of cool liquid, and allow it to "bloom"—that is, to soften—for 5 minutes. Then add the warm liquid, stirring it with a whisk until the gelatin is fully dissolved.

Grease the insides of 6 ramekins (or other molds) lightly with butter. Pour 6 ounces of the molten panna cotta mixture into each of the ramekins, and put them in the refrigerator to set up overnight (or for at least 6 hours).

Assembly:

After the panna cotta has set up, dip each ramekin into a bowl of hot water for about 30 seconds to warm the outside. Flip the ramekin upside down, and position it slightly off-center on a serving plate. The panna cotta should slide out easily. (If it does not, flip the ramekin back over, run the tip of a knife around the outside edge of the panna cotta, and then try again.)

Cut the Bosc pears in half, remove their cores, and cut each half into about 10 slices. Arrange the slices from one of the pear halves on each plate, next to and on top of the panna cotta.

Crumble a few toasted walnuts and about 1 tablespoon of Danish blue cheese over each salad. In a mixing bowl, toss the petite mache with just enough of the pear cider gastrique to coat the leaves lightly. Place a small bunch of petite mache on top of each panna cotta. Season the top of each salad with fresh cracked black pepper, and drizzle a bit more pear cider gastrique on each plate.

The New Scenic Café

gold beets & citrus

yield: 4 servings

Chefs often enjoy making dishes that offer an alluring variety of colors. It can be a gratifying challenge as well to go the other route and work within a monotone palette, keeping all of the colors in a dish within a more narrow range. I've taken up that challenge in this dish, in which I focus on warm oranges and yellows. Rather than using standard red beets, which bleed and mark the plate, I use gold beets, and once in a while a few chioggia beets, which turn a pale pink color when cooked. I roast and peel the beets, cool them, and cut them into quarters for a pleasing wedge shape.

To bring acidity and a hint of bitterness to the plate, I add candied kumquats. Candying softens and sweetens the kumquats, giving them a flavor similar to orange marmalade. Because many people are not familiar with kumquats, trying them in this dish at the Café has allowed our guests to experience the fruit without too big a leap into the unknown. To the mix, I also add citrus supremes, made of orange and ruby red grapefruit that I have cut into "supreme" wedges to deliver only the pure, brilliant meat of the fruit. They add acidity to the plate as well as a cool, juicy "burst." I toss these ingredients in a vanilla vinaigrette, divide it onto serving plates, and finish with slivers of raw shallot and a few tiny edible flowers. It is an enjoyable plate to look at and eat and makes a particularly fine fall dish.

Method:

Vanilla Vinaigrette:

Put all of the ingredients except the water and oil in a blender, and puree them thoroughly. Add the water, and blend the mixture. With the blender running on low speed, slowly add the canola oil in a steady stream, to emulsify the ingredients. Store the vinaigrette in the refrigerator, saving any extra for other uses.

Assembly:

Roast and peel the baby gold beets ahead of time. Allow them to cool completely, and cut them into quarters, yielding small wedges.

"Supreme" the orange and ruby red grapefruit by cutting off both ends of the fruits, setting each on one of its cut ends, and slicing off all of the peel to expose the fruit. Carefully slice directly alongside the membrane that separates the sections of each fruit. You can then remove perfect wedges of citrus, with no skin or pith attached.

In a mixing bowl, toss the beets and candied kumquats gently in about 6 tablespoons of the vinaigrette, and then divide them onto four plates. Scatter the thinly-sliced shallots over the beets, and place segments of both citrus fruits over the top.

Using the extra vinaigrette from the bowl, pour a bit more vinaigrette lightly over each plate. Over the top, finish the salads with a pinch of micro edible flowers and fresh cracked black pepper.

Ingredients:

Vanilla Vinaigrette:

1	T	Dijon mustard
2	T	minced shallot
1	T	minced garlic
1/4	c	vanilla extract
1/2	c	apple cider vinegar
1	t	kosher salt
1/2	t	cracked black pepper
2	T	granulated sugar
2	T	poppy seeds
1	c	water
2	c	canola oil

Other:

4	C	roasted baby gold beets (p. 369)
1	each	orange
1	each	ruby red grapefruit
2	C	candied kumquats (p. 363)
1	oz	shallot (thinly sliced)
1/2	C	micro edible flowers

red belgian endive

yield: 4 servings

At the great San Francisco restaurant Boulevard, I once saw an amazing endive salad, the striking visual pattern of the cut on the endive showing lovely crescent moons in stacks. I knew I had to create an endive salad of my own. In this recipe, I coat the endive leaves in creamy buttermilk dressing made with buttermilk, yogurt, lemon juice, poppy seeds, grated Pecorino Romano cheese, and spices. To give it a bit of smoky flavor, I grill asparagus over charcoal and stack the asparagus spears amidst the endive. Then I add apple-wood-smoked bacon lardons, cut large enough to grab with a fork. On top, I shave Mimolette cheese. I considered using cheddar, but the aged Mimolette has a more mature and earthy flavor. Plus, it shaves beautifully and holds a baby-sized curl that allows me to mound it and create the appearance of a lavish amount of cheese when, in reality, there is not a lot—just the right amount to add flavor and visual appeal. This salad is tight in presentation, with many contrasting shapes, colors and textures. It is almost like a chef's salad, with its crunchy, tart, cheesy, and smoky flavors all pulled together in what I think of as an "all-American" combination.

Ingredients:

Buttermilk Vinaigrette:

1	C	buttermilk
1/3	C	plain Greek yogurt
1/2	T	fresh lemon juice
1	t	poppy seeds
1/4	C	Pecorino Romano cheese (finely grated)
1	t	kosher salt
1	pinch	ground black pepper
1/2	T	granulated sugar
1/2	t	dill weed
1	t	fresh chives (chopped)

Other:

1	C	bacon lardons (p. 362)
20	spears	asparagus (pencil-thin)
2	T	olive oil
4	heads	red Belgian endive
6	oz	aged Mimolette cheese

Method:

Buttermilk Vinaigrette:
Combine all of the ingredients in a mixing bowl, and whisk them together until they are smooth. You will use only a little more than 1 cup of the dressing for the 4 servings of endive salad, but don't worry—it's so delicious, you'll eventually use it all. Save the remainder in the refrigerator for your next green salad.

Assembly:
Prepare the bacon lardons ahead of time, and then rewarm them just before assembling the salads.

Trim off the woody ends of the asparagus spears, and discard the ends. In a small dish, gently toss the asparagus with just enough olive oil to coat it, and then season the asparagus with salt and pepper. Grill the asparagus over a charcoal or gas grill until it is slightly cooked but still green and crisp. (You can also cook the asparagus on a griddle or in a sauté pan.)

Cut off the root end of the endive, and peel away each leaf, cutting more of the stem as needed. Place the leaves in a large mixing bowl, pour 1/2 cup of the buttermilk dressing over them, and toss them until they are coated evenly.

Reconstruct the leaves by piling them into 8 stacks of approximately 8 leaves each. Place two of the endive stacks in the center of each of the 4 plates, side by side with the curved sides up, and then pour 1 to 2 more tablespoons of buttermilk dressing over each pair of endive stacks.

Place 5 spears of grilled asparagus on top of and between each pair of endive stacks. Then spoon the warmed bacon lardons over the top of the asparagus. (Some of the lardons might fall to the sides, which is fine.)

Using a microplane or other grater, shave a mound of Mimolette cheese over the top of each salad.

The New Scenic Café

148

roasted red beets

yield: 4 servings

I love the sweet flavor of beets, so at the New Scenic Café I enjoy offering a variety of beet salads and appetizers. One of the most popular beet dishes I've created includes Danish blue cheese, haricots verts, and mache greens. In this salad, I take things in a bit of a different direction. I toss the roasted beets in tangy apple cider gastrique, which acts as a flavor enhancer by bringing sweetness from the cider and sharpness from the vinegar, and then I warm the beets in a sauté pan. To achieve the classic pairing of beets and goat cheese, I make panko-crusted goat cheese "coins" by crushing balls of goat cheese in panko bread crumbs, sautéing them, and placing them atop the beets. The crumbs add crunch and also allow me to warm the cheese without melting it. I add haricots verts that have been cooked in browned butter and then "dainty" the dish up with lacey frisée greens. The slightly bitter flavor of the frisée marries well with the sweetness of the beets. I finish the dish with shaved hazelnuts and a sprinkling of the apple cider gastrique.

Method:

Roast and peel the red baby beets ahead of time, and cut them into halves or quarters.

You'll also want to prepare the panko-crusted goat cheese "coins" in advance. Let the goat cheese warm to room temperature, and portion it into four 1 1/2-ounce balls. Press the balls into the panko bread crumbs until they are coated on all sides, shape them into "coins" that are approximately 2 inches in diameter, and refrigerate them until they are firm.

In a sauté pan, combine the beets with 1/4 cup of apple cider gastrique and 2 tablespoons of browned butter. Salt and pepper the beets, and put the pan over medium-low heat, stirring until the beets are heated through.

In a second sauté pan, heat the olive oil over medium-high heat. Place the goat cheese "coins" carefully in the pan, and brown one side lightly. Use a spatula to flip them over, and brown the other side.

Place the haricots verts and the remaining browned butter in a small sauce pot over medium heat, and season them with salt and pepper. Heat the haricots verts just enough to warm them through and soften them a bit.

Place a portion of warmed beets in the center of each of 4 large dinner plates. Then put the pan-fried goat cheese "coins" gently atop the beets, and place the haricots verts over the cheese.

Use a knife to cut the frisée into thin shavings that are about 2 inches long. Put the shaved frisée in a mixing bowl, dress it with the cream sherry vinaigrette, and pile a nicely-mounded peak of the greens on top of each salad.

Using a microplane grater, shave one hazelnut over the top of each salad. Finish by pouring a few drops of apple cider gastrique on the plate, around the outside of the salad.

Ingredients:

4	C	roasted red baby beets (roasted, peeled, & halved) (p. 369)
6	oz	goat cheese (soft, chevre)
1/2	C	panko bread crumbs
1/2	C	apple cider gastrique (p. 362)
1/3	C	browned butter (p. 363)
2	each	frisée heads
2	T	olive oil
24	each	haricots verts
2	oz	cream sherry vinaigrette (p. 365)
4	each	hazelnuts (toasted)

roasted mushrooms

yield: 4 servings

My goal in creating this dish was to make a salad that was not based on greens, and this dish has become a feature and a favorite of the Café's winter menu. I start with a variety of mushrooms, including criminis, shitakes, oysters, morels, and hon shimejis and prepare each type in a way that heightens its unique flavors. I roast the criminis, sauté the shitakes, oysters, and morels, and marinate the hon shimejis. I also incorporate cipollini onions, beets, and some amazing carrots that I get from Paul's Memorial Orchard, a local grower just up the road in Two Harbors, Minnesota. Their carrots are some of the best I have ever tasted. (And they also grow wonderful apples, beets, green beans, and garlic scapes.) I cook the cipollini onions slowly in olive oil, which gives them an almost decadent richness and sweetness and makes them glisten on the plate. And roasting the cipollinis allows me to store them long-term. The celery heart leaves are pale green in color, with an intense celery flavor that is earthy, herbaceous, and light. I toss them in white truffle oil and place them atop the mushrooms and onions. I also add shaved Belper Knolle cheese from Switzerland. The Belper Knolle looks like a little, black truffle, although it is actually a small, round nodule of cheese that has been coated in black pepper. I shave it on a truffle slicer, which gives it the appearance of truffle slices. Then I finish the plate with a carrot purée, bringing a vibrant carrot flavor and color to the dish. This salad's composition evokes the natural alterations we see along the shores of Lake Superior as the fall season changes to winter.

Ingredients:

Carrot Purée:

2	C	carrots
1	qt	water
2	t	kosher salt
4	T	butter

Other:

1/2	C	crimini mushrooms
1	C	shiitake mushrooms
1/2	C	oyster mushrooms
1/2	C	morel mushrooms
1	C	marinated hon shimeji mushrooms (p. 367)
4	each	roasted chioggia baby beets (p. 369)
2	each	small carrots (roasted)
10	pieces	cipollini onion confit (p. 364)
1	C	celery heart leaves
1	t	white truffle oil
1/4	oz	Belper Knolle cheese
		olive oil

Method:

Carrot Purée:

Roughly chop the carrots, and put them in a small pot with the water and salt. Bring it to a boil, and cook the carrots until they are soft all the way through but not mushy. Strain out the carrots, put them in a blender along with the butter, and puree the mixture until it is completely smooth. You can use the carrot purée immediately or allow it to cool and then store it in the refrigerator.

Assembly:

Preheat the oven to 350 degrees. Cut the crimini mushrooms into quarters, toss them with just enough olive oil to coat them, and season them with salt and pepper. Roast the criminis on a sheet pan for about 5 minutes, or until they are just cooked through and the edges begin to brown. Remove them from the oven, and set them aside.

Slice the shiitake mushrooms into strips, tear the oyster mushrooms into bite-size pieces, and leave the morels whole. In a large sauté pan over high heat, sauté the shiitakes, oysters, and morels for about 5 minutes, along with olive oil and a little salt and pepper. After the mushrooms are cooked, reduce the heat to medium, and add the criminis, hon shimejis, chioggia beets, and carrots. Continue to heat the mixture, stirring occasionally, until all the vegetables are warm.

Meanwhile, in separate small pots warm the cipollini onions and the carrot purée gently over low heat.

(continued on page 151)

(continued from page 150)

On 4 large plates, arrange the mushroom mixture in a line across the middle from left to right. Then place the cipollini onions randomly on top of and next to the mushrooms.

In a small bowl, toss the celery heart leaves with the truffle oil, salt, and pepper. Place a bunch of the dressed leaves on top of the mushrooms and onions on each of the plates, directly in the middle. Shave 5 or 6 slices of the Belper Knolle cheese over each salad. (If needed, you can substitute shavings of aged parmesan or Pecorino Romano cheese.) Using a spoon, drop and pull a smear of the carrot purée on the plate at the front of each salad.

Serve the salads immediately, while the mushrooms and other ingredients are still nicely warm.

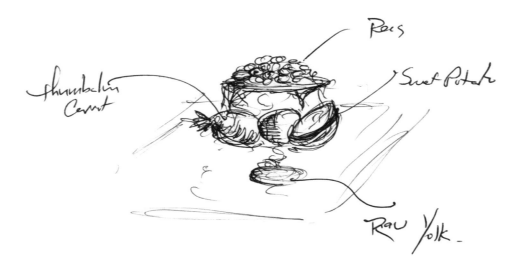

Roes

Suet Potato

thumbelina Carrot

Raw Yolk.

Entrées

The New Scenic Café

The New Scenic Café

sea bass & asparagus flan

yield: 4 servings

Sea bass is a flavorful and attractive fish that works well with a variety of recipes and sauces. It is also highly sought after and sometimes limited in availability. I serve this wonderful fish with a savory asparagus flan and a light and tangy sauce vierge. At the Café, we often make good use of cut-off asparagus ends remaining from other recipes to create the flan. In the sauce vierge, which is a French term that literally means "virgin sauce," I include olive oil, shallots, tomatoes, capers, and lemon, among other ingredients. I sear the sea bass in olive oil, with only salt and pepper for seasoning, and then roast the fish in the oven until it is cooked through and just beginning to flake apart. I serve the sea bass atop the asparagus flan, pour a bit of the sauce vierge over it to finish, and garnish the dish with buttery peas and fresh, aromatic fennel fronds.

Method:

Note that for the most flavorful results, you might prefer to prepare the sauce vierge the day before you plan to serve this dish, to give the flavors in the sauce time to meld fully.

Asparagus Flan:

Bring a large pot of salted water to a boil. Chop the asparagus, blanch it in the boiling water for 15 seconds, transfer it into ice water, and then drain it well. Dice the white onion, and melt the butter in a medium-size pot over medium heat. Add the onion and "sweat" it, stirring frequently until it is soft and translucent. Allow the onion to cool, and then mix it with the asparagus, thyme, parsley, and chives. Purée this mixture in a blender until it is completely smooth.

Crack the eggs into a large bowl, and beat them lightly by hand until they are mixed. Add the heavy cream, along with the asparagus purée, and stir all the ingredients until they are blended evenly. Strain the mixture through a fine mesh strainer to remove any remaining solids. Using a fine microplane grater, grate the Pecorino Romano to create tiny, light shavings, and then add the grated Romano, kosher salt, and white pepper to the mixture and stir.

Preheat the oven to 300 degrees. For the flan molds, you can use many different types of vessels, as long as they are ovenproof. I usually make our flans in coffee cups that have rounded bottoms so the finished flans have a half-dome appearance. I have also made them in ramekins, cannelé molds, and other small dishes.

To prepare your flan molds, spray them with a light layer of pan release, dust the insides with all-purpose flour (or for a gluten-free alternative, use corn masa), and then spray them again with pan release.

(continued on page 158)

Ingredients:

Asparagus Flan:

3/4	lb	asparagus
1	each	white onion
1/4	C	butter
1/2	T	fresh thyme (chopped)
1	T	fresh parsley (chopped)
1	T	fresh chives (chopped)
6	each	eggs (beaten)
1 1/2	C	heavy cream
1/4	C	Pecorino Romano (grated)
1/2	T	kosher salt
1/2	t	white pepper

Sauce Vierge:

1/4	C	shallot (brunoise cut)
1	T	garlic (brunoise cut)
1/3	C	fennel (brunoise cut)
1/2	C	tomato (brunoise cut)
1	t	fresh basil (minced)
1	t	fresh parsley (minced)
1	t	fresh chives (cross-cut)
1	T	capers (cut in half)
1/2	C	olive oil
1/2	T	lemon juice
1	t	white truffle oil
1/4	t	kosher salt
1	pinch	cracked black pepper

Sea Bass:

24	oz	sea bass (without skin)
4	T	olive oil

Other:

1/2	C	English or green peas
1	T	butter
12	each	fresh fennel fronds

(continued from page 157)

Set the molds inside a baking pan, and pour in the flan mixture, filling the molds to about 2 inches deep. Fill the baking pan with hot water up to 2 inches, to match the level of the flan mixture in the molds. Cover the entire pan with aluminum foil, and poke multiple small vent holes in the foil. Transfer the pan to the oven, being careful not to tilt it or splash water into the molds.

Visually check the flans after 30 minutes, and then check them every 5 minutes until they are done. They will be firm all the way through, with no liquid in the center, and will have a slightly domed top with perhaps a few browned areas. Remove the molds from the pan to cool. Let them sit at room temperature for about 10 minutes, and then place the molds in the refrigerator so the flans cool completely.

Sauce Vierge:
To prepare this piquant sauce takes some time, but the end result is worth the effort. Take the time to cut all of the ingredients carefully; they will be easily visible in the finished sauce.

Cut the shallot, garlic, fennel, and tomato into a "brunoise" cut of tiny 1/8-inch cubes. Mince the basil and parsley, and cross-cut the chives into 1/8-inch pieces. Drain the capers, and cut them in half. Combine those ingredients with the olive oil, lemon juice, white truffle oil, kosher salt, and cracked black pepper, and stir them together. If time permits, let the sauce sit in the refrigerator overnight for the flavors to meld.

Sea Bass:
Preheat the oven to 400 degrees. Cut the sea bass into 4 thick and blocky pieces (not thin and flat pieces), each weighing about 6 ounces. Season the fish with salt and pepper, and put the olive oil in a large sauté pan on high heat. When the pan begins to smoke, set the fish carefully in the pan. Sear one side of the sea bass until it has a golden-brown crust.

Flip the sea bass over, and transfer the sauté pan to the oven. (If your sauté pan is not ovenproof, move the fish onto a small baking pan that has been coated lightly with pan release.) Bake the sea bass until it is cooked all the way through, about 10 minutes.

Assembly:
About 45 minutes before you plan to serve this dish, remove the asparagus flans and the sauce vierge from the refrigerator. Set them in a relatively warm location so they can warm to room temperature. Stir the sauce vierge before you use it, to be sure it is mixed well.

To remove each flan, hold a mold in your hand, and use your fingers to pull the outside edge of the flan gently away from the side of the cup, all the way around. Then flip the cup over to release the flan onto the center of a plate. If the flan does not release on its own, shake the cup gently to help release it. If it still does not come out, run a small knife around the flan's outside edge to help free it, and try again. (You might also try dipping the cup in hot water to help the release.)

Warm the peas gently in a small pot with the butter, and season them with salt and pepper. Be careful not to overcook the peas; they should be bright green and plump.

Spoon about 2 tablespoons of the sauce around the outside of each flan. Then spoon another tablespoon of it on top of each flan. Scatter about a dozen peas around the outside of each flan as well, so the peas are resting in the sauce vierge. Set one piece of sea bass on top of each flan, and spoon a little more sauce vierge on top of the fish. Garnish each dish with 3 fresh, feathery fennel fronds.

rabbit confit, roulade, & rack

yield: 4 servings

With the light flavor of the rabbit, the freshness of the pea tendril and radish salad, and the tender English peas, this dish exemplifies spring. You'll find that to be so even with the hearty flavors of the accompanying sweet potato and foie gras. In this recipe, it's acquiring the rabbit that takes some planning. It is possible to purchase rabbit legs and loins separately, but it is virtually impossible to locate rabbit racks because they are so small and so time-consuming to clean. The best and most economical route is to buy whole rabbits and do the butchery yourself. You'll find there are many guides available online, in books, and in other publications to take you through the process. I suggest that when removing the loins, you keep the belly flaps attached. Often, they are so thin they have no apparent value and are discarded. But rolling them up along with the loins is a great way to make use of the meat they contain and better round out this flavorful dish. Rendered duck fat is expensive, but it can be reused many times. You can find it at gourmet food stores (and perhaps you know of a restaurant that might be willing to sell you some).

Method:

Keep in mind when you prepare this recipe that the rabbit legs are marinated in spices in the refrigerator for two days, so plan ahead.

Rabbit Confit:

Use a spice grinder to grind the toasted fennel and coriander coarsely, and then mix them with the salt and pepper in a small mixing bowl. In the bottom of a wide dish or pan, sprinkle half of the seasoning mixture and half of the minced garlic and sliced shallots. Arrange the rabbit legs in a single layer over those ingredients, and then coat the rabbit with the remaining seasoning, garlic, and shallots. Cover the rabbit, and refrigerate it for 2 days.

Preheat the oven to 250 degrees. Brush the majority of the spices, garlic, and shallots from the rabbit legs, and then move them to a roasting pan. Melt the duck fat in a pot over low heat, and pour it over the legs. Cover the pan with aluminum foil, and place it in the oven for 2 to 3 hours, until the meat can be pulled gently from the bones.

Remove the pan from the oven, and allow it to cool. If you plan to use the legs right away, remove them from the duck fat. Otherwise, place the entire pan in the refrigerator, allow the fat to solidify, and then cover the pan.

Before serving, heat the rabbit legs in a 350-degree oven for 10 minutes. Glaze the top of each with 2 tablespoons of fennel & coriander honey glaze, and then return them to the oven for an additional 5 minutes.

(continued on page 160)

Ingredients:

Rabbit Confit:

2	t	fennel seed (toasted)
2	t	coriander seed (toasted)
2	T	kosher salt
2	t	cracked black pepper
1	T	minced garlic
2	T	sliced shallots
4	each	rabbit hind legs
4	C	rendered duck fat

Rabbit Roulades:

4	each	rabbit loins (with belly flaps attached)
4	each	green cabbage leaves
8	slices	prosciutto

Rabbit Racks:

4	each	rabbit racks (French-cut)

Other:

8	each	fingerling sweet potatoes
1/2	C	English peas
1/2	C	cream sherry & foie gras sauce (p. 365)
4	each	French breakfast radishes
4	oz	pea tendrils
2	T	cream sherry vinaigrette (p. 365)
1/2	C	fennel & coriander honey glaze (p. 366)

(continued from page 159)

Rabbit Roulades:

Lay one rabbit loin on a clean work surface, with the belly flap faced down and stretched out flat. Season it with salt and pepper. Cut a cabbage leaf to fit the size of the belly flap, and lay the leaf on top of the flap. Roll the loin, together with the cabbage leaf, inside the belly flap. On a cutting board, lay two slices of prosciutto so that they are side by side but with the edges overlapping about 1/2 inch. From a roll of 12-inch-wide plastic wrap, tear off a piece that is about 12 inches long, and lay it flat on the counter.

Place the rolled loin on the prosciutto, at a bit of an angle near one end. Roll the loin and the prosciutto up tightly, like a "cigar," working carefully because the prosciutto can tear easily. Pick up the rolled loin and prosciutto, place it along one edge of the plastic wrap, and roll it tightly and evenly in the plastic wrap. Then pinch the air out of both ends, and twist them like the ends of a candy wrapper. Keep twisting until the plastic wrap is tight and firm and the roll is evenly cylindrical. Fold the ends of the plastic wrap under so that they stick to each other and keep the roll from unraveling.

Repeat this process with the other 3 rabbit loins, let the four roulades rest in the refrigerator for at least 2 hours (or, preferably, overnight), and then remove them from the plastic wrap gently. Put 2 to 3 tablespoons of olive oil in a large sauté pan, and heat it over high heat. Place the roulades in the pan, and sear them on all sides until the prosciutto is nicely browned and crisp and the rabbit is cooked through.

Rabbit Racks:

To French-cut the rabbit racks, use a small knife to trim away and scrape as much meat as possible from the bones, leaving the larger piece of meat attached along the bottom. Be careful as you work because the bones are extremely small and break easily. Season the meat lightly with salt and pepper. Heat 2 tablespoons of olive oil in a small sauté pan over high heat. Add the racks to the pan, meat side down, and sear them until they are golden brown. Flip them over, and continue to cook them an additional 30 seconds. They should be cooked to medium-well, so that they are slightly pink in the center.

Assembly:

Preheat the oven to 250 degrees. Coat the potatoes lightly with olive oil, and season them with salt and pepper. Roast them on a sheet pan for about 20 minutes, until they are "knife tender." Let them cool, and then cut each potato into 2 to 4 small pieces, depending on their size. Just before serving, roast them in a 350-degree oven for 6 to 7 minutes to brown their outsides.

Bring a small pot of water to a simmer, add the English peas, and cook them until they are tender and bright green. Pour off any excess water, leaving the peas in the warm pan. Add the cream sherry & foie gras sauce to the pan, and stir continuously as the sauce melts. Do not place the pan back on the heat.

Shave thin slices of the French breakfast radishes using a knife or mandoline, and cut the pea tendrils into 3-inch lengths. Toss the tendrils and radishes gently with just enough cream sherry vinaigrette to coat them.

Trim the ends of the roulades so they are flat, and then cut each roulade in half diagonally. Stand two of the halves on end on each plate. Place 3 to 4 pieces of sweet potato next to each pair of roulades, and then set a rabbit leg on top of the potatoes.

Nestle a handful of the radish salad next to the roulades, and lean one of the seared rabbit racks against each of the salads. Drizzle a bit of fennel & coriander honey glaze over the top of each rack. Spoon some of the peas, along with the cream sherry & foie gras sauce, over the top of each the rabbit legs. Serve immediately while the dish is warm and fresh.

seared sea scallops
yield: 4 servings

This simple, summery dish brings together the rich flavor of fresh scallops seared to a caramel brown and lightly-cooked asparagus. I cut the blunt ends of the jumbo asparagus spears to tapered points, mimicking the asparagus tips so that both ends are appealingly pointed, and then poach them gently in butter. To the plate of scallops and asparagus, I add a few applewood-smoked bacon lardons and some toasted walnuts and then finish with a bit of walnut oil and baby greens. This recipe also works nicely with large shrimp.

Method:

Seared Sea Scallops:

Most fresh scallops come with the "foot" still attached. It is a small piece of muscle on the side of the scallop that is edible but a bit tough and can be peeled away easily.

Just before you cook them, lay the scallops on a paper towel and blot them on all sides to be sure they are dry. (Drying the scallops will help them sear properly.) Then season them on both sides with kosher salt and black pepper.

Put 2 to 3 tablespoons of olive oil in a large sauté pan, and heat it over high heat. When you add the scallops, be sure there is plenty of room around each of them and that they are not touching when cooking. You might need to sear the scallops in 2 or 3 batches or use more than one sauté pan.

After the oil begins to show wisps of smoke, use a pair of tongs to set each scallop gently in the pan, being careful not to drop them and splash the hot oil. Keep the pan on high heat, and occasionally tilt it to move the oil around.

The scallops will likely stick to the pan as soon as you set them in it, but resist the temptation to move them prematurely. When the scallops are properly seared, they will release themselves.

Let the scallops sear until there is an even caramel crust across the entire surface of their bottom sides. Then turn the heat off, and flip them over in the pan. Allow the other side to cook for about 30 seconds, remove the scallops from the pan, and set them on a paper towel to rest for a minute or two.

(continued on page 164)

Ingredients:

Seared Sea Scallops:

16	each	sea scallops (U10 size)
		kosher salt
		cracked black pepper
2 - 3	T	olive oil

Asparagus Tips:

30	each	jumbo asparagus spears
1	C	butter

Other:

8	oz	bacon lardons (p. 362)
1/2	C	walnut halves & pieces (toasted)
4	t	walnut oil
1/2	C	baby greens (baby mache, arugula, micro-greens)

(continued from page 163)

Asparagus Tips:

For this dish, use only the beautiful tips of the asparagus—about the top 2 1/2 to 3 inches. Use a knife to shave the cut end of each tip to a sharp point, as if sharpening a pencil, to create beautiful asparagus tips that have two pointed ends. I save the remaining asparagus stems for asparagus flan (page 157) or to add to a soup.

Heat the butter in a small- or medium-size pot. Add the asparagus tips, and poach them gently over medium heat for about 5 minutes, until they soften but are still bright green. Remove the pot from the heat.

Assembly:

Add the bacon lardons and the toasted walnuts to the same pan you used to sear the scallops, while the pan is still hot, and toss them together to warm them. If necessary, return the pan to a burner for a minute.

Use a spoon or a pair of tongs to divide the bacon and walnuts among the 4 plates. Strain the asparagus tips out of the warm butter, and place 6 to 8 pieces on each plate. Then nestle 4 scallops on top of each set. Finish by pouring 1 teaspoon of walnut oil across the top of each dish, and garnish the plate with a few baby greens.

hot-smoked skuna bay salmon

yield: 4 servings

The inspiration for this dish came from the former executive chef of Aquavit Restaurant in New York, Christer Larsson of Sweden. While working with him at a retreat lodge in northern Wisconsin, I had the opportunity to observe his delicate technique for smoking salmon and went on to incorporate his method in this recipe. I marinate the fish in a Thai chile marinade, hot-smoke it over mesquite wood chips, and then finish cooking it to a nice medium rare. In the past, I have used Norwegian salmon, but I recently began using Skuna Bay craft-raised salmon. Skuna Bay raises their salmon in a natural open ocean environment, off the coast of Vancouver Island in the Pacific. The quality of the salmon is outstanding, and Skuna Bay's practices are sustainable and environmentally conscious. Pairing smoked fish with something salty like cheese is a common approach, but I find that sweetness also balances well with smokiness, so I serve it with sweet roasted Parisian (Thumbelina) carrots and baby beets. I coat the carrots and beets with a sauce of mustard seed and cream, top them on each plate with the hot-smoked salmon, and finish the dish with a touch of fresh cilantro.

Method:

You will want to keep in mind as you prepare to cook this dish that it requires marinating the salmon overnight (or for at least 6 hours) and that the wood chips must be soaked for at least 2 hours before you use them.

Thai Chile Marinade:

Bring a small pot of salted water to a boil, blanch the cilantro in it quickly, and then plunge the cilantro into an ice water bath. Squeeze as much water out of the cilantro as you can, and chop it.

In a blender, combine the cilantro with the remaining ingredients, and purée them. Add small amounts of additional oil if needed to keep the mixture moving, blending on high speed until the mixture is the consistency of a thick pesto. (It will not be perfectly smooth; you will see small pieces of cilantro.) Use the marinade immediately, or store it in the refrigerator.

(continued on page 167)

Ingredients:

Thai Chile Marinade:

1	bunch	cilantro
3	each	Thai chiles
1/4	t	kosher salt
1	t	minced garlic
2+	T	olive oil

Salmon:

24	oz	salmon (skin on)
1/2	C	mesquite wood chips

Sauté:

2	T	olive oil
4	T	shallots (sliced)
4	t	garlic (minced)
1 1/2	C	Parisian carrots (cooked)
1 1/2	C	roasted baby beets (p. 369)
4	T	mustard seed mix (p. 368)
1/2	C	heavy cream
4	T	beet purée (p. 363)

Other:

1/2	C	green peas
1	T	butter
4	dozen	dried wild blueberries
1/2	C	micro cilantro or cilantro leaves

The New Scenic Café

(continued from page 165)

Salmon:

Leave the skin on the salmon, and cut it into 4 equal portions, each about 6 ounces. Coat the flesh side of each portion of salmon with 2 to 3 tablespoons of the Thai chile marinade, and refrigerate it overnight (or for at least 6 hours). Submerge the mesquite wood chips in water and soak them for at least 2 hours.

Preheat the oven to 350 degrees, and line a sheet pan with parchment paper.

Drain any excess water from the wood chips, and place them in the bottom of a small pan over which a bamboo steamer will fit. Spray the steamer lightly with pan release.

Place one of the 4 pieces of salmon, skin side down, in the bamboo steamer, and cover it with a lid. Set the pan on a burner over medium-high heat until the wood chips begin to smoke, remove the pan from the heat for a few moments to prevent the wood chips from scorching, and then return it to the heat again.

Continue to repeat this procedure, smoking the salmon over the burner until the outer layer of the flesh turns opaque and tiny amounts of the white albumin begin to seep out. Then transfer the salmon to the parchment-lined sheet pan. Repeat this process until you have smoked all 4 pieces of the salmon and placed them on the pan.

Put the sheet pan in the oven for 5 to 7 minutes to finish cooking the salmon to medium-rare.

Sauté:

In a large sauté pan, heat the olive oil over medium heat. Add the shallots and garlic, and sweat them until they are translucent. Add the cooked carrots and beets, and then the mustard seed mix, heavy cream, and beet purée. Simmer until the vegetables are warm and the sauce has reduced and coats the vegetables evenly. Season it to taste with salt and pepper.

Assembly:

In a small pot, gently warm the green peas with a little bit of water, butter, salt, and pepper.

Divide the carrot and beet mixture evenly among the 4 plates, placing them in the center of each. Sprinkle about a dozen dried wild blueberries on each portion, followed by roughly the same amount of warmed peas.

For each piece of salmon, use a thin spatula to remove the salmon from its skin, and place the salmon on top of the vegetables and blueberries. Garnish the plates with micro cilantro or fresh cilantro leaves.

miso-marinated sea bass

yield: 4 servings

With this soba noodle salad on the menu at the New Scenic Café, I am able to bring a delicious cold salad to the table, finished with a wonderful piece of fish. Soba noodles are a Japanese style of noodle made from buckwheat flour. If you can locate green tea soba noodles, you will find the flavor of the green tea a nice addition, although standard soba noodles also work well. I considered simply grilling the sea bass for this dish. But marinating the fish in the miso marinade and then roasting it in a very hot oven gives it a beautiful caramelized appearance and flavor. The sea bass is the only part of this dish that is hot. All of the other components are served either chilled or at room temperature, so if you like you can prepare them well in advance.

Ingredients:

Soba Noodle Salad:

3	T	kosher salt
8	oz	green tea soba noodles (dry weight)
2	t	sesame oil
1/2	bunch	cilantro
1/2	each	poblano pepper
1	each	large shallot
1	each	cucumber linguini (p. 365)
1/2	C	marinated hon shimeji mushrooms (p. 367)
1/2	C	sesame soy sauce (p. 370)

Sea Bass:

24	oz	fresh sea bass
1	C	miso marinade (p. 368)

Other:

1	C	elephant garlic chips (p. 366)

Method:

As you plan this meal, keep in mind that the sea bass is marinated for three hours before cooking. So plan ahead—it will be worth it!

Soba Noodle Salad:
Add 1 gallon of water and the kosher salt to a large pot, and bring it to a boil. Put the dry soba noodles into the boiling water, scattering them in slowly. (If you add them all at once, they might clump and stick together.) Stir the noodles every couple of minutes, and check them until they are cooked "al dente." They usually take about 7 to 9 minutes to cook.

Strain the noodles, rinse them thoroughly with cold running water, let them drain well, and then toss them with the sesame oil. Keep the noodles in the refrigerator until you are ready to use them.

Pluck the cilantro leaves off of the stems, and discard the stems. Remove the core and seeds from the poblano pepper, peel the shallot, and slice both of them into very thin slivers. The thin slicing allows them to curl and blend into the noodle salad and to provide a subtle background flavor.

In a large mixing bowl, combine the soba noodles and the cucumber linguini, being sure the linguini has been strained from its marinade. Add the poblano pepper, shallot, hon shimeji mushrooms, cilantro leaves, and sesame soy sauce. Toss the mixture gently by hand until it is combined evenly and dressed with the sesame soy sauce.

Most of the vegetables will tend to fall to the bottom of the mixing bowl, so be sure you mix them in well. Taste the noodle salad. If it seems under-seasoned, add small amounts of sesame soy sauce, mix it in well, and taste the salad again.

(continued on page 169)

(continued from page 168)

Sea Bass:

If the skin is still on the sea bass, remove and discard it. Cut the sea bass into 4 thick, cube-shape portions, each weighing about 6 ounces. Pour the miso marinade over the pieces of fish, toss them in the marinade so they are coated on all sides, and let them marinate in the refrigerator for 3 hours.

Preheat the oven to 450 degrees. (If you have one, a convection oven works particularly well.) Spray a sheet pan lightly with pan release, remove the pieces of sea bass from the marinade, and set them on the sheet pan.

Put the pan in the oven, and bake the fish for 12 to 15 minutes, until it is cooked all the way through and the sugars in the marinade begin to caramelize on the outside of the sea bass. Don't worry if some of the edges of each piece of fish even become a bit charred.

Assembly:

This dish is best served in large, shallow bowls (although plates with rims that contain any liquid also work well).

Using a pair of tongs, lift a portion of noodle salad over the center of each bowl. As you lower the noodles, twirl the tongs so that rather than spreading out flat the noodles create a mound.

Scatter a generous handful of elephant garlic chips around the perimeter of the mound of noodles in each bowl. Then, when the sea bass is finished cooking remove it from the oven and place one piece directly in the center of each plate, on top of the noodle salad. Serve the dish immediately while the fish is hot.

ahi tuna nicoise

yield: 4 portions

For this rich, slightly decadent dish, I use the best tuna possible, Maguro. It can be seared in a pan, but grilling the tuna adds a wonderful smoky flavor. I take a standard approach to the other components of a classic salad Nicoise, using potatoes, asparagus, olives, and capers. On top of a stack of tender baby greens, I place the grilled tuna and then alongside it the 2 halves of a soft-center egg, letting the luxuriously fluid yolk bring a "sexy" element to the plate. I finish the dish with brilliantly-colored grape tomatoes and a bit of tangy lemon aioli.

Method:

Fingerling Potatoes:

In a medium-size pot, bring 2 quarts of water to a boil, and add the kosher salt, black peppercorns, and bay leaves. Add the potatoes, and cook them until they are just tender, about 10 minutes. Remove the pot from the heat, drain the potatoes, and cool them in cold water. Cut each potato into 4 to 6 thin wedges.

Asparagus:

Coat the asparagus with olive oil, and season it with salt and pepper. Char the asparagus over a grill, or sear it in a very hot sauté pan or cast-iron skillet.

Tuna:

Cut the tuna into 4 steaks, each about 6 ounces. Rub the outsides lightly with olive oil, and season them with kosher salt and black pepper. Grill the tuna for about 20 seconds on each side (or sear it in a hot sauté pan). The tuna will be rare, with a thin cooked layer on each side.

Assembly:

If you made the soft-center eggs in advance and they are now cold, reheat them for 2 to 3 minutes in a pot of simmering water.

Use a spoon to dress the 4 serving plates in an abstract fashion with 2 to 3 tablespoons of lemon aioli apiece. Lay 6 spears of asparagus neatly across the center of each plate.

In a mixing bowl, dress the baby mache greens very lightly with lemon aioli. Place 1 cup of dressed mache on each plate in a tight pile directly on the cut ends of the asparagus. Slice each piece of cooked tuna into 2 pieces, and set the 2 pieces on top of the mache.

Use a knife to split each soft-center egg in half, turning the two halves quickly cut-side-up before the yolk has a chance to flow out. Set two halves on top of, or next to, the asparagus on each plate, and season the eggs with a touch of salt and pepper.

Place 4 kalamata olives, 4 grape tomato halves, a few capers, and the cut pieces of one fingerling potato randomly but neatly on each of the 4 plates. Use a spoon to place 1 tablespoon of lemon aioli on top of each piece of seared tuna, and garnish the tuna with a couple sprigs of mache.

Ingredients:

Fingerling Potatoes:

2	T	kosher salt
1	t	whole black peppercorns
2	each	bay leaves
4	each	fingerling potatoes

Asparagus:

24	spears	asparagus (pencil-thin)
1	T	olive oil

Tuna:

24	oz	sashimi-grade tuna
4	t	olive oil

Other:

1	C	lemon aioli (p. 367)
4	C	baby mache greens
4	each	soft-center eggs (p. 370)
16	each	kalamata olives
8	each	grape tomatoes (halved)
2	T	capers (drained)

ratatouille lasagna

yield: 4 servings

I named this dish "ratatouille lasagna" as a play on its ingredients and construction. It is a "ratatouille" because it includes the classic ratatouille elements—zucchini, eggplant, and garlic—and "lasagna" because I build it in layers of freshly-sautéed vegetables and soft, warm goat cheese. Though this is not the standard lasagna made of noodles, red sauce, and cheese, it is one of the Café's most popular vegetarian dishes. To create a menu-worthy vegetarian dish, I do not simply take the meat out of a recipe. I create it specifically to be vegetarian, giving the freshest locally-grown vegetables center stage. This dish is in part a fond tribute to a small farm in Herbster, Wisconsin called Roode Food that supplies us with amazing produce, including the zucchini, Chinese eggplant, and tomatoes highlighted in this colorful entrée.

Ingredients:

2	C	quinoa (cooked) (p. 369)
2	each	zucchini
2	each	Chinese eggplant
1/2	C	olive oil
24	spears	asparagus
2	each	large ripe tomatoes
1/4	C	balsamic reduction (p. 362)
1/2	C	soft goat cheese (chevre)
1	C	elephant garlic chips (p. 366)
4	sprigs	fresh oregano

Method:

On low heat, warm the quinoa in a small pot, stirring occasionally so it heats evenly.

Cut the zucchini and Chinese eggplant into approximately 5-inch lengths. Using a mandoline slicer or sharp knife, slice the lengths into strips that are about 1/8-inch thick. (Per serving, you will need 5 to 6 strips each of the zucchini and the eggplant.)

On a flat surface, shingle each set of 5 to 6 strips of zucchini or eggplant by laying them so that they are parallel but overlapping and spread over a 4- to 5-inch width. Pour a small amount of olive oil over all of the slices, and season them with salt and pepper. Trim the asparagus spears so they are about 6 inches long, and toss them with olive oil, salt, and black pepper.

Heat 2 large sauté pans over medium heat. Gently place the composed sets of sliced zucchini and eggplant in one pan and the asparagus in the other pan. (If all the vegetables do not fit in the pans at one time, you can cook them in batches or in more pans.) Sear the vegetables until they just begin to soften, using a spatula to flip them over partway through.

Slice the tomatoes into round slices that are each about 1/4-inch thick. Shingle the slices into 4 overlapping sets of 3 slices each and season them with salt and pepper. Coat the bottom of a separate sauté pan with olive oil, and heat it over medium heat. Place the sets of tomatoes in the pan, and heat them just long enough to warm them through, being sure not to cook them too long (or they will become overly soft).

Using a squeeze bottle with a fine tip or a small spoon, drizzle several thin lines or circles of balsamic reduction on the 4 plates.

Spoon the warm quinoa onto the centers of the plates, lay 6 spears of asparagus evenly across the quinoa, and place the tomatoes on top of the asparagus. Crumble the soft goat cheese across the tops of the tomato slices, and then lay the eggplant slices over the goat cheese. Place the zucchini slices over the eggplant, nestle a small mound of elephant garlic chips on top of each dish, and garnish the top with a sprig of fresh oregano. Serve it immediately.

174

manhattan strip loin

yield: 4 servings

You'll enjoy the French flair of the thyme and lavender in this light dish—and its relatively straightforward preparation. I use a Manhattan strip loin, which is cut twice as thick but half as wide as a New York strip loin. The thicker cut is more stout in its presentation, cooks more evenly, and is similar in appearance to beef tenderloin. I grill the strip loin to give its outside a tasty sear, finish it in the oven, and then before serving toss it with dried lavender buds and fresh thyme leaves. To accompany the meat, I slow-cook cipollini onions in olive oil, warm English peas with butter and truffle oil, and sauté chanterelle mushrooms. After arranging them all with the strip loin, I finish the plate with a touch of veal demi-glace and some delicate greens or colorful edible flowers.

Method:

Manhattan Strip Loin:

Preheat the oven to 400 degrees. Set the un-cut strip loin on a cutting board with the thick layer of fat facing up. Cut it in half in one direction, and then cut it in half again in the other direction, resulting in 4 thick, almost cube-shaped steaks.

Season the steaks on all sides generously with salt and pepper, and then rub them with olive oil. Either on a grill or in a hot sauté pan, sear the outsides of the steaks on all sides. Transfer them to a sheet pan, and cook them in the oven to the desired temperature.

Mix the dried lavender buds and fresh thyme leaves together in a small mixing bowl. After removing the steaks from the oven, roll them in the lavender and thyme mixture so that it sticks to their sides.

Assembly:

Put the English peas in a small pot with 2 tablespoons of butter, and season them with salt and pepper. Heat them gently over low heat until they are hot and bright green but still firm. Stir in 1 teaspoon of white truffle oil just before serving them.

In a large sauté pan, heat 2 tablespoons of olive oil over high heat until wisps of smoke form from the pan. Add the chanterelle mushrooms, and season them with salt and pepper. Sauté the mushrooms until they are softened and a bit caramelized.

Warm the cipollini onion confit in one small pot and the demi-glace in another. Set one of the steaks on each plate, nestle 3 cipollini onions next to each steak, and arrange the English peas at the base. Spoon the chanterelle mushrooms on top of the steaks, and then spoon 1 to 2 tablespoons of veal demi-glace over the tops so that it runs down the sides and pools just a little on the plates. Garnish the dish with fresh thyme, micro greens, or even tiny edible flowers.

Ingredients:

Manhattan Strip Loin:

2	lb	beef strip loin (un-cut)
2	T	olive oil
1/4	C	dried lavender buds
1/4	C	fresh thyme leaves

Other:

1	C	English peas
2	T	butter
1	t	white truffle oil
2	T	olive oil
1	C	chanterelle mushrooms
12	pieces	cipollini onion confit (p. 364)
1/4	C	veal demi-glace (p. 371)
few	sprigs	fresh thyme, micro greens, or tiny edible flowers

grilled pheasant breast

yield: 4 servings

This dish is the big brother to the famous Southern "chicken and waffles." Along with much of the other poultry I cook, the pheasant is locally sourced and raised in a natural environment at the Wild Acres game farm in Pequot Lakes, Minnesota. I brine the pheasant breast for 1 to 2 days, grill it, and place it atop a buckwheat Belgian waffle, which has a more earthy texture and flavor than a typical Belgian waffle. For added richness, I make a small fondue out of Taleggio cheese and heavy cream and pour it into the waffle's pockets. Then I slice an apple thinly, fan the slices out to create a lovely and flavorful garnish, and finish the plate with a soft-center egg, blueberries, and maple syrup. This entrée is breakfast-like, but the quantity and composition of the food lend it the air of a sumptuous, Southern-inspired dinner.

Ingredients:

Pheasant Breasts:

4	C	apple cider
1/4	C	kosher salt
1/4	C	granulated sugar
4	each	pheasant breasts
2	T	olive oil

Buckwheat Belgian Waffles:

1	each	egg
1	each	egg yolk
1	C	warm water
8	oz	buckwheat pancake mix
1/4	C	melted butter

Taleggio Fonduta:

4	oz	Taleggio cheese
4	oz	heavy cream

Other:

1	each	honeycrisp apple
4	each	soft-center eggs (p. 370)
1	C	fresh blueberries
1/2	C	pure maple syrup
4	t	white truffle oil

Method:

Note that this recipe requires 1 to 2 days of prior preparation for brining the pheasant breasts.

Pheasant Breasts:
In a large bowl or pan, mix together the apple cider, kosher salt, and granulated sugar. Submerge the pheasant breasts in this brine, and put them in the refrigerator for 1 to 2 days. Remove the pheasant from the brine, and pat it dry with a clean cloth or paper towel.

Rub the breasts with olive oil, and season them on both sides with salt and pepper. Either grill the pheasant to completion or mark the breasts quickly on a grill for the smoky flavor and then roast them in a 350-degree oven until they are cooked through, about 15 minutes.

Buckwheat Belgian Waffles:
Crack the egg into a mixing bowl, add the egg yolk and warm water, and mix them together. Add the buckwheat pancake mix, and stir the ingredients until they are even and smooth. Add the melted butter, and stir the mixture again. Cook the batter in a waffle iron according to the iron's instructions, to make the 4 waffles. If you prefer, you can make the waffles ahead of time and warm them in a 350-degree oven for a few minutes just before serving them.

Taleggio Fonduta:
In a small pot, combine the Taleggio cheese and heavy cream. Warm them on low heat, stirring occasionally until the cheese and cream melt together completely.

Assembly:
You can have fun being creative when plating this dish. On each plate, I place a waffle and use a spoon to fill in its pockets with the Taleggio fonduta. Then I set a grilled pheasant breast on top. Cut off one side of the apple, lay it flat, and slice it wafer-thin. Fan the slices into a semi-circle, and lean one grouping of apple slices against each pheasant breast.

Prop a soft-center egg on each waffle. Scatter 1/4 cup of fresh blueberries per dish, and pour 2 tablespoons of maple syrup over them. Drip 1 teaspoon of white truffle oil on each soft-center egg, and season the eggs with salt and pepper.

The New Scenic Café

grilled pork tenderloin

yield: 4 servings

Among the pork tenderloin entrées I've created for the New Scenic Café, this dish is a favorite. It blends the sweetness of the apple cider-brined pork with the creamy richness of the corn masa. Masa cooks to a consistency similar to hot cereal or mashed potatoes and in this recipe includes a bit of gouda cheese, some whole milk, and sliced scallions. To accompany the pork, I roast a butternut squash, cut it into half-moon slices, and lay the squash atop the masa, followed by slices of the pork and some red chile adobo sauce. I add finely-diced Spanish chorizo and corn kernels fresh off of the cob, topping it with a salad made of scallion slices and micro cilantro that has been dressed with olive oil and freshly-squeezed lime juice. This dish draws on the Oaxacan cuisine so favored from that part of Mexico, dressed up a bit in haute cuisine style.

Method:

Note that this recipe requires 1 to 2 days of prior preparation to brine the pork tenderloin.

Pork Tenderloin:
Clean the membrane, or "silverskin," off of the pork tenderloin, along with any excess fat. In a large bowl or pan, stir together the apple cider, salt, and sugar to create a brine. Submerge the pork in the brine, cover it, and refrigerate it for 1 to 2 full days.

Remove the pork from the brine, and pat it dry with a paper towel. Cook it on a grill (charcoal preferred) for about 20 minutes, until it reaches an internal center temperature of 145 degrees. While grilling the pork, brush it lightly with the red chile adobo several times to create a glaze. Remove the pork from the grill, and allow it to rest for 5 to 10 minutes before you slice it.

Butternut Squash:
Preheat the oven to 300 degrees. Cut off the larger end of the squash—the end that contains the seeds. (You can roast that part of the squash, if you wish, to use it in soup or another dish, but it won't be used in this recipe.)

Cut the remainder of the squash lengthwise down the center, and set both halves (flat sides down) on a sheet pan lined with parchment paper. Place the pan in the oven, and roast the squash for about 30 minutes or until it is "knife-tender." (That is, a small knife will penetrate through the center of the squash with relative ease, but it should still be fairly firm.)

(continued on page 180)

Ingredients:

Pork Tenderloin:

24	oz	pork tenderloin
4	C	apple cider
3	T	kosher salt
4	T	granulated sugar
1	C	red chile adobo (p. 369)

Butternut Squash:

1	each	butternut squash

Corn Masa:

1/4	C	gouda cheese (shredded)
1/4	C	scallions (sliced)
2	C	milk
1/2	T	chicken base
1	t	vegetable base
1	C	water
2	C	corn masa
1/4	C	corn kernels
1/4	lb	butter
1/4	t	kosher salt
1/4	t	cracked black pepper

Other:

1	oz	Spanish chorizo
1	ear	sweet corn
1	each	scallion
1/2	C	cilantro leaves
1	T	olive oil
1	each	lime

(continued from page 179)

Remove the pan from the oven, and allow the squash to cool to room temperature. It can be refrigerated, if necessary. Cut the skin carefully off of each half of the squash, and then cut the squash into 1/4-inch thick slices, each in the shape of a half-moon.

Corn Masa:

Shred the gouda cheese with a grater, and cross-cut the scallions into thin, round slices. Combine the milk, chicken base, vegetable base, and water in a large pot, and whisk them together until the chicken base and vegetable base are dissolved. Add the corn masa, and stir it in thoroughly.

Put the pot over low-to-medium heat, and bring it slowly to a simmer. Allow the ingredients to cook, stirring continuously until the masa reaches a consistency similar to thick cream of wheat. Add the corn kernels, gouda cheese, butter, salt, and pepper. Continue stirring until the cheese and butter have melted and are completely incorporated. Stir in the sliced scallions, and turn off the heat.

Assembly:

Cut the chorizo into a small dice (less than 1/4 inch on all sides), and slice the fresh corn off of the cob. It is not necessary to cook the corn. Good, fresh sweet corn has a delightfully sugary crunch that is pleasing in the right context.

If it is not still hot, warm the corn masa slowly over low heat, stirring it frequently. Add small amounts of water, by the tablespoon, if the masa has become too thick, until it returns to the consistency of thick cream of wheat.

To heat the squash, fan out the slices on a sheet pan, and season them with salt and pepper. Drizzle a little olive oil over their tops, and warm the squash in the oven for a few minutes at 300 degrees.

Spoon about 1/2 cup of the warm corn masa in the center of each plate. Divide the butternut squash into 4 portions, and fan out the slices on top of the corn masa.

Cut the pork tenderloin into thin slices, and fan them out on each plate on top of the butternut squash, spooning a bit more red chile adobo over the meat. Then scatter the diced Spanish chorizo and fresh corn kernels around the plate.

For the final garnish, slice the scallion into thin slivers, combine it with the cilantro leaves, and dress them with a bit of olive oil, a squeeze of fresh lime juice, and a pinch of salt and pepper. Nestle this delicate salad on top of the pork.

seared duck breast & amarena cherries

yield: 4 servings

Searing duck breasts properly so they are tasty and moist with crisp skin is not difficult, but it does require time and a bit of patience. I begin by laying the breasts on a plate and seasoning them with salt and pepper. Then I coat a large sauté pan with olive oil, lay the duck breasts in the pan skin side down, and cook them slowly. The skin becomes golden brown and crisp, without the layer of chewy fat that can result if the duck is cooked too fast and the fat is not allowed to fully render out. I turn the breasts over, cook them for a couple minutes longer, and then remove them from the pan and let them rest so the juices will remain inside when the meat is sliced.

In this recipe, I serve the seared duck breast with roasted fingerling potatoes and haricots verts, which are slim, tender green beans I cook in butter. Then I finish the dish with a variety of flavors to complement the richness of the duck: sliced figs, sour amarena cherries, a drizzle of fragrant "green oil," syrup from the cherries, and a garnish of fresh thyme.

Method:

Duck Breasts:

Lay the duck breasts on a plate, and season both sides with kosher salt and cracked black pepper.

Pour the olive oil into a large sauté pan, and move the pan around to coat the bottom. (The skin of the duck does contain quite a bit of fat, but adding a little oil helps get the cooking process started.) Lay the duck breasts in the pan, skin side down, and place the pan over medium-low heat, cooking the skin slowly so the fat renders out into the pan. Move the duck around every few minutes, lifting it to look underneath to be sure the breasts are cooking evenly. It will take 15 to 20 minutes for the fat to render out and the skin to become golden brown and crisp.

Flip the breasts over, and cook them on the other side for about 2 minutes more. Then remove them from the pan, and set them on a paper towel to rest for 5 to 7 minutes. Save the rendered fat.

While searing, the duck breasts appear to shrink because the meat and skin tighten as they cook. If you were to cut them immediately after removing them from the pan, they would most likely still be rare in the center and much of their juice would drain onto the cutting board. Allowing the duck breasts to rest allows them to continue to cook a bit more, the meat and skin to relax, and most of the juice to remain inside when you slice the breasts.

Lay the breasts, skin side down, on a cutting board, and use a knife to cut thin slices, taking care not to cut all the way through the skin. The breast will fan open like an accordion, and you should have 12 to 14 slices on each duck breast.

(continued on page 182)

Ingredients:

Duck Breasts:

4	each	duck breasts (6 - 8 oz each)
2	T	olive oil

Fingerling Sweet Potato Coins:

8	each	fingerling sweet potatoes
2	T	olive oil
1/2	C	rendered duck fat

Haricot Verts:

8	oz	haricots verts
1	T	butter

Other:

4	each	black mission figs
12	each	canned amarena cherries
2	T	syrup from the cherries
2	T	green oil (p. 366)
4	sprigs	fresh thyme

(continued from page 181)

Fingerling Sweet Potato Coins:
Preheat the oven to 250 degrees. Toss the fingerling potatoes with the olive oil to coat them, and then season them with salt and pepper. Lay the potatoes on a baking sheet, and roast them for about 30 minutes—or until they are cooked through but still firm. Remove the potatoes from the oven, and place them in the refrigerator to cool fully.

Slice the potatoes into thin rings, or "coins." In a large sauté pan, heat the rendered duck fat over high heat until it begins to smoke. Add the fingerling coins, and fry them until they are golden brown and crisp, tossing them to fry both sides. Remove the potatoes from the pan, and drain them on a paper towel.

Haricots Verts:
Warm the haricots verts gently in a small pot with the butter, 1 tablespoon of water, and a bit of salt and pepper, moving them around in the pan periodically so they heat evenly. Cook them until they are bright green and just beginning to soften.

Assembly:
Place the fried fingerling coins in a small pile in the center of each plate. Using a pair of tongs, gather the haricots verts so they are parallel, and place them on top of the fingerling coins.

Set a sliced duck breast across the haricots verts, with the skin side facing down. The duck should curl over the vegetables a bit, with the slices fanning open.

Cut each fig into quarters, put 4 pieces around the outside of each duck breast, and then add 3 amarena cherries. Using a squeeze bottle or a small spoon, drizzle a bit of cherry syrup and green oil over the duck breast and around the outside edge of the plate. Garnish the dish with a sprig of fresh thyme.

The New Scenic Café

The New Scenic Café

seared duck breast & creamed leek tartlet

yield: 4 servings

I was inspired to create this dish by the work of well-known chef Charlie Trotter, who created a recipe that has a similar composition of flavors. With its bright colors and tastes, it has turned out to be one of the New Scenic Café's favorites. I simmer dried apricots along with cream sherry, saffron, curry, and other spices and then purée them, to create a sauce with a brilliant orange color that looks lovely on the plate. Accompanying the thinly-sliced duck breast is a small tartlet, made of creamed leeks and a bit of blue & goat cheese mousse. I finish the plate with a small salad of microgreens, fresh strawberries, and Arya pistachios, which are grown in California but originate from Iran (though you can certainly use any pistachios). The rich flavor of Arya pistachios and their intensely bright-green color give this summery dish its final dash of seasonal look and taste.

Method:

Apricot Curry Purée:

Combine all of the ingredients in a small pot, place the pot over low heat, and cover it with a lid. Warm the mixture slowly to a low boil, and then turn the heat down slightly, letting the mixture simmer for 15 minutes. Pour it into a blender, and purée it until it is completely smooth. (This sauce can be refrigerated and reheated as needed.)

Seared Duck Breasts:

See "seared duck breast & amarena cherries" on page 181 for detailed instructions on how to sear the duck breasts. For this recipe, also season the sides of the breasts that do not have skin with garam masala—but only the non-skin sides. If you sprinkle the garam masala on the skin sides, the spices tend to burn during cooking.

Creamed Leek Tartlets:

While the duck is cooking, preheat the broiler in your oven, and warm the creamed leeks gently in a small pot over low heat. Put the blue cheese & goat cheese mousse into a small ziplock bag, and cut about 1/4 inch off one corner of the bag. Spoon the creamed leeks into the tartlet shells, and squeeze the ziplock to pipe about 1 tablespoon of the mousse on top of each tartlet.

Place the tartlets on a sheet pan, and set the pan under the broiler. Broil the tartlets for about 1 minute or until the mousse melts and just begins to brown.

(continued on page 186)

Ingredients:

Apricot Curry Purée:

1/2	C	dried apricots (diced)
1	C	water
1 1/2	T	cream sherry
4	threads	saffron
1/2	t	curry powder
1	t	red curry paste
1	T	brown sugar
3	oz	crystallized ginger
1	pinch	garam masala (p. 366)
1	t	vegetable base
1/2	T	kosher salt

Seared Duck Breasts:

4	each	duck breasts (6 - 8 oz each)
4	t	garam masala (p. 366)
2	T	olive oil

Creamed Leek Tartlets:

1/4	C	creamed leeks (p. 365)
4	each	tartlet shells (2") (p. 371)
1/4	C	blue cheese & goat cheese mousse (p. 363)

Other:

4	C	microgreens
1/4	C	cream sherry vinaigrette (p. 365)
2	each	strawberries
2	T	Arya pistachios (hulled)

(continued from page 185)

Assembly:

In a small pot, warm the apricot curry purée gently on low heat. Use a spoon to "paint" each plate with the purée, experimenting with the appearance of the sauce on the plate, if you like, to produce a fun and beautiful design. (This colorful dish looks especially appealing on a white plate). If the purée is too thick, stir in a small amount of additional water, 1 tablespoon at a time, to thin it.

Set the seared duck breasts on a cutting board, skin side down (they are much easier to slice evenly this way). Using a sharp knife, slice each breast into 12 to 14 thin, round slices. Fan the slices out a little, and then set a duck breast on each of the plates, positioning it slightly off-center.

Set one of the creamed leek tartlets on each plate, opposite the sliced duck breast. In a small mixing bowl, dress the greens lightly with the cream sherry vinaigrette. Using your hands, create a "ball" of dressed greens and place one in the center of every plate, between the duck and the tartlet. Dice the strawberries and chop the pistachios, and then scatter them around the outside edge of the dish.

grilled quail

yield: 4 servings

Many years ago, I had dinner at Minnesota chef Tim McKee's restaurant La Belle Vie, when it was still located in Stillwater, Minnesota. This dish was inspired by that memorable meal. I roast sweet potatoes, cool and dice them, sauté them with diced kielbasa and minced shallots, press the mixture into a ring mold to create a cylinder for the center of the dinner plate, and release the mold onto the plate. Then I make a ring of puréed Medjool dates and cumin around the outside of the pressed mixture, adding a bit of warm, rich chicken stock as well. Atop the sweet potatoes, I place two quail that have been grilled to the proper temperature so they are succulent and tender. I finish the dish with an apricot saffron sauce and a sprig of microgreens or fresh herbs. This easy and delicious autumn meal also works well with other white wild fowl, including Cornish game hen and pheasant.

Method:

As you plan your meal, keep in mind you'll need to marinate the quail for three hours prior to cooking.

Quail Marinade:

Combine all of the ingredients in a medium-sized mixing bowl. Use a whisk to stir them vigorously until they are evenly combined. Set the marinade aside for a few minutes.

Grilled Quail:

This recipe uses "semi-boneless" quail, which have had the rib cage removed but are otherwise intact and still have wing and leg bones. (The semi-boneless quail broil nicely and present particularly well on the plate, but you can use quail with the bones in. If you do so, you will need to increase their cooking time slightly.)

Put the quail into a container, and pour the quail marinade over the top, moving the quail around in the marinade to coat them on all sides. Put the container in the refrigerator, and let the quail marinate for about 3 hours.

Remove the quail, draining off any excess marinade, and grill them for 5 to 7 minutes on each side, until they are cooked to medium or medium-well. (Cooking the quail on a grill works especially well, but you can also sear them for a few minutes on each side in olive oil, in a hot sauté pan.)

Sweet Potatoes:

Preheat the oven to 250 degrees. Place the sweet potatoes on a sheet pan, and put them in the oven. Roast them slowly, for about 45 minutes or until a fork or knife tip can be inserted easily all the way through. Remove the sweet potatoes from the oven, and allow them to cool.

(continued on page 188)

Ingredients:

Quail Marinade:

1/4	C	brown rice vinegar
1/3	C	olive oil
2	T	soy sauce
2	T	apple cider vinegar
1	t	sesame oil
1	t	toasted ground cumin
1	t	toasted ground coriander
2	T	dried chives
1	pinch	dried thyme
1	pinch	crushed red pepper
1	t	parsley flakes
1/2	T	garlic (minced)
2	T	brown sugar
1	T	Dijon mustard
1	T	vegetable base
1/2	T	cream sherry

Grilled Quail:

8	each	semi-boneless quail (whole, 4 - 5 oz each)

Sweet Potatoes:

2	each	sweet potatoes (medium size)
8	oz	kielbasa sausage
2	T	olive oil
2	T	shallots (minced)

Other:

1	C	Medjool date & cumin purée (p. 367)
1/2	C	chicken stock (p. 364)
1	C	apricot saffron sauce (p. 362)
4	sprigs	microgreens or fresh herbs

(continued from page 187)

When the sweet potatoes are still warm but cool enough to handle, peel off and discard their skins. Dice the sweet potatoes into 1/2-inch cubes. Slice the kielbasa sausage lengthwise into quarters, and then cross-cut the quarters into small pieces that are about the same size as the cubes of sweet potato.

In a large sauté pan, heat the olive oil over medium heat. Add the diced kielbasa and minced shallots, and sauté them until the kielbasa begins to brown and the shallots are soft and translucent. Add the diced sweet potatoes, and season the mixture with salt and pepper, stirring frequently but gently to mix the sweet potatoes evenly with the kielbasa and shallots without mashing the potatoes. Continue to heat the mixture slowly until it is hot all the way through.

Assembly:
Warm the Medjool date & cumin purée, apricot saffron sauce, and chicken stock gently in separate small pots over low heat.

Spoon 1/4 cup of the Medjool date & cumin purée onto the center of each of 4 plates, and then use the back side of the spoon to push the purée into a ring large enough that your ring mold can be set inside it, with a 1/4-inch gap all the way around the mold.

For each of the 4 plates, place the ring mold in the center of the plate, and fill it with the sweet potato, kielbasa, and shallot mixture to a height of 2 1/2 inches, using a spoon to press it into the mold. Then slide the ring mold carefully up and off to release a cylinder of sweet potato and kielbasa on the plate. (To plate this dish exactly as we do at the New Scenic Café, you will need a ring mold that is 3 inches in diameter and at least 2 1/2 inches tall. If you do not have one, you can adjust your plating technique as you like to create an equally attractive presentation.)

Using a spoon, fill the gap carefully between the date puree and the sweet potato cylinder with the warm chicken stock, creating a "moat" of stock all the way around.

Lay 2 grilled quail on top of the sweet potatoes on each plate, one quail on top of the other, so that the legs rest over the side of the mound of potatoes. Pour 1/4 cup of warm apricot saffron sauce over the top of each pair of quail; some of the pieces of diced apricot should stay on top of the quail, and some will fall over the sides. Garnish the top of each pair of quail with a sprig of microgreens or fresh herbs.

seared alaskan salmon

yield: 4 servings

This dish embodies the kind of "northern Minnesota cuisine" I love to work with, created from the bounty and the people of this region. It begins with salmon caught by local resident, Dave Rogotzke, who owns Simple Gifts Syrup and Salmon. He operates a salmon boat in Alaska, and I buy a lot of his wonderful king and sockeye salmon. He also has a maple forest and sugar shack in the Duluth area, and I use his hand-crafted syrup to finish the seared salmon in this dish. Nestled beneath the salmon on the plate are spears of lightly-cooked asparagus. And resting beneath it all is hand-harvested and wood-parched wild rice, another northern Minnesota staple, which I buy from local harvester, Sherry Rovig. You can certainly use other wild rice for this recipe, but her rice is more golden in color than standard wild rice and has a distinctly nutty, toasty taste. I cook the wild rice with a bit of mirepoix, garlic, dried cranberries, white wine, and chicken stock, to create a delicious flavor partner for the salmon and the buttery asparagus. This dish celebrates the values and work of the people in this region who catch the fish, tap the maple trees, harvest the wild rice, and produce the many other local foods we use with pride at the New Scenic Café.

Ingredients:

Wild Rice:

1	C	hand-harvested, wood-parched wild rice
1	t	kosher salt
1/3	C	dried cranberries
1/3	C	carrot (brunoise cut)
1/3	C	red onion (brunoise cut)
1/3	C	celery (brunoise cut)
2	T	olive oil
3	t	garlic (minced)
1/4	C	white wine (dry)
1/2	C	chicken stock (p. 364)

Seared Salmon:

24	oz	Alaskan sockeye salmon
3	T	olive oil

Asparagus:

36	spears	asparagus
2	T	melted butter

Other:

1/4	C	pure maple syrup
1/2	C	microgreens

Method:

Wild Rice:

If you use "parched" wild rice, the cooking time for the rice is greatly reduced. (If you use rice that is not parched, follow the cooking instructions for that type of rice.)

Put the parched wild rice in a medium-size pot, along with 2 1/2 cups of cold water and the kosher salt. Put a tight-fitting lid on the pot, and place it over high heat. Bring it to a boil, and allow it to boil rapidly for about 5 minutes. Turn off the heat, but leave the pot on the burner. Let the pot rest for 15 minutes, and then remove the lid. If any water remains in the pot, put the lid back on, and let the rice continue to sit until it soaks up the remaining water.

Pour boiling water over the dried cranberries, let them soak for 5 minutes until they become plump, and then drain off the excess water.

Cut the carrot, red onion, and celery into a "brunoise" cut of tiny cubes that are 1/8 inch on all sides. (The French term for this flavor-base mix of vegetables is "mirepoix.") It is worth taking time to cut these vegetables as nicely as you can. The visual impact of the perfect, tiny cubes adds greatly to this dish. Plus, making the brunoise cuts is great practice for your knife skills.

Put the olive oil in a large sauté pan, and place the pan over high heat. When the oil is just beginning to smoke, add the mirepoix (carrot, onion, celery) to the pan. Sauté the vegetables until they begin to soften, and then add the minced garlic and sauté the mixture for another minute.

Deglaze the pan with the white wine, and cook the vegetables until the wine has evaporated. Add 2 cups of cooked wild rice to the pan, along with the chicken stock, and stir them thoroughly. Continue to cook the rice mixture over high heat until most of the chicken stock has been absorbed. Mix in the dried cranberries, and season the mixture to taste with salt and pepper.

(continued on page 191)

(continued from page 190)

Seared Salmon:
If the salmon still has the skin on, remove and discard it. Then cut the fish into 4 portions of about 6 ounces each, and season the salmon on both sides with kosher salt and black pepper.

Put the olive oil in a large sauté pan, and heat it over medium heat until shimmering. Then lay the pieces of salmon in the pan, with the non-skin sides down. (You can also grill the salmon, if you prefer. I have done so many times when making this dish for outdoor catering events, and it works well for this dish.)

You can observe the progress of the searing by watching the change in color that occurs around the salmon's edges. The edges will lighten, in contrast to the coloring of the uncooked center of the fish. After about 5 minutes, when the edges of the salmon have changed color and the cooking appears to be about halfway finished according to your preference, use a spatula to carefully flip each piece over. Cook the salmon for about 5 minutes longer, and remove it from the pan.

(If you like your salmon cooked all the way through, you can choose to leave it in the pan for a few minutes more. But good-quality salmon is great when it is cooked to medium or even medium-rare, when it will appear a bit soft and translucent in the center.)

Asparagus:
You can prepare the asparagus in any number of ways, including in a steamer basket, over a grill, in a sauté pan, or on a roasting pan in the oven. More important than the method you use, though, is making sure you do not overcook the asparagus, which can leave it mushy, brown, and stringy. Asparagus that is cooked properly will be a nice, bright green, with just a bit of crunch as you bite through its center. After you cook the asparagus, dress it with the melted butter, and season it with salt and pepper.

Assembly:
Divide the wild rice mixture evenly onto the centers of 4 plates, and then across the top of each mound of rice arrange 9 asparagus spears, lined up nicely. Set a piece of salmon on top of the asparagus on each plate, and pour about 1 tablespoon of maple syrup across the top of each piece of fish. Garnish the salmon as you prefer. I use a small tuft of microgreens, which adds a nice bit of height to the dish.

braised lamb shank & parsnips

yield: 4 servings

Ingredients:

Lamb Shanks:

4	each	lamb shanks (12 oz each)
1	C	all-purpose flour
1 1/2	C	olive oil
2	C	chopped carrot
2	C	chopped onion
2	C	chopped celery
2	T	minced garlic
28	oz	crushed tomatoes
1	C	red wine
1	T	oregano
1	t	dried thyme leaves
2	each	bay leaves
1/2	T	fennel seed
1	t	celery seed
1/2	t	ground nutmeg
2	each	whole star anise pods
1/2	T	dried dill weed
1/2	C	vegetable base
1/2	T	kosher salt

Parsnips:

8	each	small parsnips

Orange Gremolata:

8	oz	Italian flat-leaf parsley
1	each	zest of orange
1/4	C	olive oil
1	t	kosher salt
1	pinch	white pepper
2	t	minced garlic
1/2	C	toasted bread crumbs

Other:

1	C	green peas
1/2	C	pearl onions

Braised lamb shanks provide a rich and versatile foundation for a variety of dishes, and over the years at the Café I have served them in many different ways. This recipe brings braised lamb shanks together with parsnips, green peas, pearl onions, and a gremolata, which is a condiment traditionally made from parsley, lemon zest, garlic, and olive oil. I substitute orange zest for the lemon zest to smooth the flavors and just before serving add coarse toasted breadcrumbs to the mixture for a bit of crunch. This hearty, tangy dish is great for late summer or early fall.

Method:

Lamb Shanks:

Roll the lamb shanks in the flour until they are coated well, and heat the olive oil in a large pot until wisps of smoke begin to form. Using a long pair of tongs, set the four lamb shanks carefully in the hot oil. Allow the shanks to sear until they are browned thoroughly on one side, and then turn them over to the next side. Continue cooking them until they are browned evenly all the way around. Remove the lamb shanks from the pot, and arrange them in one layer in a roasting pan.

To create a braising liquid, add the mire poix (mixture of carrot, onion, and celery) to the pot you just used to sear the lamb, and cook the vegetables on medium heat, stirring them frequently, until the onions are soft and translucent. Add all of the remaining ingredients, and simmer the mixture for 30 minutes.

Preheat the oven to 275 degrees. Pour the hot braising liquid over the lamb shanks in the roasting pan, adding a bit of water, if necessary, to be sure the shanks are submerged. Cover the roasting pan tightly with plastic wrap and then aluminum foil, and place it in the oven. Braise the shanks in the oven for 2 to 3 hours. After 2 hours, begin checking them every 10 to 15 minutes. You will know the lamb shanks are done when you can pull the meat apart gently using a fork or tongs (but they should not fall apart on their own when you pick them up). Remove the pan from the oven.

Cool the shanks at room temperature for at least 30 minutes. Remove them from the braising liquid, and place them in the refrigerator to cool completely.

Parsnips:

Using a vegetable peeler, peel the parsnips. Submerge them in the roasting pan of hot braising liquid that was used for the lamb shanks, and return the pan to the oven.

(continued on page 193)

(continued from page 192)

Braise the parsnips in the oven for 10 to 15 minutes. You will know they are done when you can slip the tip of a small knife easily into the center of their thickest part. Check the parsnips often to avoid overcooking them. Remove them from the liquid, taking care because they will be soft and fragile. Cool the parsnips in the refrigerator, along with the lamb shanks.

Pour the braising liquid through a fine-mesh strainer and into a large pot, and discard the solids. You will use the liquid to rewarm the lamb shanks and to create a sauce with the parsnips, green peas, and pearl onions.

Orange Gremolata:

Pull the parsley leaves off of the stems, and discard the stems. Chop the parsley finely, and put it in a mixing bowl. Use a microplane grater to remove all of the zest from the orange, and add the orange zest to the chopped parsley, along with the olive oil, kosher salt, white pepper, and minced garlic. Stir the ingredients together until they are mixed evenly. Just before you serve your meal, add the toasted breadcrumbs to the gremolata, using your fingers to stir the crumbs until they are coated lightly with oil.

Assembly:

Heat the pot of braising liquid to a simmer, and add the braised lamb shanks. (If the shanks are cold, you can speed things up by heating each shank in the microwave for a minute or two.) Simmer the shanks for 10 to 15 minutes, until they are hot all the way through.

Lay the braised parsnips in a large sauté pan, and add 3 cups of braising liquid from the pot where you are warming the shanks. Heat the sauté pan over medium heat until the parsnips are warmed through and the liquid has reduced by about 20 percent. Add the green peas and pearl onions, and simmer them until they are hot.

Large bowls that are shallow and wide work well for serving this dish, so that the sauce can pool around the bottom of the bowl. Place one lamb shank in the middle of each bowl, and lay 2 parsnips next to it. Sprinkle a couple spoonfuls of green peas and pearl onions across the top of each shank, and pour about 1/2 cup of the reduced liquid from the sauté pan into each bowl. Then scatter a handful of the orange gremolata and breadcrumb mixture over the top, and serve the dish right away, while it is hot and fresh.

The New Scenic Café

potato gnocchi

yield: 4 servings

This deliciously decadent vegetarian dish offers a simple marriage of ingredients, with the focal point being the gnocchi itself. Mastering the process of making gnocchi takes practice. But the more you make it, the more you will develop a feel for subtly adjusting the dough to produce a gnocchi that is airy and soft. I've tried a number of methods, and this is the best I've found. I roast russet potatoes, put them through a ricer, sprinkle them with Pecorino Romano cheese, and cut them with flour and eggs, to create a beautifully light gnocchi dough that I roll and slice and then cook in boiling water. I sauté the cooked gnocchi and toss it with roasted kalamata olives and grape tomatoes as well as béchamel, a white sauce with a touch of nutmeg. The plate is finished with an artichoke heart, fried capers, fresh oregano, and lemon zest. This is a simple and honest dish that captures the flair of the Mediterranean.

Method:

Gnocchi:

Preheat the oven to 350 degrees. Bake the potatoes on a sheet pan for 1 hour, which will remove much of their moisture. They should be fully cooked, with the skins dry and crunchy. While the potatoes are baking, measure the other gnocchi ingredients so they will be ready. You will need a clean and wide-open counter on which to work.

Remove the potatoes from the oven, and immediately cut them in half lengthwise. Working quickly, before the potatoes cool and become sticky or lumpy, scoop the insides of the potatoes out of the skins, and push them through a ricer or food mill. The total yield of riced potatoes should be about 2 pounds. Spread the potatoes on a sheet pan or on the counter, and allow them to sit until they are only slightly warmer than room temperature.

While the potatoes are cooling, fill a large pot with water and bring it to a boil. Add 3 tablespoons of kosher salt for every gallon of water in the pot. Make a cold bath as well by filling a large bowl with ice water.

Sprinkle the kosher salt, white pepper, and grated Pecorino Romano cheese over the potatoes. Crack the eggs into a small bowl, and whisk them with a fork. Pour the eggs evenly over the potatoes, and spread the flour over the top. Using a bench knife, make repeated vertical chopping strokes, going back and forth in different directions, to combine the ingredients without "working" the flour. (Mixing gently in this way ensures the dough will be light and airy.)

After you've mixed the flour in evenly, gather the dough with your hands, and begin pressing it gently into a ball. Keep kneading it until it comes together in a uniform dough. Test the readiness of the dough by pressing a spot lightly with the tip of your finger. Watch closely, and though the fingerprint will still be visible you should be able to see the spot you pressed bounce back a bit. If it does not, keep kneading the dough, and test it again.

(continued on page 196)

Ingredients:

Gnocchi:

3	lb	russet potatoes (large)
2	T	kosher salt
1	t	white pepper
2	T	Pecorino Romano cheese (grated)
2	each	eggs
2	C	all-purpose flour (plus extra for dusting)

Fried Capers:

2	C	canola oil
1/4	C	capers

Other:

4	each	long-stem marinated artichoke hearts (whole)
4	T	butter (melted)
20	each	kalamata olives
20	each	grape tomatoes
1/4	C	olive oil
2	C	béchamel sauce (p. 362)
4	sprigs	fresh oregano
2	t	lemon zest

(continued from page 195)

Shape the dough into a log, and lay a clean, dry towel over it. Let it rest for about 5 minutes, and then use the bench knife to cut the dough into 3 or 4 pieces.

Dust the dough and the work surface lightly with flour. Using both hands, roll each piece of dough back and forth until it elongates into a "snake" that is about 1/2 inch in diameter. Use the bench knife to chop the long pieces into 1-inch segments, and then dust them with flour to keep them from sticking together.

Scoop up about 2 cups of the gnocchi, and place them carefully in the lightly boiling water. (Be sure the water is not boiling rapidly or the gnocchi could be at risk of falling apart.) After a few seconds, use a spoon to stir the gnocchi gently, since they often stick to the bottom of the pot when they first begin cooking. Let the gnocchi cook in the boiling water until they rise and float, about 5 minutes.

Scoop up the gnocchi with a strainer, and drop them in the cold bath to stop them from cooking further. Repeat this process until all the gnocchi have been cooked and placed in the ice water. (You may need to add more ice periodically to keep the water cold.) Drain the gnocchi well, and toss them with just enough olive oil to coat them. Place them in the refrigerator until you are ready to use them. (The gnocchi can be refrigerated for up to 2 days.)

Fried capers:
In a small pot, heat the canola oil to 350 degrees. Drain the capers, and pat them dry with a paper towel. Drop about 1 tablespoon of capers at a time into the hot oil, and fry them for about 60 seconds, until they are crisp. Use a small strainer or a slotted spoon to retrieve them from the oil, and then place them on a paper towel to drain. (They will stay fresh and ready to use for a couple of hours.)

Assembly:
Preheat the oven to 400 degrees. Cut the stem off each artichoke heart so it has a flat base. Chop the stems into small pieces, and set them aside. Place the hearts on a sheet pan, and pour the melted butter over them so the butter fills in the cracks. (If you are especially ambitious and want to use fresh artichokes instead, you will need to steam them and remove the hearts.)

In a small bowl, toss the kalamata olives and grape tomatoes in just enough olive oil to coat them. Place the olives and tomatoes on the sheet pan next to the artichoke hearts, and roast them for 5 to 7 minutes, until they are hot and just beginning to soften.

Put the olive oil in a large sauté pan, and heat it on high heat until small wisps of smoke form. Add the gnocchi to the pan, and sauté them, tossing them every minute or so until they are brown and crisp. Remove the pan from the heat, and drain off any excess oil.

Add the roasted olives and tomatoes to the sauté pan, along with the chopped artichoke stems and the béchamel sauce, and toss them with the gnocchi. Keep the pan off the heat. Enough residual heat from the ingredients will remain to melt the béchamel, which is susceptible to "breaking," or separating into its components, if it is overheated.

This dish is best served in large, shallow bowls, but flat plates will work if you prefer. Divide the sautéed gnocchi mixture among the 4 plates, placing it in the middle. Set one of the roasted artichoke hearts atop the center of each serving of gnocchi, and scatter about one tablespoon of fried capers over each plate. Garnish the dish with fresh oregano and lemon zest.

cumin-scented pork tenderloin

yield: 4 servings

To create the most flavorful, moist pork tenderloin for this dish, I first brine the tenderloin. Then I rub it with a cumin-based spice rub, cook it over a charcoal grill to give it that delicious smoky flavor, and slice it thinly. Atop the pork slices, I spoon browned butter, a bit of apple cider gastrique, and port-fortified dried cherries, to bring a sweet fruit flavor to the plate. These are tart cherries that I simmer slowly in tawny port wine, along with garlic and thyme, until the cherries absorb the liquid and take on the port's distinctive flavor. The dried cherries I use come from two places known for producing some of the best: Door County, Wisconsin and northern Michigan. Along with the pork, I serve a smooth purée of rich Yukon Gold potatoes (or, in fall or winter, puréed rutabagas make a delicious alternative). The dish is garnished with thin slices of fresh, crisp scallions.

Method:

Note that this recipe requires 1 to 2 days of prior preparation to brine the pork tenderloin.

Cumin Rub:

Heat a small sauté pan over high heat. Add the whole cumin seeds (no oil needed), and shake the pan constantly until the seeds begin to darken, about 1 minute. Put the seeds in a spice grinder and pulse them just enough to crack them—but do not grind them finely. Then mix the cumin seeds with the remaining Cumin Rub ingredients.

Pork Tenderloin:

Clean the membrane, or "silverskin," off of the pork tenderloin, along with any excess fat. In a large bowl or pan, stir together the apple cider, kosher salt, and granulated sugar to create a brine. Submerge the pork in the brine, cover it, and refrigerate it for at least one full day (two days is even better).

Remove the tenderloin from the brine, and pat it dry with paper towels. Cut it into 4 portions of about 6 ounces each, coat the tenderloin chunks with the cumin rub, and set them in the refrigerator until you are ready to cook them.

If you can, cook the pork over a charcoal grill. The smokiness of the charcoal will add a lot to the flavor. (You can use a gas grill instead or sear the pork in a sauté pan and then roast it in the oven to finish it.) Cook the pork until it is medium, 145 degrees at the center. Its center will still be a bit pink.

Port-Fortified Dried Cherries:
To cook the cherries, you will need to create a makeshift double boiler, using a metal bowl that is the right size to rest on top of a small or medium-size pot.

(continued on page 198)

Ingredients:

Cumin Rub:

1/4	C	cumin seeds
1	T	kosher salt
1/4	C	dried chives
1/2	T	dried thyme leaves
1	t	crushed red pepper flakes
2	T	brown sugar

Pork Tenderloin:

24	oz	pork tenderloin
4	C	apple cider
3	T	kosher salt
4	T	granulated sugar

Port-Fortified Dried Cherries:

4	oz	dried cherries
1/2	C	tawny port
1	sprig	fresh thyme
1/2	clove	garlic
1	pinch	cracked black pepper

Yukon Gold Potato Purée:

3	lb	Yukon Gold potatoes
1	C	butter
1	C	heavy cream
1	T	kosher salt
1/2	t	white pepper

Other:

8	each	scallions
4	T	browned butter (p. 363)
4	T	apple cider gastrique (p. 362)

(continued from page 197)

Fill the pot with water (but not so full that the water will touch the bottom of the bowl when you place it on top). Heat the water to a simmer.

Combine all of the ingredients in the bowl, and cover it tightly with plastic wrap. Poke one small vent hole in the center of the plastic wrap, and place the bowl on top of the pot of simmering water. Allow the cherry mixture to cook slowly for up to 2 hours, until the cherries have absorbed most of the liquid.

Yukon Gold Potato Purée:
Peel the potatoes, and boil them until they are "fork tender" all the way through. Melt the butter and heavy cream together in a small pot, and set the pot aside. Drain the potatoes, and push them through a potato ricer or a food mill back into the pot you cooked them in. (If you do not have a ricer or food mill, you can use a potato masher or even a large fork to crush them, though they will not be quite as smooth.)

Add the mixture of melted butter and heavy cream to the potatoes, as well as the kosher salt and white pepper, and whisk the ingredients together. The potatoes are best when served immediately.

Assembly:
On a steep angle, slice the scallions as thinly as you can, to create long, thin slivers. Then put them in an ice-water bath. They will curl a bit and become more firm. Just before you are ready to serve, pull the scallions from the ice water, shake off as much water as you can, and drain them on a paper towel.

Place about 2/3 cup of potato purée in the center of each of the 4 plates. Lay a portion of the thin slices of pork across each serving of the potatoes, overlapping the slices like a stack of fallen dominoes.

Pour 1 tablespoon of browned butter and 1 tablespoon of apple cider gastrique across each portion of pork, followed by about 2 tablespoons of port-fortified dried cherries. Then divide the scallions into neat piles atop each plate, for a lively green accent.

beef tenderloin

yield: 4 servings

Working with the cuisine of Mexico's Oaxacan region was one of my first loves as a new chef, and today I still enjoy bringing components of that fare into the dishes I create, including the chocolate mole I incorporate in this dish. I start with a beautiful portion of beef tenderloin, grill it to start, and finish it in the oven. For an accompaniment, I candy multi-colored heirloom baby carrots in a sauté pan with butter and sugar. I plate this dish by first spooning a pool of chocolate mole for each serving. Mole is a chile sauce of Oaxacan origin that is flavored with nuts, seeds, and bittersweet chocolate. I also add a smear of cashew whip to the plates, which I make from cashews, vanilla, and hand-crafted syrup from local sugar-shack operator Dave Rogotzke. I lay the cooked tenderloin on top of the mole and top the steak with a sfogliatelle, which is a coiled Italian pastry. Rather than filling them with the more traditional pastry cream, marzipan, or ricotta, I fill the sfogliatelle with a Medjool date mixture that includes Thai chiles, giving the pastry a zesty flavor that serves as an excellent complement to the beef tenderloin.

Method:

Note that making the sfogliatelle and the chocolate mole can take a bit of time, so plan to start on those two elements 1 to 2 days in advance.

Cashew Whip:

Place all of the ingredients in a blender, and purée them on high speed until they are completely smooth, pausing periodically to stir them with a spatula if necessary. The cashew whip can be held at room temperature for 1 day or kept for a longer period in the refrigerator.

Candied Carrots:

Baby heirloom carrots come in a variety of lovely colors, including orange, yellow, white, and purple, and are usually about 6 inches long and 1/2 inch in diameter at the thick end. Whole baby carrots look great on the plate, so use them if possible. Otherwise, find the best-tasting carrots you can, and cut them into pieces that are about that same size.

Heat a large pot of salted water to a boil, and blanch the carrots until they are just cooked through, about 2 to 3 minutes. Remove the carrots from the water, and plunge them immediately into ice water. After the carrots are chilled, remove them from the ice water and drain them.

Heat a large sauté pan over medium heat, and add the butter, granulated sugar, and 1 tablespoon of water, cooking the ingredients until the butter melts and the sugar is mostly dissolved. Add the carrots to the pan, and toss them until the sugar becomes bubbly and caramelized and coats the carrots with a glaze. Season the carrots with a pinch of kosher salt and black pepper.

(continued on page 202)

Ingredients:

Cashew Whip:

1	C	cashews
6	T	hot water
1/2	T	maple syrup
1/4	t	vanilla extract
1	pinch	kosher salt

Candied Carrots:

12	each	heirloom baby carrots (multi-color)
2	T	butter
1/4	C	granulated sugar

Beef Tenderloin:

32	oz	beef tenderloin
2	T	kosher salt
1	T	fresh cracked black pepper
2	T	olive oil

Other:

4	each	Medjool date-filled sfogliatelle (p. 92)
1	C	chocolate mole (p. 364)
4	sprigs	cilantro or other fresh herb

(continued from page 201)

Beef Tenderloin:

I buy whole beef tenderloins, which can weigh well over 5 pounds, and then I clean and portion them. If you are buying your meat from a butcher, see if you can get a piece from the "barrel" of a tenderloin. The barrel is the center section, which is round and even. You might have to pay a little more for that cut, but having steaks that are of a uniform size and shape makes cooking them easier. (You can also substitute a different cut of steak for this recipe or even use another red meat, such as lamb, venison, or veal.)

Preheat the oven to 400 degrees. Cut the tenderloin into 4 cylindrical portions, each weighing about 8 ounces. Season them liberally with kosher salt and fresh cracked black pepper, and rub them with olive oil.

Put the steaks on a hot grill, and leave them on just long enough to mark them, about 1 minute per side. (If you are not using a grill, sear them with olive oil in a hot sauté pan, about 1 minute per side.) Then put the steaks on a sheet pan.

Place the sheet pan in the oven, and roast the steaks to the desired doneness, using an instant-read digital thermometer to check the center temperature of each steak. Medium-rare is 130 degrees, medium is 140 degrees, and medium-well is 150 degrees. Remove the steaks from the oven, and allow them to rest for a few minutes. (Keep in mind the temperature will continue to rise by a few degrees after you take the steaks out of the oven, so pull them out a bit before they reach the temperature you want.)

Assembly:

While the steaks are resting, put the sfogliatelle in the oven to reheat them to a flaky golden brown. It will take 7 or 8 minutes. In a small pot over low heat, gently warm the chocolate mole as well.

Spoon 2 to 3 tablespoons of chocolate mole onto each of the 4 plates, to create a pool that is slightly off-center. Use another spoon to drop a large dollop of cashew whip off to the side, pulling the edge of the spoon through it to create an attractive smear.

Set a piece of tenderloin in the center of each pool of chocolate mole. Then stack 3 carrots on top of each steak, taking the time needed to be sure the carrots stay in place.

Pick up the sfogliatelle, and bend it gently into a curl so that it can be set on top of the carrots and will curve over them and stay in place. You will have to work with each sfogliatelle for a bit, teasing the layers gently to get them to move slightly. Finish the dish with a bright garnish of fresh herbs or cilantro.

lamb meatloaf

yield: 4 servings

Lamb has always been my favorite red meat, but when I was growing up it was served at home only for special occasions. At the café, I have looked for cost-effective and approachable yet exciting ways to bring lamb to the table, serving it over the years in many dishes, from braised shanks, to chops, to meatballs. I have found that this lamb dish captures a particularly pleasing combination of flavors and colors that diners love. I use fresh ground lamb, to which I introduce a bit of beef fat that I glean from trimming ribeye steaks, to add loft and lightness to the lamb. Each individual portion of meatloaf is baked atop a thick slice of red onion, which caramelizes beautifully and brings a delightful flavor to the meat. I pair the lamb with three small root vegetables—Parisian carrots, baby red potatoes, and fingerling sweet potatoes—that have been glazed in a bit of butter: Covering the lamb are green peas that I toss in a cream sherry & foie gras sauce, adding a rich, gravy-like texture to the plate. To the side of the meatloaf, I place a raw egg yolk, for body and a creamy, smooth element. I top the dish with braised cabbage and black truffle oil, which pulls the meal together nicely, and then garnish it with fresh frisee leaves. This dish can be served as I do at the Café, in individual portions, or can be modified easily to create a traditional meatloaf that you cut into slices. The rich flavors and colors of this dish make it the perfect meal for autumn.

Method:

Lamb Meatloaf:

Preheat the oven to 400 degrees. To form each portion of meatloaf, weigh 7 ounces of meatloaf mix, and press it into a 3-inch diameter ring mold that has been coated lightly with oil. Cut four cross-section slices of red onion that are each about 1/4-inch thick, and lay them individually on a sheet pan.

Set the ring mold that you have filled with the meatloaf mix on top of one of the onion slices. (The slices of onion keep the meatloaf from sticking to the pan and are nicely caramelized and flavorful by the time the meatloaf is cooked.) Use your fingers or a spoon to hold down the center of the meatloaf while you slide the ring mold up and off carefully. Repeat this process for the other 3 meatloaf portions.

Place the meatloaf in the oven, and bake it for about 20 minutes, using an instant-read digital thermometer to check the center temperature of each portion. When the thermometer reads 150 degrees, the meatloaf is done. Remove the meatloaf from the oven, and allow it to rest.

Root Vegetables:

You can choose to prepare the root vegetables in advance and then reheat them or make them and serve them immediately.

Put the baby red potatoes in a medium-size pot, and cover them with cold water. Add about 2 tablespoons of salt to the water, bring it to a boil over high heat, and let the potatoes boil for 2 minutes. Turn off the heat, and leave the potatoes in the hot water for 10 more minutes. Check that they are cooked through by poking them with a knife or fork. Then drain off the water.

(continued on page 204)

Ingredients:

Lamb Meatloaf:

28	oz	lamb meatloaf mix (p. 367)
1	each	red onion

Root Vegetables:

4	each	baby red potatoes
2 - 4	each	Parisian carrots ("Thumbelina carrots")
2	each	fingerling sweet potatoes (or 1 regular sweet potato)
1	T	olive oil
4	T	butter

Other:

1/2	C	green peas
1/2	C	cream sherry & foie gras sauce (p. 365)
1	C	savoy cabbage (cut into 1" squares)
2	t	black truffle oil
4	each	eggs
1	C	frisee leaves

(continued from page 203)

Parisian carrots, sometimes called "Thumbelina carrots," and are short, fat, and round. They are similar in shape to a radish, baby beet, or baby turnip. To cook them, bring a pot of salted water to a boil. If they are small, leave the carrots whole. Otherwise, split them in half or even in quarters. Blanch the carrots for 5 to 7 minutes in the boiling water, until inserting a knife or fork indicates they are just cooked through, and then remove them from the boiling water and put them immediately into an ice-water bath.

Preheat the oven to 250 degrees for the fingerling sweet potatoes. (If you cannot locate fingerlings, you can roast a regular-size sweet potato for approximately 1 hour and cut it into smaller pieces after it is cooked.) Coat the potatoes with the olive oil, and season them with salt and pepper. Lay the fingerlings on a sheet pan, and roast them for about 20 minutes, checking them frequently by poking them with a small knife, which should penetrate to the center of the potato with relative ease. Cut the fingerling potatoes in half on an angle. (If you are using a regular-size sweet potato, cut it into pieces that are similar in size to the red potatoes and carrots.)

Just before serving the root vegetables, combine them in a medium-size pot with the butter and 2 tablespoons of water. Put a lid on the pot, and heat it on medium heat, stirring the vegetables frequently. The water will steam the vegetables to help them get hot without burning, and the butter will glaze them nicely. Season the vegetables with salt and pepper.

Assembly:

Warm the peas in a small pot, along with a few tablespoons of water to keep them from burning. When the peas are hot, drain off any excess water, and add the cream sherry & foie gras sauce. Stir the mixture until the sauce is melted.

Cut the cabbage into postage-stamp-size squares, about 1 inch by 1 inch. Put the cabbage in a small pot along with 2 tablespoons of water, 1 teaspoon of salt, and a pinch of black pepper, and place it on medium heat. Cook the cabbage until it has wilted but is still green, about 5 minutes. If any water remains, drain it off, and then pour the black truffle oil on the cabbage.

Use a spatula to move each portion of meatloaf, with the onion still underneath, onto the center of a plate. Scoop a couple of spoonfuls of peas with cream sherry & foie gras sauce on top of the meatloaf. Some of the peas will fall to the sides, but try to get most of them to stay on top.

Stack about 12 pieces of braised cabbage on top of the peas. Place one baby red potato, one Parisian carrot, and one piece of sweet potato next to the meatloaf. For each plate, crack open an egg, and separate the yolk from the white, taking time to remove all of the white. Then set the yolk gently on the plate, and season its top with salt and pepper. Garnish the top of the meatloaf with a small handful of frisee leaves and a few more drops of black truffle oil.

ostrich en croute

yield: 4 servings

Ingredients:

Duxelle:

4	oz	crimini mushrooms
4	oz	shiitake mushrooms
1	T	olive oil
2	T	shallot (minced)
2	T	garlic (minced)
1/4	t	dried thyme
1/2	t	dried chives
1/2	t	dried parsley flakes
1	pinch	rubbed sage
1/2	t	kosher salt
1	pinch	cracked black pepper
2	T	pistachios (ground)
1	T	butter
1	T	white wine

Ostrich en Croute:

16	oz	ostrich fan filets
3	T	olive oil
8	pieces	puff pastry (cut 3" x 6")

Huckleberry Demi-glace:

1/2	C	veal demi-glace (p. 371)
1/4	C	frozen huckleberries

Candied Root Vegetables:

8	each	Parisian carrots
8	each	baby turnips
2	C	milk
1/2	C	sugar
6	T	butter
8	each	roasted baby beets (p. 369)

Other:

4	each	fresh rosemary sprigs

This recipe was born from an elk en croute entrée I prepared on New Year's Eve years ago, which was a hit. That following Valentine's Day, I modified the recipe to use ostrich instead and found it was an even bigger hit. Ostrich is exceptionally tender, deep in color, and lean. I grill the ostrich lightly to give it a nice smoky flavor, cut it into small cubes, and mix it with a duxelle, which is prepared from wild mushrooms, herbs and spices, and some pistachios, butter, and wine. Then I encrust that mixture with puff pastry and bake it. Using puff pastry, as in this recipe, creates a larger form for the ostrich entrée. For a smaller form, I have used filo dough to create a pouch like a small purse with a gathering at the top, tied with a chive. I serve the pastry-enrobed ostrich with a huckleberry demi-glace and candied root vegetables. If you prefer an alternative to ostrich, you will get excellent results using venison, beef tenderloin, or elk as a substitute in this savory entrée.

Method:

Duxelle:

Mince the mushrooms finely in a food processor. In a large sauté pan, heat the olive oil over high heat, and then add the minced shallots and garlic. Sauté them until they have caramelized. Reduce the heat to medium, and add the minced mushrooms and all of the herbs and spices. Continue cooking the mixture, stirring it constantly, until the mushrooms have released their liquid and have begun to caramelize.

Add the ground pistachios, butter, and white wine to the sauté pan, and continue cooking them until the duxelle becomes stiff, about 3 minutes. Spread it on a sheet pan, and cool it in the refrigerator.

Ostrich en Croute:

Season the ostrich filets with salt and pepper, and rub them with about 2 tablespoons of olive oil. On a charcoal grill, sear the outsides for just 1 minute per side, to give the meat a smoky flavor, which adds nicely to the dish. The meat should essentially still be raw. (If necessary, you can instead sear the ostrich on high heat in a sauté pan, for 1 minute per side.) Cut the meat into 1/2-inch cubes.

Preheat the oven to 400 degrees. Blend the ostrich meat, duxelle, and 1 tablespoon olive oil in a mixing bowl. On a floured work surface, use a rolling pin to roll out and elongate the strips of puff pastry until they are 12 inches in length.

Dust a 3-inch ring mold generously with flour. Lay one strip of puff pastry inside the ring, pushing the center all the way down to your work surface and pressing the pastry flat inside the ring.

(continued on page 207)

(continued from page 206)

Lay a second pastry strip perpendicular to the first one, pressing it down in the same way. The two strips should cover the inside of the ring mold completely.

Fill the mold to the top with the ostrich and duxelle mixture (approximately 6 ounces). Fold over the ends of the puff pastry strips, trimming them if they are too long but leaving enough length so they overlap. With the palm of your hand, press down firmly on them to seal the ends of the puff pastry together. Flip the filled pastry over so that the ends of the puff pastry are now on the bottom, and slide the ring mold carefully up and off. Repeat this process for the other 3 servings.

Cover a sheet pan with parchment paper, and set the 4 portions on the pan. Bake the ostrich en croute for 25 to 30 minutes, rotating them part way through the baking time so they bake evenly. Use an instant-read digital thermometer to check the center temperatures. When the temperature reaches 145 degrees, remove them from the oven, and allow them to rest.

Huckleberry Demi-glace:
Warm the veal demi-glace and frozen huckleberries together in a small pot. Bring the mixture to a simmer for about 5 minutes, stirring thoroughly, and season it to taste with salt and pepper.

Candied Root Vegetables:
Bring a large pot of salted water to a boil. Blanch the Parisian carrots in the boiling water for 5 to 7 minutes, until inserting a knife or fork indicates they are just cooked through. Then remove them from the boiling water, and put them immediately into an ice-water bath to cool. Drain the carrots well.

Peel the baby turnips, and trim their stems to 1/4 inch. Place the baby turnips, milk, sugar, and 2 tablespoons butter in a small pot, and simmer them over medium heat, until the turnips are tender. Strain the turnips, and put them in the refrigerator to cool.

In a large sauté pan, heat 4 tablespoons of butter over medium heat until the butter is sizzling hot but has not yet begun to turn brown. Add the carrots, turnips, and roasted and peeled baby beets, and sprinkle them with 2 tablespoons of sugar.

With one hand, tilt the sauté pan toward you, keeping it over the burner, and use a large spoon to baste the hot butter and sugar over the root vegetables. Turn them over occasionally, and continue basting them until the vegetables have begun to brown slightly and a thin glaze has formed.

Assembly:
This dish is best served in a large, shallow bowl, so that the sauce pools in the center. Place the baked ostrich en croute in the middle of the bowl, and then nestle 2 each of the candied carrots, turnips, and beets up against it all the way around. Spoon 2 tablespoons of huckleberry demi-glace on top of the ostrich en croute, so that it runs over its side and collects around the outside while some huckleberries remain on top. Garnish each dish with a sprig of fresh rosemary.

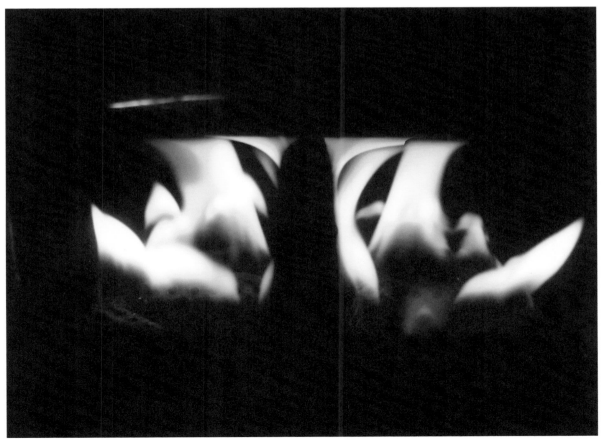

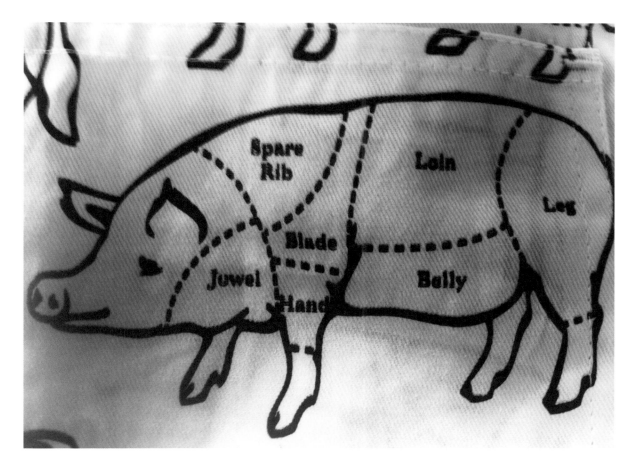

Desserts

The New Scenic Café

fruit pies

yield: 7 - 8 servings (9" pie)

I originally made our pie crusts with lard because it offers such excellent flavor and texture. But we began getting requests at the Café from vegetarians asking us to use shortening instead so that they, too, could enjoy our pies. I made the switch, found great success with my crust recipe, and never looked back. Non-vegetarians are surprised to hear our flaky crusts are made with shortening, and vegetarians and vegans are delighted to find out they can partake. For the pie fillings, I particularly enjoy creating recipes that use berries. I buy fresh berries from small berry farms in the region, including Lakewood Berry Farm in Duluth, Minnesota and Shary's Berries in Two Harbors, Minnesota. Then I freeze the berries. Using frozen berries in a pie filling helps keep the filling firm when it is being mixed and when it is poured into the pie crust. And freezing the berries also allows me to have delicious berries available all year!

Ingredients:

Pie Crust:

3/4	C	vegetable shortening
1 3/4	C	all-purpose flour
1	t	kosher salt
5	fl oz	ice-cold water

Other:

3	lb	fruit pie filling (p. 228)
1	T	granulated sugar

Method:

Pie Crust:

Before beginning, chill the vegetable shortening in the refrigerator. Combine the all-purpose flour and kosher salt in a mixing bowl, and use a pastry blender to incorporate the shortening, until the shortening pieces are no larger than the size of peas.

Add the ice-cold water to the mixture, using a fork to blend it together lightly until the dough looks evenly damp. You should still be able to see small clumps of shortening in the dough. Put the dough on a floured work surface. With floured hands, form the dough into a ball, and divide it into 2 equal parts. Shape each part gently into a smooth, round disc, and wrap each disc tightly with plastic wrap. Refrigerate the dough for at least 30 minutes.

Assembly:

Remove one of the dough discs from the refrigerator, place it on a floured work surface, and use a floured rolling pin to roll the dough out so that it is just wider than the outer rim of the pie pan. Transfer the dough into the pie pan, and press it into the pan's corners, making sure the edge of the crust just barely hangs over the rim of the pan all the way around. Refrigerate the pie pan and bottom crust while you prepare the pie filling.

Preheat the oven to 350 degrees, and prepare the fruit filling. Roll the second dough disc to the same size as the first. Remove the pie pan and bottom crust from the refrigerator, fill it with the fruit filling, and set the top crust in place, making sure there are no air pockets between the filling and the top crust. Roll and crimp the edges of the dough to seal the two crusts together. Using the tip of a knife, cut several vent holes in the top crust, and dust it with granulated sugar.

Bake the pie for 15 minutes. Turn the oven down to 300 degrees, bake it for another 35 minutes, and use a thermometer to check the temperature of the pie's center. Continue baking the pie and checking it every few minutes until the thermometer reads 170 degrees, which is when the flour in the filling will properly thicken. Any juices that have bubbled out should appear clear rather than cloudy, indicating doneness, and the crust should be a light golden brown. Remove the pie from the oven, place it on a cooling rack, and allow it to cool at room temperature for at least 60 minutes before slicing.

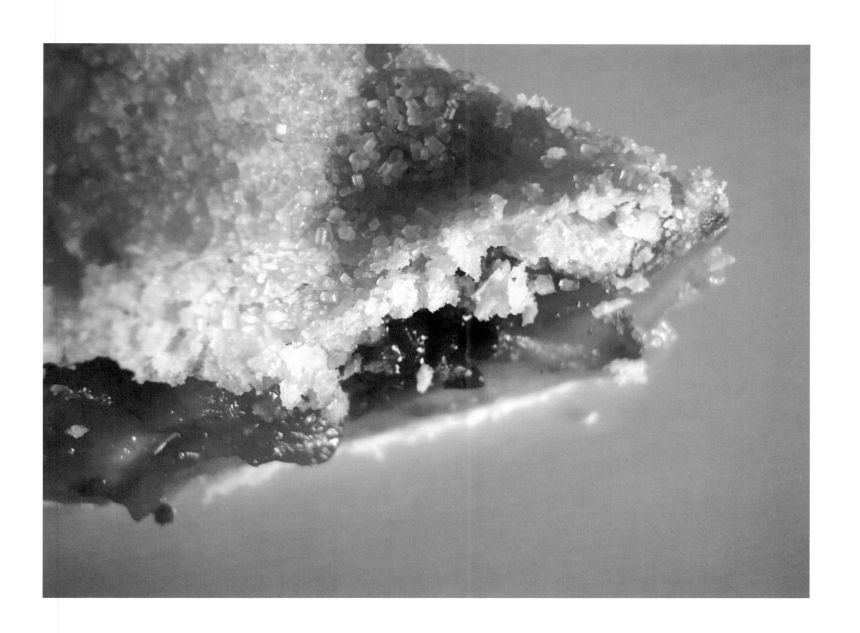

triple-berry pie filling

When we first opened the Café, my business partner Rita and I looked for the right combination of mixed berries for our pies, and after much delectable testing settled on a blend of blackberries, blueberries, and raspberries. Over time, we found ourselves simply sticking with the name "triple-berry," and this pie has become our flagship. One key to its success is the wild Maine blueberries that I use, which are smaller and more intense in color and flavor than standard blueberries. But whatever blueberries you use, you'll find this triple-berry pie a real treat.

Ingredients:

12	oz	frozen blackberries
16	oz	frozen blueberries
8	oz	frozen raspberries
1/2	C	all-purpose flour
1 1/4	C	granulated sugar

Method:

Combine all of the berries in a mixing bowl, allowing them to defrost about halfway and soften a little. Add the all-purpose flour and granulated sugar, and stir the mixture to combine the ingredients. The partially frozen fruit helps make the process easier because it keeps the filling stiff while you put it in the crust, add the top crust, and crimp the edges. (The more the berries melt and become liquid, the more challenging they can be to work with.)

blackberry peach pie filling

Another favorite among our "fleet" of pies is blackberry peach pie, which I retained on the menu when I took over the Café, though I gave the original recipe my own taste twist. I loved peach pie when I was a young child, and I love it still. In fact, it is a family tradition that I receive a peach pie each year on my birthday. But you don't need to wait for a special occasion to enjoy this tasty dessert.

Ingredients:

28	oz	frozen peaches
8	oz	frozen blackberries
1/4	t	vanilla extract
1/2	C	all-purpose flour
1 1/3	C	granulated sugar
1/4	t	ground nutmeg

Method:

Allow the peaches to defrost completely, and then cut them into 1-inch pieces. Put the pieces in a mixing bowl, add the frozen blackberries and the vanilla extract, and stir the mixture. Whisk together the all-purpose flour, granulated sugar, and ground nutmeg, making sure the nutmeg is distributed evenly. Add the dry ingredients to the fruit mixture, and stir them until they are combined evenly. Pour the pie filling into the pie crust quickly, while the filling is still somewhat stiff. (It becomes more liquid as it sits, making the filling and crimping of the pie crust a bit more challenging.)

raspberry rhubarb pie filling

Our raspberry rhubarb pie is another sought-after treat at the New Scenic Café. I have always enjoyed the tart and bitter flavor of rhubarb, and it is traditional to use it in desserts in Minnesota, though I add just enough sugar to soften the rhubarb's singular impact. When it is in season, I use as much fresh rhubarb as I can get my hands on. Use fresh for this recipe, if it's available, but frozen rhubarb also works well.

Ingredients:

24	oz	rhubarb (fresh or frozen)
12	oz	frozen raspberries
1/2	C	all-purpose flour
1 1/3	C	granulated sugar

Method:

If you are using frozen rhubarb, allow it to defrost fully (though the raspberries should remain frozen). For fresh rhubarb, clean the stalks and chop them into small pieces that are about 1/4-inch thick. Put the rhubarb and raspberries in a mixing bowl, add the all-purpose flour and granulated sugar, and stir them until they are mixed evenly. Pour the filling into the pie crust right away, before the frozen berries in the filling defrost completely and become soft and liquid.

goat cheese cake
yield: 4 servings

The primary flavoring for this creamy goat cheese cake is orange blossom water, which has a floral softness that works perfectly in this recipe. (Orange oil is another option, but it has a much stronger flavor and is quite acidic.) I blend the orange blossom water with the soft goat cheese, cream cheese, butter, heavy cream, and other ingredients, whip the mixture, and put it in a pastry bag to fill the cake rings. I then top each chilled cake with candied kumquats and add "fairy floss," or Pashmak, to give the cakes a soft, sweet appearance. Pashmak is an Iranian product made from spun sugar. It is similar to cotton candy but has delicate strands that are lined up almost like glossy, fine hair. I acquire the Pashmak through an import company based in Australia, called Pariya. Alongside the finished cake on the plate, I place one more candied kumquat to give this dessert a final flair of sweetness and color.

Method:

Goat Cheese Cake:

I have found that I can shape these cakes successfully and unmold them cleanly by using strips of acetate film to form ring molds. I order sheets of acetate online, from a company called JB Prince, and cut it into strips.

To make the 4 cake molds, cut strips of acetate film that are 2 1/2 inches wide and 10 inches long, roll them into 2 1/2-inch diameter rings, and secure each ring with one small piece of tape. Then line a sheet pan with parchment paper, and spray the paper very lightly with pan release. Arrange the 4 acetate rings on the parchment, leaving space between them.

Allow the goat cheese, cream cheese, and butter to soften at room temperature. Then blend them with an electric mixer, using its paddle attachment. Mix in the powdered sugar, vanilla extract, and orange blossom water, and whip the mixture on high speed for 2 minutes.

In a medium-size metal bowl, "bloom," or soften, the sheets of silver gelatin by pouring the cold water over them. Then warm the softened gelatin gently by placing the metal bowl over a simmering pot of water, stirring the gelatin until it is completely melted. Set the gelatin aside.

Switch the attachment on the electric mixer to a whisk, add the heavy cream to the goat cheese mixture, and whip it for 3 minutes on medium speed. Remove about 1 cup of the batter, and stir it into the melted gelatin. Then pour that gelatin mixture back into the batter, and continue to whip it on medium speed until soft peaks form.

Transfer the mixture to a pastry bag. (You can also put it in a ziplock bag from which you have trimmed off about 1/2 inch of one corner.) Use the pastry bag to fill each of the 4 acetate rings to about 3/4 full. Set the pan of goat cheese cakes in the refrigerator for several hours to set up completely.

(continued on page 231)

Ingredients:

Goat Cheese Cake:

1	lb	goat cheese (soft chevre)
1/4	lb	cream cheese
1	oz	butter
1/2	C	powdered sugar
1/4	t	vanilla extract
2	drops	orange blossom water
3	sheets	silver gelatin
1/4	C	cold water
4 1/2	C	heavy cream

Other:

16	each	candied kumquats (p. 363)
4	tufts	pistachio Pashmak

The New Scenic Café

(continued from page 229)

Assembly:

Remove the goat cheese cakes from the refrigerator, and with the acetate still attached, transfer them carefully from the sheet pan to the serving plates. Then use the tip of a small knife to cut the tape holding each acetate ring together. Peel the acetate gently off of each cake, and discard it.

Using the back of a spoon, press an indentation into the tops of the cakes. Place 3 whole candied kumquats in the indentation in each cake, and pour a little of the kumquat syrup over them, allowing it to drip slightly over the sides.

With clean, dry hands, pick up a small amount of the pistachio Pashmak, using your fingers to pull it gently into a light and airy "tuft." Place the tuft directly on top of the kumquats, pulling the Pashmak up a little so that it looks a bit like a flame.

You'll want to move quickly at this juncture, since the moisture from the kumquats will begin dissolving the Pashmak as it sits. Place another kumquat off to the side on the plate as a garnish, and then serve the dessert immediately.

ice cream sundae
yield: 4 sundaes

A bit of excess is something we can all use once in a while, and I created this bounty of sweetness and flavor with that sentiment in mind. I had found some lovely old pewter goblets, and somehow they spoke "ice cream sundae" to me. I filled them with homemade vanilla bean ice cream and then added more homemade sweets: crushed hazelnut tuile, chocolate ganache, browned butter caramel, hand-crafted marshmallows, and fresh whipped cream. On top, I placed a nest of spun sugar "glass," made up of fine strands of hard sugar, and then popped in a celebratory sparkling candle. And, of course, it is finished with cherries! I serve this sundae with two spoons, in the hope that it will bring people together in the enjoyment of the quintessential ice cream sundae.

Ingredients:

Vanilla Bean Ice Cream:

2	C	2% milk
1	C	granulated sugar
1/3	C	honey
4 1/2	C	heavy cream
2	each	vanilla beans
12	each	egg yolks
1/4	t	kosher salt

Marshmallows:

1/4	C	powdered sugar
5 1/2	sheets	silver gelatin
1/3	C	cold water
1	C	granulated sugar
1 1/2	T	light corn syrup
1/2	C	water
1	pinch	kosher salt
1	each	egg white

Other:

1/4	C	hazelnut tuile (p. 366)
1/4	C	chocolate ganache (p. 364)
1/4	C	browned butter caramel (p. 363)
1	C	whipped cream (p. 371)
2	C	spun sugar "glass" (p. 370)
4 - 8	each	candied amarena cherries

Method:

Note that you will need to prepare this recipe one day ahead, to allow time to refrigerate the ice cream mixture overnight.

Vanilla Bean Ice Cream:
Combine the 2% milk, granulated sugar, honey, and half of the heavy cream in a large pot. Split the vanilla beans in half lengthwise, scrape out the seeds using the tip of a small knife, and then add the seeds and pods to the mixture in the pot. Place the pot over medium heat, stirring frequently until the mixture just comes to a boil, and then remove it from the heat.

Put the egg yolks in a large mixing bowl, and beat them using a whisk or fork until they are mixed evenly. Temper the yolks by whisking in small amounts of the hot cream mixture until you have added about 1 cup of it. Then slowly pour and whisk the egg mixture back into the pot of hot cream.

Place the pot over low heat. Whisking constantly, bring the temperature of the mixture up to 185 degrees (using an instant-read digital thermometer for best accuracy). Remove the pot from the heat, and add the other half of the heavy cream. Stir the salt in thoroughly.

Transfer the mixture to a storage container, and refrigerate it overnight to allow the flavors to develop further. The next day, strain the cream mixture through a fine mesh strainer to remove the vanilla pods. Pour it into an ice cream maker, and follow the maker's instructions to finish creating your vanilla bean ice cream.

(continued on page 234)

(continued from page 232)

Marshmallows:
Line a sheet pan with parchment paper, and dust the parchment generously with powdered sugar. Set it aside.

In a small bowl, pour the cold water over the sheets of silver gelatin, and allow the gelatin to "bloom," or soften. In a sauce pot, combine the granulated sugar, corn syrup, water, and salt, and heat it over high heat until it reaches exactly 238 degrees.

Place the egg white in the bowl of an electric mixer, and, using the whisk attachment, begin whipping the egg white on high speed until it becomes foamy. With the mixer running, pour the hot sugar mixture slowly into the egg white, and then add the gelatin. The residual heat from the hot sugar will melt the gelatin and allow it to mix evenly. Continue to whip the mixture on high speed until it begins to cool and soft peaks form.

Transfer the marshmallow batter immediately into a piping bag that has a 1/2-inch round tip. Pipe small "kiss"-shaped drops of the marshmallow onto the sheet pan that has been lined with parchment paper and sprinkled with powdered sugar. You will want to work quickly because the marshmallows will set up quickly. Dust the tops of the marshmallows with additional powdered sugar, and allow them to cool and set up for several hours at room temperature before you use them (or you can store them in an airtight container). For an extra touch, you can use a brûlée torch to gently toast the outsides of the marshmallows.

Assembly:
Place a couple of generous scoops of vanilla bean ice cream into a sizable bowl or cup. Then top the ice cream with a bounty of homemade sweets that you can find recipes for in this book: crushed bits of hazelnut tuile, chocolate ganache, browned butter caramel, hand-crafted marshmallows, fresh whipped cream, spun sugar "glass," and, of course, cherries (in this recipe, delicious candied amarena cherries). Or go wild by piling on any sweet treats you like. Don't be afraid to build your sundaes to a nice height! And for a festive flair, try some sparkling candles.

passionfruit panna cotta

yield: 4 servings

Panna cotta is similar to a light custard, but unlike custard it is not made with eggs. It contains a bit of milk or cream, sugar, and flavoring, and it is the gelatin that holds it together. I make this panna cotta with passionfruit, which is a wonderful fruit that has an intense, unique citrus flavor and can be purchased in puréed form. I buy the French brand, Boiron, but any fruit purée will work, including homemade purées. You will need to stick with puréed fruit, though; jam or jelly is not a good substitute. Panna cotta can be put into forms or molds and then released, but it can also simply be made and served in individual dishes. It also functions well as a palate cleanser, presented in tiny one- or two-bite servings. I like to highlight cucumber as well as fresh pineapple, mango, papaya, or melon with the passionfruit panna cotta, and in this recipe I serve it with pineapple crisps as well. This is a nice, refreshing dessert that is perfect for summer. If ever there were such a thing as a healthy dessert, other than a simple piece of fruit, this just might be it.

Method:

Panna Cotta:

If the passionfruit purée is frozen, allow it to thaw and warm to room temperature. And if you are using a brand other than Boiron, note that the level of sweetness in the fruit might vary. It is also important to note that many fresh fruits, especially tropical fruits like passionfruit, contain an enzyme that destroys the gelling properties of gelatin. If you plan to use fresh passionfruit in this recipe, you will need to kill the enzyme by heating the fruit above 185 degrees. Commercial frozen-fruit purées have typically been heat-pasteurized, however, and are ready to use.

Cut the sheets of silver gelatin into small pieces, and then, in a small bowl, add the gelatin to the cold water. Add one piece of gelatin at a time so that the pieces don't stick together. Allow the gelatin to "bloom," or soften, until it is supple and has absorbed almost all of the water.

Combine the heavy cream and granulated sugar in a sauce pot, and heat them over medium heat, stirring the mixture occasionally until it comes to a low boil. Remove the pot from the heat, and allow the cream and sugar mixture to cool to between 95 and 105 degrees. Use an instant-read digital thermometer to ensure accuracy. Gelatin begins to degrade if it is exposed over a prolonged period to temperatures higher than 105 degrees, but do not cool the mixture below 95 degrees because you will need the heat to melt the gelatin.

Add the bloomed gelatin and water to the warm cream and sugar mixture, and stir it until the gelatin has dissolved. Then add the passionfruit purée, and stir the mixture thoroughly. Pour it into the molds quickly because the gelatin might begin to set up. (If needed, the mixture can be re-warmed gently to keep it liquid.) Small dishes, such as ramekins, or even wide, shallow cups work best. Place the filled molds in the refrigerator for at least 2 hours to set completely.

If you have any extra passionfruit mixture, you can store it in a sealed container in the refrigerator and reheat it later to pour into additional molds.

(continued on page 236)

Ingredients:

Panna Cotta:

14	oz	passionfruit purée
3	sheets	silver gelatin
3	T	cold water
2	C	heavy cream
3/4	C	granulated sugar

Pineapple Crisps:

1/4	each	fresh pineapple
1/4	C	powdered sugar

Garnish:

1/4	C	fresh fruit (pineapple, mango, papaya, melon)
1/4	C	cucumber

(continued from page 235)

Pineapple Crisps:
Preheat the oven to 170 degrees.

You will need to cut very thin slices of pineapple for the crisps. At the Café, we make full, round cross-section pineapple slices using a commercial rotary slicer. At home, you can use a sharp mandoline slicer, but the pineapple core can be tough to cut through. You might find it easier to cut the pineapple into rectangles, half-moons, or other shapes of any size, making sure the slices are as thin as possible.

Use a fine-mesh sieve to sprinkle an even layer of powdered sugar on the surface of a sheet pan lined with a silicone baking mat. Then lay the pineapple slices on the powdered sugar, with space between them, and sprinkle more powdered sugar lightly over their tops until a thin coating covers them.

Bake the pineapple until it becomes crisp when cooled. The baking might require a couple of hours, depending on how thin the slices are. (You can test a slice for doneness by removing it from the oven, laying it on a cool surface for 20 to 30 seconds, and then taking a bite of it or using your fingers to try to snap it.) When the pineapple is done, remove it from the silicone mat as quickly as possible so it does not stick as it cools. You can peel the pineapple slices off the mat carefully using your fingers or slide a thin spatula underneath the slices and lift them off.

Garnish:
I like to use some combination of fresh pineapple, mango, papaya, or melon for this recipe, but you could use any fruit you prefer. The fresh flavor and crisp texture of cucumber is also pleasantly surprising. Take your time, and cut the fruit and cucumber into a precise 1/4-inch dice. The visual impact you will achieve with perfectly-cut, small cubes is worth the effort.

Assembly:
Serve the passionfruit panna cotta cold—directly out of the refrigerator—to ensure that it has a nice, firm texture. I usually serve this panna cotta right in the dish I've chilled it in, but if you prefer to unmold your panna cotta, warm the outside first by setting the dish in warm water for 15-20 seconds. Then flip the dish upside-down onto a serving plate, and the panna cotta should slide out. (If it does not, set the dish back in the warm water for a few more seconds, and try again.) Spoon 2 tablespoons of diced fruit and cucumber onto the center of each panna cotta, and then stick one or more pieces of pineapple crisp into it so that the crisps stand straight up. Serve this summery treat with a spoon.

lemon poppyseed bundt cake

yield: 16 servings (10" cake)

Pies and cookies were always my favorite desserts growing up, much more than cake. But my Aunt "Rita B," co-founder with me of the New Scenic Café, made a lemon poppyseed cake that has rivaled other desserts for my affections. She made it in the form of a bundt cake and then finished it with velvety lemon curd that was mixed with whipped cream. Over the years, I have altered the cake recipe by cutting sour cream into the cake batter and baking the cake at a lower temperature, yielding a moister and denser poppyseed cake. I serve thin slices of the cake on spoonfuls of blueberry sauce and then top it with lemon curd whipped cream and, for a lighter flair, a slice of candied orange and a sprinkling of sugared blueberries.

Method:

Cake:

Preheat the oven to 300 degrees. Spray the inside of a 10-inch (12 cup) bundt pan with pan release, and then dust it with flour. Combine the all-purpose flour, kosher salt, baking soda, and poppy seeds in a large bowl, mix them thoroughly, and set them aside.

Using the paddle attachment of an electric mixer, beat the unsalted butter, granulated sugar, vanilla extract, and lemon zest on high speed until the mixture is light and fluffy. Mix the eggs in one at a time, stopping the mixer occasionally to scrape the sides of the bowl.

Add the dry ingredients and the sour cream to the mixture, and blend it on low speed until all the ingredients are combined evenly, still continuing to stop the mixer now and then to scrape the bowl's sides.

Pour the cake batter into the prepared bundt pan, and bake it for 45 minutes or until a toothpick inserted into the thickest part of the cake comes out clean. Remove the cake from the oven, and cool it at room temperature.

Blueberry Sauce:

Put all of the ingredients in a small sauce pot, and bring the mixture to a low boil. Reduce the heat, let it simmer for 10 minutes, and then transfer the mixture to a blender. Purée it on high speed until it is completely smooth. Cool and store the sauce in the refrigerator.

(continued on page 240)

Ingredients:

Cake:

2 1/2	C	all-purpose flour
1/2	t	kosher salt
1/2	T	baking soda
3	T	poppy seeds
1	C	unsalted butter (softened)
1 1/2	C	granulated sugar
1/2	T	vanilla extract
2	T	lemon zest
5	each	eggs
1 1/2	C	sour cream

Blueberry Sauce:

1 1/2	C	blueberries (fresh or frozen)
1/4	C	water
1/4	C	granulated sugar
1	t	lemon zest
1	pinch	kosher salt

Lemon Curd Whipped Cream:

2	C	heavy cream
2	T	granulated sugar
1/2	C	lemon curd (p. 367)

Candied Orange Slices:

1/4	C	powdered sugar
1	each	orange

Other:

130	each	sugared blueberries (p. 370) (approx. 130 berries)

(continued from page 239)

Lemon Curd Whipped Cream:
Using an electric mixer, whip the heavy cream and granulated sugar on medium speed until very soft peaks form. Change to low speed, and incorporate the lemon curd slowly. Then whip the mixture on medium speed until stiff peaks form, and store the lemon curd whipped cream in the refrigerator.

Candied Orange Slices:
Preheat the oven to 175 degrees. Using a sharp mandoline slicer, cut cross-section slices of orange that are 1/16 inch wide. Then use a fine-mesh sieve to sprinkle an even layer of powdered sugar on the surface of a sheet pan lined with a silicone baking mat, tapping the side of the sieve with your hand as you go to release the sugar. Lay the orange slices on the powdered sugar, with space between the slices, and sprinkle more powdered sugar over their tops. Slide the sheet pan into the oven.

Allow the orange slices to bake as long as needed to dehydrate them—it might take an hour or even longer. (An oven that has a fan works best.) You can test their doneness by removing a slice from the pan, setting it on a cool surface for about 20 seconds, and biting it to see if it is crisp or using your fingers to try to snap it. When the orange slices are done, remove them from the silicone mat immediately so they will not stick as they cool.

Assembly:
In the center of each plate, put 2 or 3 tablespoons of blueberry sauce. Then cut two thin wedges of cake, stack them together, and set them in the blueberry sauce. Use an ice cream scoop or large spoon to place a generous dollop of lemon curd whipped cream on top of the cake slices. Perch one slice of candied orange horizontally on the whipped cream, scatter 6 to 8 sugared blueberries on and around the cake, and dust the top with powdered sugar.

chocolate ganache tart

yield: 4 servings

I use a cookie crumb crust for these rich, chocolaty tarts, by forming the crust mixture in flan rings and then pouring in the chocolate ganache. (If you prefer, a standard tart crust or even a pie crust would work well.) I also make thin Florentine cookies that are the same diameter as the tarts and place a cookie upright in each tart, cutting it in so it looks like a rising moon. The tart is finished with a couple of large fresh berries, a creamy butterscotch sauce, and a few grains of coarse sea salt. I typically use marion blackberries because they are big and juicy and work well with the chocolate and the Florentine, but any blackberry or large berry will be a tasty addition to this eye-catching dessert.

Method:

Chocolate Ganache Tarts:

To make these tarts, I have found it works best to use 3-inch diameter flan ring molds. They are stainless steel, bottomless rings that have rolled edges and smooth seams, making it relatively easy to remove the finished product.

Set the flan ring molds on a sheet pan lined with parchment paper. The sheet pan must be smooth and flat, not warped or dented, to ensure that the ganache does leak out the edges of the molds.

Preheat the oven to 300 degrees. Put the all-purpose flour and granulated sugar in a food processor, and pulse it once or twice to combine the ingredients. Cut the chilled butter into small pieces, and drop them into the food processor. Pulse it again until the butter is incorporated but the mixture is still powdery in texture.

Put 4 tablespoons of the crust mix inside each flan ring mold, using the back side of a spoon to press the crust mix into an even, flat, 1/8-inch thick layer across only the bottom of the mold (not up its sides). Place the sheet pan in the oven, and bake the tart crusts for 5 to 6 minutes, until they just begin to brown. Remove the sheet pan from the oven, and leave the ring molds on the pan as the crusts cool to room temperature.

Heat the chocolate ganache until it is just warm enough that it will pour easily and "self-level." (The warmer the ganache is, the runnier it is and therefore the more likely it is to seep out the bottom edges of the molds.)

After the tart crusts have cooled, fill the flan rings the rest of the way with the molten ganache. Allow the tarts to sit until the ganache cools to room temperature, and then place the entire sheet pan in the refrigerator so the tarts can cool further. (If you place the filled tarts in the refrigerator while the ganache is still warm, the ganache will shrink too quickly, and cracks will form on its surface.)

(continued on page 242)

Ingredients:

Chocolate Ganache Tarts:

1	C	all-purpose flour
2	T	granulated sugar
4	oz	butter (chilled)
2 1/2	C	chocolate ganache (p. 364)

Florentines:

1/3	C	butter
1/4	C	light brown sugar
2	T	granulated sugar
2	T	light corn syrup
1	t	vanilla extract
1/3	C	all-purpose flour
1/2	C	ground almonds
1	T	hot water

Butterscotch Sauce:

4	oz	butter
3/4	C	granulated sugar
3	T	water
1	C	heavy cream
1/2	t	vanilla extract
1	oz	Scotch whisky

Other:

8	each	fresh marion blackberries
1	t	coarse sea salt

(continued from page 241)

After the tarts have cooled in the refrigerator for at least an hour, take the flan ring molds out of the refrigerator one at a time. If you have a brûlée torch, use it to briefly warm the outside of the metal ring. The chocolate will melt just enough to allow you to slide the ring up and off. If you don't have a torch, run a small, thin knife under hot water, and then slide it around the outside edge of the tart to free it from the ring. Place the tart back on the sheet pan in the refrigerator, and continue releasing the other tarts.

Florentines:

Preheat the oven to 350 degrees. Combine the butter, light brown sugar, granulated sugar, and light corn syrup in a small pot. Place it over low heat, stirring the mixture frequently until the sugars have dissolved completely. Increase the heat to medium, and, stirring constantly, bring the mixture just to a boil and then remove it immediately from the heat. Stir in the vanilla extract, and add the all-purpose flour, stirring until the mixture is smooth, and then mix in the ground almonds. Add the hot water, and stir the mixture until all the ingredients are completely incorporated.

Use a small scoop or spoon to drop 1/4-ounce portions of the batter onto a sheet pan lined with a silicone baking mat. Leave at least 3 inches of space between each cookie because Florentines spread a lot as they bake. (This recipe will make more Florentines than are needed for the tart, but it is never a bad thing to have extra on hand!)

Place the pan in the oven, and bake the Florentines for 8 to 10 minutes, until they are thin and a deep golden brown. Remove the pan from the oven, and allow the cookies to cool completely before removing them carefully from the silicone mat. They should have many little holes in them and be very thin, crisp, and translucent. Store the cooled Florentines in an airtight container.

Butterscotch Sauce:

Put the butter in a medium-size sauce pan, and cook it over medium heat, stirring frequently, until the milk solids turn brown. Add the granulated sugar and water, and stir the ingredients to combine them thoroughly. Increase the heat to medium-high, and cook the mixture until the sugar caramelizes to a medium-brown color.

Remove the pot from the heat, and immediately pour in the heavy cream very quickly, all at once. The caramel will bubble up, but the coldness of the cream will stop the bubbling. Return the pot to the heat, bring the mixture to a boil, and then remove it from the heat to let the caramel cool. Add the vanilla extract and Scotch whisky, and stir to combine them completely. (The Scotch can be eliminated, if desired, resulting in a buttery caramel sauce that is still delicious.)

Assembly:

The ganache tarts are much better served at room temperature than cold, but they are difficult to move after they have warmed because they become soft. You can work around this easily by placing the tarts on serving plates while they are cold and allowing them to warm slowly.

After the tarts have warmed to room temperature, press one Florentine cookie upright in each one, positioning the Florentine toward the back of the tart so that it looks a bit like the back of a chair and leaves most of the surface of the ganache visible.

Set 2 whole blackberries on top of each tart. Then use a small squeeze bottle or a spoon to drizzle butterscotch sauce over the berries and the tart, allowing the sauce to drip a bit over the sides. Sprinkle a few grains of coarse sea salt over the top of the tart, and serve it immediately.

mille-feuille

yield: 4 servings

Translated literally, mille-feuille means, "thousand layers." This dessert is often made with multiple layers of puff pastry, but I prefer the crispness of baked sheets of filo dough. I brush the filo with butter, top it with sugar, and put it under a broiler until the sugar caramelizes and the filo is baked to a golden brown. It is a process similar to that of caramelizing sugar on top of a crème brûlée, but instead of custard as the base, here it is the filo. To assemble the mille-feuille, I create layer after layer to build structure and add new elements. I begin with a base of blackberry puree, lemon curd, and pastry cream, and continue to build, adding sugared blueberries, more pastry cream and lemon curd, and more layers of crispy filo. Then I garnish the mille-feuille with delicate edible flowers or microgreens. You can easily alter this dessert by using such ingredients as bananas, chocolate mousse, or even fresh figs in place of the berry and lemon flavors.

Method:

Blackberry Purée:
In a small pot, combine all of the ingredients, and begin cooking them over low heat. Increase the heat to bring the mixture just to a boil, and then reduce it again to simmer it for 10 minutes. Transfer the berry mixture to a blender, purée it until it is smooth, and push the purée through a fine mesh strainer to remove any seeds. Store the purée in the refrigerator.

Mille-feuille Layers:
Preheat the oven broiler. (Or, you can use a brûlée torch instead.) Create a stack of 5 individual layers of filo dough, and then cut the stack into 2-inch-by-4-inch rectangles. Cut a total of 12 of these 5-layer rectangles, and lay each stack on a sheet pan. Brush the tops of the filo stacks with the melted butter, and coat them lightly with granulated sugar.

Place the sheet pan beneath the hot broiler for about 30 seconds, until the sugar caramelizes and the filo is crisp and golden. (If you are using a brûlée torch, move the flame constantly back-and-forth across the sugar on each piece until the sugar is caramelized evenly.)

Assembly:
Put the lemon curd and pastry cream into separate squeeze bottles. (You can also create a pastry bag by cutting the tip off a corner of a ziplock bag.) On a flat plate, create a rounded rectangle of blackberry purée that is 4 inches long and 1 inch wide. On top of the blackberry purée, create a stripe of lemon curd that is 1/2-inch wide and runs the length of the purée. Next to the lemon curd, create an identical stripe of pastry cream.

Place a filo rectangle on top of the lemon curd and pastry cream. Squeeze a 1/4-inch thick, zigzagged layer of lemon curd over the filo, filling it to within 1/4 inch of the filo's edges. Place 10 sugared blueberries on the lemon curd, and then squeeze 3 dots of pastry cream in a line on top of the blueberries, making each dot of cream the size of a quarter and about 1 inch tall.

Set another rectangle of filo on top, and then squeeze 3 more dots of pastry cream on it, followed by a third layer of filo. Garnish the top of the filo with edible flowers or microgreens.

Ingredients:

Blackberry Purée:

9	oz	blackberries (frozen)
2	oz	granulated sugar
1/2	C	water
1/2	t	vanilla extract

Mille-feuille Layers:

12	pieces	filo dough (cut 2" x 4", with 5 layers per stack)
1/2	C	butter (melted)
1	C	granulated sugar

Other:

1	C	lemon curd (p. 367)
1	C	pastry cream (p. 368)
1	C	sugared blueberries (p. 370) (approx. 40 berries)
4	pinches	edible flowers or microgreens

black-bottom banana cream tart

yield: 4 servings

I originally prepared this dessert as a whole banana cream pie, with chocolate ganache on the bottom, topped by pastry cream, bananas, and whipped cream. Over time, I turned the recipe into individual tarts that were like little one-serving cream pies, and diners loved having one all to themselves. I also began topping the bananas with sugar and caramelizing them with a brûlée torch, which added the new dimension of a delicious caramelized crunch to the dessert. Pie. Fruit. Chocolate. Cream. Crunch. What could be more perfect?!

Ingredients:

Tart shells:

1/2	C	all-purpose flour
1	t	granulated sugar
1/2	C	butter (chilled)
1/2	C	heavy cream

Other:

1	C	chocolate ganache (p. 364)
2	C	pastry cream (p. 368)
2+	each	bananas
1/2	C	granulated sugar
2	C	whipped cream (p. 371)

Method:

Tart shells:

Combine the all-purpose flour and granulated sugar in a food processor. Pulse it twice to blend the ingredients together. Cut the cold butter into small pieces, and drop it in the processor, pulsing it again until the butter is incorporated but the mixture is still powdery. Add the heavy cream slowly, pulsing the mixture until the dough clumps together. Remove it from the food processor, and shape it into 4 equal discs. Wrap each disc in plastic wrap, and refrigerate the discs for 1 hour.

Preheat the oven to 400 degrees. On a floured work surface, use a rolling pin to roll each piece of dough into a circle that is about 1/8 inch thick. Place each circle in a 4-inch tart pan.

Press down the bottom, and then work your way to the edges, forming the dough up the sides of the pan. Trim any excess dough that extends beyond the edge of the pan. Bake the tart shells for 8 to 10 minutes, until they are golden brown. Remove the shells from the oven, and allow them to cool to room temperature before removing them from the tart pans.

Assembly:

Melt the chocolate ganache gently. Pour enough ganache into each tart shell to coat the bottom generously, about 1/4 cup per shell. Set the shells aside until the ganache is cool and firm.

When you are ready to serve the tarts, use a spoon or a pastry bag to put pastry cream on top of the ganache, filling the shells the rest of the way.

Cut the bananas into thin slices, cutting at a 45-degree angle so the slices are long ovals (rather than small circles). Working on a heat-proof surface, such as a sheet pan, arrange the banana slices into 4-inch circles, overlapping and fanning out the slices as you go. Create 4 circles, using about one-half of a banana for each.

Sprinkle the granulated sugar over the banana slices until they are coated evenly. Then use a brûlée torch to caramelize the sugar, moving the flame constantly back and forth until the sugar forms an evenly brown, crisp layer. Let the bananas rest for a minute as the sugar cools and hardens, and then use a thin spatula to transfer one circle of bananas carefully on top of the pastry cream in each tart. Finish the tarts with a generous scoop of whipped cream in the center, and serve them while the bananas are still warm.

The New Scenic Café

chocolate terrine

yield: 32 portions (9" x 13" terrine)

This delightfully decadent dessert is built in stages as a large, single dish. Then it is cut into individual portions, showing off the beauty of the terrine that comes from the striation and the simplicity of its layers. I build the terrine with a base of chocolate praline, to which I've added pailleté feuilletine, which is a crunchy, flaky wheat product that looks like extra-thin corn flakes and stays crunchy even when mixed in melted chocolate. On top of the praline, I add dark chocolate mousse, and then a layer of chocolate cake, followed by milk chocolate mousse, and then chocolate ganache. Using both dark and milk chocolate allows me to combine bitterness and sweetness together for a more complex, rich flavor. I serve the terrine with a few fresh raspberries, to bring some fresh, juicy acidity to the plate. And I top it with bright green Arya pistachios. Terrines are not complex in concept, but the richness of the varied chocolates in the recipe gives this terrine a unique twist on delicious decadence.

Method:

This dessert is built using a sheet pan and a 4-inch-tall pan "extender." The extender is a rectangular frame that fits inside the edges of the sheet pan, creating a 4-inch-high wall that makes it easier to remove the finished product than it would be if one were using a deep pan. It also creates a terrine that has perfectly square edges, resulting in less waste.

Pan extenders that are 4 inches tall are readily available for larger sheet pans, such as 13-by-18-inch pans or 18-by-26-inch pans. It is difficult, however, to find an extender of that height for a standard 9-by-13-inch pan. Pan extenders that are 2 inches high are easier to find, so you could use two 2-inch pan extenders by fastening them together, which we have done at the Cafe. Alternatively, you could prepare this dessert in a standard 4-inch-deep pan.

I have noted the quantities here for use with a 9-by-13-inch pan, but you can scale the quantities to accommodate any size pan, including a bread pan or a deep, round cake pan. This recipe makes a generous quantity of chocolate terrine. So if you have extra, it's easy to save it for use later by wrapping it tightly and keeping it in the freezer.

Chocolate Sheet Cake:

Preheat the oven to 300 degrees. Prepare the cake batter as directed on the box, and divide the batter between 2 sheet pans that have been lined with parchment paper and sprayed with pan release. Spread the batter to form a 1/4-inch thick layer in each pan. It will bake to a thickness of 3/8 inch. (You will only need 1 sheet cake for this recipe, but make the extra in case of breakage.)

Bake the sheet cakes for about 10 minutes, until a toothpick inserted in their centers comes out clean. Allow them to cool to room temperature, and then cover the cakes and refrigerate them.

(continued on page 248)

Ingredients:

Chocolate Sheet Cake:

1	box	good quality devil's food cake mix (18.25 oz)

Praline Sheet:

6 1/2	oz	milk chocolate
7 1/2	oz	hazelnut paste
5	oz	pailleté feuilletine flakes

Dark Chocolate Mousse:

2	T	granulated sugar
1/2	C	half & half
4	each	egg yolks
9	oz	dark chocolate
1 1/4	C	soft whipped cream (p. 371)

Milk Chocolate Mousse:

2	T	granulated sugar
1/2	C	half & half
4	each	egg yolks
9	oz	milk chocolate
1 1/4	C	soft whipped cream (p. 371)

Other:

3	C	chocolate ganache (p. 364)
1/2	C	fresh raspberries
1/4	C	Arya pistachios

(continued from page 247)

Praline Sheet:
In a small pot over low heat, melt the milk chocolate until it reaches 120 degrees, and mix in the hazelnut paste. You can purchase good-quality hazelnut paste at specialty food stores, or you can make your own by grinding toasted hazelnuts in a food processor and slowly adding oil to create a thick liquid that resembles soft peanut butter.

Mix in the pailleté feuilletine flakes, which you can also buy at specialty food stores or online. Line a 9-by-13-inch sheet pan with parchment paper, and fit it with a 4-inch-tall sheet pan extender. Spray the parchment and the inside of the pan extender lightly with pan release. Pour the praline mixture into the pan, and spread it evenly. This forms the first layer of the terrine. Put it in the refrigerator to harden for 10 to 15 minutes, when you will remove it to pour the next layer on top, the dark chocolate mousse.

Dark Chocolate Mousse:
Combine the granulated sugar and the half & half in a small pot, and bring it just to a boil, stirring frequently. Put the egg yolks in a small mixing bowl, and beat them using a whisk or fork until they are mixed evenly. Then temper the yolks by whisking in small amounts of the hot liquid until you have added about 1/4 cup of it. Pour the yolk mixture slowly back into the pot, whisking it to combine the ingredients. Heat it over low heat, stirring constantly, until its temperature reaches 185 degrees.

If the dark chocolate is in bar form, chop it, and then put it in a heat-proof mixing bowl. Pour the hot half & half and egg mixture through a fine mesh strainer over the chocolate, and stir the mixture until the chocolate is melted thoroughly. Allow it to cool to room temperature. Then fold the soft whipped cream into the cooled chocolate mixture.

Pour the dark chocolate mousse on top of the praline sheet, inside the sheet pan extender, spreading it evenly. Then place a chocolate sheet cake that has been cut to the exact size of the extender on top of the dark chocolate mousse. Put the pan in the refrigerator while you prepare the milk chocolate mousse.

Milk Chocolate Mousse:
For the milk chocolate mousse, follow the same process you did to make the dark chocolate mousse but using milk chocolate. Remove the extended sheet pan from the refrigerator, and pour the milk chocolate mousse over the layer of chocolate cake, spreading it evenly. Then return the pan to the refrigerator.

Chocolate Ganache:
Warm the chocolate ganache gently to 95 degrees, so that it is warm enough to be liquid but not so warm it will melt the mousse. Pour the ganache evenly over the layer of milk chocolate mousse. Then put the terrine into the freezer to harden fully.

Assembly:
Remove the terrine from the freezer. While the terrine is still frozen, hold the blade of a long, thin knife under hot water to heat it, and run it around the inside of the pan extender frame. Reheat the blade as often as needed until you have run the knife all the way around the pan. Then slide the pan extender up and off the terrine.

Transfer the terrine to a cutting board, and heat the knife again to cut the terrine in half the long way. Then cross-cut each half into 3/4-inch slices, cutting only as many slices as you intend to serve. (Wrap the remaining terrine tightly in plastic wrap, and store it in the freezer for later use.) Lay the terrine slices individually on a pan or platter lined with parchment paper, cover the slices, and place them in the refrigerator to thaw.

To serve the chocolate terrine, transfer each slice of terrine to a plate, and garnish it with fresh raspberries and coarsely-chopped Arya pistachios.

sweet potato chiffon

yield: 4 - 6 servings

This dessert offers a delicious and elegant way to introduce the less-familiar sweet potato in pie form, rather than using the typical pumpkin. The sweet potato is uniquely sweet, with its large amount of natural sugar, and it is pleasingly creamy and smooth when puréed. I initially made sweet potato pies in the traditional fashion, at full size and inside a pie crust, but I have switched to creating individual portions without a crust. I find that the individual portions look more clean and elegant on the plates. I make a sweet potato chiffon, using the pumpkin pie spices of cinnamon, nutmeg, ginger, allspice, cloves, and cardamom and form it in individual ring molds lined with acetate film. On the plate, I finish the chiffon with browned butter caramel, whipped cream, and toasted pecans, and then add the crunch a crust normally provides by serving the dessert with a thin ginger tuile cookie. Because it can be a bit of a challenge to keep sweet potato chiffon intact and looking lovely for a long period of time, it's best to serve it as soon as possible after you prepare it.

Ingredients:

Sweet Potato Chiffon:

1	lb	sweet potatoes
1 1/2	sheets	silver gelatin
2	T	cold water
1/4	C	heavy cream
2	each	egg yolks
4	T	granulated sugar
1/2	T	vanilla extract
1/2	t	pumpkin pie spice (p. 369)
1/4	t	kosher salt
2	each	egg whites

Ginger Tuile:

6 1/2	T	butter (softened)
13	T	powdered sugar
1	t	ground ginger
1/4	t	lemon zest
2	T	molasses
2	each	egg whites
3/4	C + 1T	all-purpose flour

Other:

1/2	C	browned butter caramel (p. 363)
1	C	whipped cream (p. 371)
1/4	C	toasted pecans

Method:

Note that the sweet potato chiffon will need to set up in the refrigerator for at least a few hours, or overnight, before serving.

Sweet Potato Chiffon:
Prepare the molds ahead of time, using 3-inch metal entremet rings or any round ring molds of that approximate diameter. Even tall, round cookie or biscuit cutters will work as long as they do not have handles. Cut strips of acetate film long enough to line the insides of the ring molds, with the ends overlapping. (I order sheets of acetate online, from a company called JB Prince.)

Bring a large pot of water to a boil. Add the sweet potatoes, with their skins on, and boil them until they are soft all the way through, about 30 minutes. Remove the skins, chop the sweet potatoes into large pieces, and put them in a food processor while they are still hot. Purée them until they are completely smooth, and set them aside.

Cut the sheets of silver gelatin into small pieces, and then, in a small bowl, add the gelatin to the cold water. Add one piece of gelatin at a time so the pieces don't stick together, allowing the gelatin to "bloom," or soften, until it is supple and has absorbed almost all of the water.

Heat the heavy cream in a small pot until a few bubbles begin to form around the edges. Remove the pot from the heat, and place a lid on it to keep the cream warm.

Using an electric mixer with a whisk attachment, whip the egg yolks on high speed until they are light in color and thick. Add 2 tablespoons of the granulated sugar, and continue to whip the egg yolks and sugar until they are very thick, about 5 minutes. Reduce the mixer's speed to low, and add the warm cream slowly. Then transfer the egg yolk mixture to a large metal mixing bowl or a heat-proof glass mixing bowl.

(continued on page 251)

(continued from page 250)

Fill a medium-size pot with 1 inch of water, and bring it to a simmer. Set the bowl of egg yolk mixture over the simmering water, and cook it, stirring constantly, until the yolks thicken further and an instant-read digital thermometer reads 170 degrees. Remove the bowl from the pan of water, add the softened gelatin to the egg yolk mixture, and stir it until the gelatin is dissolved completely. Then add the puréed sweet potatoes, vanilla extract, pumpkin pie spice, and kosher salt, and stir the mixture. Set it aside.

In a clean, heat-proof mixing bowl, combine the egg whites and the remaining 2 tablespoons of granulated sugar. Set the bowl over the simmering water, and cook the egg white mixture, stirring constantly, until the instant-read digital thermometer reads 160 degrees. Remove the bowl from the pan of water, and, using an electric mixer with a clean whisk attachment, whip the egg whites on high speed until they are stiff and glossy.

Use a rubber spatula to fold the egg whites into the sweet potato mixture until they are combined evenly. Transfer the mixture to a pastry bag (or to a ziplock bag with one corner cut off), and pipe it into the acetate-lined ring molds, filling them to the top. Place the ring molds in the refrigerator.

Ginger Tuile:
Make the tuiles in advance, and keep them in an airtight container unless you use them immediately. You will need to find or make a stencil that you can use to shape the tuiles. A clean sheet of thin cardboard works for a one-time use; plastic works great if you want to reuse the form. (Plastic that is 1 millimeter thick works best. I simply cut my stencil out of a semi-rigid lid from a plastic box.)

To make your stencil, cut out as many shapes as will fit on your sheet, each about 1 inch by 5 inches. At the Café, we have made stencils in the shape of crescent moons, circles, and long rectangles that we curl into bands while they are still warm.

Using an electric mixer with a paddle attachment, on high speed cream together the softened butter, powdered sugar, ground ginger, lemon zest, and molasses until they are smooth. Reduce the mixer speed to low, and incorporate the egg whites and flour.

Put the batter in the refrigerator for at least 30 minutes, and then remove it a little in advance so it can warm up enough to be pliable when you spread it. Preheat the oven to 300 degrees.

Lay the stencil on a baking sheet that has been lined with a silicone baking mat. Using a small, thin offset metal spatula, spread the tuile batter into the stencil cut-outs, scraping the batter so it is even and the same thickness as the stencil sheet. Lift the stencil carefully, and repeat the process of spreading the tuile batter into the cut-outs to create as many tuiles as you need.

Bake the tuiles for 5 to 6 minutes, until they are an even golden brown. Using a thin spatula, gently remove the tuiles from the sheet pan as soon as they come out of the oven to prevent them from continuing to cook, and set them on a counter to cool.

Assembly:
Remove the sweet potato chiffon ring molds from the refrigerator, setting each one on an individual serving plate. Slide the ring mold up and off the top of the chiffon, and then peel the acetate strip off carefully and discard it.

Use a squeeze bottle or spoon to drizzle browned butter caramel on top of each chiffon, so that it drips down the sides and pools a bit on the plate.

Then add a ball of whipped cream to the top of the dessert, using an ice cream scoop, and sprinkle toasted pecans across the plate so some pecans stay on the whipped cream and some scatter on the plate. Set a ginger tuile in the top of the dessert as a garnish, pressing it down gently because the tuile is fragile. Serve the sweet potato chiffon as soon as possible.

crème brûlée

yield: 6 servings

I see this crème brûlée as embodying touch, passion, and expertise—because it uses only five ingredients and yet produces a stellar dessert. It is the quality of the ingredients that makes the difference, along with understanding how to prepare the crème brûlée properly. A brûlée that lacks good ingredients and proper preparation can quickly turn into a curdled combination of sweetness and cream. But when it is done well, crème brûlée is rich, velvety, and flavorful. One of the keys in this recipe is baking the brûlée in a deep bowl, which provides an air cushion over the top that helps keep in the moisture. I also break away from using the standard water bath and instead bake the brûlée at a low temperature while covered by a second sheet pan. The lower temperature allows the entire custard to heat more evenly, resulting in a more uniform texture. I finish the crème brûlée by torching the sugar on top, giving this dessert the classic caramelized brûlée crust that is always so satisfying.

Ingredients:

1	qt	heavy cream
1	each	vanilla bean
9	each	egg yolks
1/2	C	granulated sugar
1/2	C	raw sugar

Method:

Preheat the oven to 190 degrees. Pour the heavy cream into a medium-size pot, and split the vanilla bean pod in half lengthwise, scraping the seeds out with the tip of a knife and then adding the seeds and pod to the cream. Bring the cream just to a boil, and turn off the heat to let the cream steep for 10 minutes. Remove the pieces of vanilla bean pod from the pot.

In the bowl of an electric mixer, combine the egg yolks and granulated sugar, whipping them on high speed using a whisk attachment until the mixture is as thick as a mousse. Turn the mixer speed to low, add the warm cream mixture slowly, and mix the ingredients until they are combined thoroughly. Pour 8 ounces of the mixture into each of 6 large (about 12 oz.) oven-proof soup bowls. Set the bowls on a sheet pan, and put them in the oven. Invert a second sheet pan, and place it on top of the bowls to form a lid.

Bake the crème brûlée for 45 minutes. Remove the sheet pan cover, reduce the oven temperature to 150 degrees, and bake them for another 15 minutes. Then turn off the heat, and leave the bowls in the oven for another 15 minutes. The brûlée should appear firm but should still jiggle like jello when the bowls are tapped on the side. Remove the bowls from the oven, and allow the crème brûlée to cool to room temperature. Then cover each one with plastic wrap, and place them in the refrigerator to cool completely, for at least 1 hour.

When you are ready to serve the crème brûlée, coat the top of each with raw sugar. Use a brûlée torch to melt the sugar, moving the flame constantly until the sugar is caramelized thoroughly.

Serve the bowls of crème brûlée with a little something extra, if you like, such as fresh berries. Or serve the brûlée completely on its own, and enjoy the simple elegance of the texture and flavor of the smooth custard and crisp caramelized sugar.

maple pot de crème

yield: 4 servings

Ingredients:

Maple Pot de Crème:

1	C	heavy cream
1/4	C	whole milk
1/2	C	pure maple syrup
1/2	each	vanilla bean
3	each	egg yolks
1/2	T	Frangelico liqueur
1	pinch	kosher salt

Parsnip Cake:

1/2	C	canola oil
4	oz	parsnips (peeled & chopped)
1/4	t	vanilla extract
1	t	lemon zest
1/2	C	granulated sugar
1/2	C	all-purpose flour
1/2	t	baking soda
1/4	t	kosher salt
1/4	t	ground ginger
1	pinch	ground nutmeg

Candied Cranberries:

1/2	C	granulated sugar
1/4	C	water
1	t	vanilla extract
3/4	C	cranberries (fresh or frozen)

Other:

1/2	C	crème anglaise (p. 365)

I buy the maple syrup I use at the Café from two wonderful local businesses: Clover Valley Forest Products, in Two Harbors, Minnesota, and Simple Gifts Syrup and Salmon, just outside Duluth, Minnesota. As a tribute to those friends, neighbors, and handcrafted maple syrup itself, I began making a maple pot de crème, with the flavor of the maple syrup its highlight. The recipe is a simple one. It follows a typical custard process but uses maple syrup in place of sugar, and the result is delicious! I originally served the maple pot de crème with a small carrot cake, but I have since moved on to a parsnip cake because it's a bit more unique and blends better with the maple flavor. Parsnip cake is similar to carrot cake, but instead of grated carrots its main ingredient is puréed parsnips. I bake the cakes in tiny individual cannelé molds that have fluted sides, although any small baking cups or a small muffin tin would also work well.

Method:

Maple Pot de Crème:

Preheat the oven to 300 degrees. In a medium-size pot, combine the heavy cream, whole milk, and pure maple syrup. Slice the half vanilla bean in half lengthwise, and use the tip of a knife to scrape out the seeds. Put the seeds and the scraped half pod into the cream mixture. Stirring frequently, bring the mixture to a simmer, and then remove it immediately from the heat and let it steep for 30 minutes. Pour the warm cream mixture through a fine mesh strainer into a mixing bowl.

In a separate mixing bowl, combine the egg yolks with the Frangelico liqueur and kosher salt, and whisk them together until they are combined thoroughly. Whisk about half of the warm cream mixture slowly into the egg yolks to temper them, and then pour the egg yolk mixture back into the rest of the cream, whisking it to combine the ingredients thoroughly.

Pour about 3 ounces of the mixture into each of 4 heatproof serving cups, and then wrap each cup tightly with plastic wrap. Set the serving cups on a sheet pan, leaving space between them, and pour warm water into the pan until it reaches halfway up the sides of the cups.

Put the sheet pan in the oven, and bake the maple pot de crème for about 40 minutes, until the custard is set but still jiggles a bit like jello. Remove the cups from the sheet pan, put them on a counter to cool to room temperature, and then place them in the refrigerator for at least 2 hours before serving.

(continued on page 255)

The New Scenic Café

(continued from page 254)

Parsnip Cake:

Preheat the oven to 300 degrees. Put the canola oil, peeled and chopped parsnips, vanilla extract, and lemon zest in a blender, and purée them until they are smooth, pausing to stir the mixture by hand, if necessary, or pulsing the blender to help keep the contents moving. In a mixing bowl, combine the remaining (dry) ingredients, and mix them together thoroughly. Add the purée to the dry mixture, and fold it in with a rubber spatula. Continue stirring until the batter is smooth and mixed evenly.

Spray 4 cannelé molds (or other small baking cups) generously with pan release. Pour the cake batter into the molds, set the molds on a sheet pan, and bake the cakes until a toothpick inserted in their centers comes out clean. Remove the cakes from the oven, and turn the cups upside-down on the sheet pan. As they cool, some of the cakes will fall out of the cups on their own. The rest should come out easily by running a thin knife around the edges to do a bit of coaxing.

Candied Cranberries:

Combine the granulated sugar and water in a small sauce pot, and bring them to a simmer over medium heat. Remove the pot from the heat, and add the vanilla extract. Then put the cranberries in a heat-proof mixing bowl, and pour the hot syrup over them. Cover the bowl with plastic wrap, and set the bowl over a pot of simmering water. Cook the mixture slowly until the cranberries are tender but not mushy, which will take 30 to 45 minutes. (Frozen cranberries will soften a bit more quickly than fresh cranberries.)

Pour the liquid through a fine strainer and then back into the pot, and return the cranberries to the bowl. Simmer the liquid over medium-low heat until it is reduced by about half. Then combine the reduced liquid with the cranberries, and place the bowl in the refrigerator to cool completely.

Assembly:

Place each cooled maple pot de crème on a serving plate, and pour about 2 tablespoons of crème anglaise over its top so that the whole surface is covered. If the parsnip cakes have cooled completely, rewarm them for just a few seconds in a microwave, and then put a cake on each serving plate next to the pot de crème. Warm the candied cranberries gently in a small pot, use a spoon to add 3 or 4 cranberries to the top of each parsnip cake, and pour a little of the cranberry syrup over the top so it runs a bit down the sides. Then serve!

chocolate espresso cake

yield: 14 servings (9" cake)

This chocolate espresso cake is a natural marriage of the flavors of rich chocolate and coffee. I start by baking a tall chocolate cake in a springform pan, rather than in separate short cake pans, to produce a cake with a tight density and small air holes. After the cake is cooled, I cut it into layers and reassemble it in the springform pan. I pour a sweet soaking liquid made of coffee, sugar, rum, and orange oil over each layer to soak the cake, as you would the ladyfingers for tiramisu, and pour a simple chocolate ganache made of semi-sweet chocolate and heavy cream between each layer as well. Using good-quality coffee in the soaking liquid really makes a difference. I get mine from Alakef Coffee, a wonderful roaster located in Duluth, Minnesota. I serve their coffee proudly in the Café, and I love having it on hand for uses just such as this, where its distinctive flavor greatly enhances the dessert's taste. Cutting the finished cake reveals layers of beautifully silky, sexy ganache and moist, dense cake–perfect layers in a simple form! I serve the chocolate espresso cake with fresh whipped cream and a few chocolate-covered espresso beans, accenting further the delicious melding of chocolate and coffee flavors.

Ingredients:

Soaking Liquid:

1/4	C	coffee grounds
1	C	water
2	T	granulated sugar
2	T	dark rum
2	drops	orange oil

Chocolate Cake:

1	box	good quality devil's food cake mix (18.25 oz)

Other:

5	C	chocolate ganache (p. 364)
4	C	whipped cream (p. 371)
28	each	chocolate covered espresso beans

Method:

Soaking Liquid:

In a small pot, combine the coffee grounds and water, and bring them to a boil. Remove the pot from the heat and let the mixture steep for 20 minutes. Strain the liquid through a fine mesh strainer or coffee filter, and discard the coffee grounds. Add the granulated sugar, rum, and orange oil, and stir it thoroughly. Put the soaking liquid in the refrigerator to cool.

Chocolate Cake:

Preheat the oven to 300 degrees. Prepare the cake batter according to the directions on the box. When using 9-inch cake pans, you would typically split the batter between 2 pans. For this recipe, however, pour all of the batter into a single 9-inch springform pan that is at least 3 inches tall. You will need to bake the cake longer, but the result will be a cake that is suited perfectly to this recipe because it is taller and denser (even though it will likely have a significant dome when it is done, but you need not be concerned about it). Bake the cake for 35 to 40 minutes or until a toothpick inserted in its center comes out clean. Remove the cake from the oven, and allow it to cool completely.

Assembly:

If it is not still warm, reheat the chocolate ganache so that as you assemble the dessert the ganache will soak into the porous cake and help hold the layers together while it cools. You can warm the ganache in brief bursts in a microwave, stirring it frequently and checking to see if it is warm enough, or you can put it in a heat-proof bowl and warm it slowly over a pot of simmering water.

Remove the outside of the springform pan, but leave the cake attached to the bottom of the pan. Use a long knife to cut off the domed top of the cake so that the top is completely flat. The easiest way to trim the dome is to hold the knife at a stationary angle and slice back and forth slowly while rotating the cake.

(continued on page 257)

(continued from page 256)

You can certainly discard the cake scrap, but at the Café, we like to eat ours in those stolen moments of sampling in which cooks are known to indulge. Or we sometimes allow cake scraps to dry and then turn them into chocolate crumbs to be sprinkled on other desserts.

Using the same technique you employed to slice off the domed top, slice the cake twice more to create three even layers. Set the top two layers aside, and reassemble the springform pan, with the bottom layer of cake still attached. Pour 1/3 cup of the soaking liquid evenly over the base layer of cake, and allow it to soak in for a minute. Then pour 12 ounces of warm chocolate ganache over that same layer. Set the second layer of cake on top, pour 1/3 cup of the soaking liquid over that layer, and then pour another 12 ounces of ganache on top. Repeat this process with the third layer of cake, pouring a little extra ganache on that last layer. The springform pan will be filled almost all the way to the top.

Put the springform pan in the refrigerator to cool the cake for at least 3 hours. Then remove the cake from the refrigerator, and hold the blade of a long, thin knife under hot water. Use the knife to cut around the entire outside of the cake, freeing it from the ring of the springform pan, which can then be removed. Run the knife under hot water repeatedly, to use it to cut the cake into as many slices as needed while the cake is still cold, and place the slices on serving plates. This is a very rich cake, so you will likely find that small slices are sufficient. Return any unused portion of the cake to the refrigerator.

Allow the slices of chocolate espresso cake to warm to room temperature. Then serve each portion with a generous scoop of fresh whipped cream and a couple of chocolate-covered espresso beans.

tiramisu

yield: 12 servings (9" x 13" pan)

Tiramisu is an Italian dessert that can be made in many different ways. I create this version on a sheet pan using crisp ladyfingers; a sweet soaking liquid made from coffee, brandy, rum, and sugar; a mascarpone cheese filling; and shaved semi-sweet chocolate. (In another version, I omit the ladyfingers and cut a thin sponge cake into circles to make individual tiramisu trifles, sprinkled with a dark chocolate cocoa powder that has just enough bitterness to balance the sweet mascarpone filling.) One of the greatest compliments I have ever received about our tiramisu was from an Italian woman who was a baker in Italy and in our area to visit her family. I was tickled when, as she departed, she announced that ours was better than any tiramisu she had eaten back home in Italy!

Ingredients:

Soaking Liquid:

3/4	C	coffee grounds
1 1/4	C	water
2	T	brandy
2	T	dark rum
1/4	C	granulated sugar

Mascarpone Cheese Filling:

10	each	egg yolks
5	each	egg whites
1/2	C	granulated sugar
1/2	T	vanilla extract
20	oz	mascarpone cheese
1	t	cream of tartar

Other:

30	each	ladyfingers (approx.)
3	oz	semi-sweet chocolate bar (chilled)
1 1/2	C	Bailey's Irish Cream (optional)
36	each	fresh berries (optional)

Method:

Note that you will need to refrigerate the tiramisu for at least 8 hours (or better yet, overnight) before serving.

Soaking Liquid:

In a small pot, combine the coffee grounds and water, bring them to a boil, and then remove the pot from the heat and let the mixture steep for 20 minutes. Strain the liquid through a fine mesh strainer or coffee filter, and discard the coffee grounds. Add the brandy, dark rum (or nonalcoholic alternatives), and granulated sugar to the liquid, and stir it until all of the sugar has dissolved. Put the soaking liquid in the refrigerator to cool.

Mascarpone Cheese Filling:

Separate the egg yolks and whites carefully, removing as much of the whites as possible from the yolks and making sure there are no traces of yolk in the whites (or they will not whip). You will need only half (5) of the egg whites for this filling.

Combine the egg yolks, 1/4 cup of the granulated sugar, and the vanilla extract, and use an electric mixer to whip them until the mixture becomes light in color and thick and mousse-like in texture. Turn off the mixer, add the mascarpone cheese, and whip the mixture on medium speed to incorporate the cheese. Then transfer it to a large mixing bowl.

Using a clean bowl and whisk, whip the 5 egg whites, along with the remaining 1/4 cup of granulated sugar and the cream of tartar, until stiff peaks form. Using a rubber spatula, fold the egg white mixture gently into the egg yolk mixture until they are just evenly mixed.

(continued on page 259)

(continued from page 258)

Assembly:

Fill the bottom of a 9-inch-by-13-inch sheet pan with ladyfingers, cutting some of them, if needed, to fill the pan completely with one even layer. (How many ladyfingers you will use will vary depending on their size.) Using a squeeze bottle with a small tip, pour half of the soaking liquid over the ladyfingers. (Or if you do not have a squeeze bottle, pour the liquid slowly from a cup.)

Use a spatula to spread half of the mascarpone cheese filling evenly across the ladyfingers. Then add a second layer of ladyfingers, pressing them in gently. Pour the remaining half of the soaking liquid over the ladyfingers, and spread the rest of the mascarpone cheese filling over the top.

Use a cheese grater or a coarse microplane grater to shave the chilled semi-sweet chocolate over the top layer of mascarpone cheese filling, until the chocolate forms a solid layer with no white spots of filling peeking through. Then put the pan in the refrigerator for at least 8 hours (overnight is even better), which will allow the ladyfingers to become saturated evenly with the soaking liquid and the mascarpone filling to firm up.

When you are ready to serve the tiramisu, remove the sheet pan from the refrigerator. Run a thin, sharp knife under hot water, and cut the tiramisu into approximately 12 even pieces (each about 3 inches by 3 inches). Using a small, square spatula, place as many pieces of tiramisu as you need on serving plates (returning any unused tiramisu to the refrigerator). It is so delicious and creamy, it can easily stand on the plate on its own, but adding a finishing touch to the plate also works beautifully. At the New Scenic Café, we serve our tiramisu over a small pool of Bailey's Irish Cream, alongside a few fresh berries.

*Variation - Lemon Tiramisu:

Lemon makes a wonderful taste as well in tiramisu, especially in the summer, when people are craving lighter, fresher flavors. This variation arose from a conversation one day when my staff and I were deciding on a weekend dessert special. I asked them if they wanted me to make something with lemon or if they wanted me to make tiramisu, and they answered, "Make lemon tiramisu!" So that's what I did.

To create this tiramisu variation, use Lemon Tiramisu Soaking Liquid (page 367) instead of the coffee-based soaking liquid presented here, and substitute white chocolate for the semi-sweet chocolate. Then serve the lemon tiramisu with fresh raspberries and a sprig of mint, for a light, summery flavor.

The New Scenic Café

B52 cake

yield: 12 servings (9 by 13-inch cake)

In the world of cocktails, a B52 is a cordial drink, or shot, made with Kahlua, Grand Marnier, and Bailey's Irish Cream liqueurs. This B52 is a dessert I make from chocolate cake layered with three soaking liquids and three buttercreams that capture the flavors of those liqueurs. I start by making a layered chocolate cake, soak the first layer with Kahlua syrup, and add a layer of Kahlua buttercream. The second layer is soaked with orange syrup and followed with a layer of orange buttercream. Then I soak the top layer with Frangelico syrup and coat it with Bailey's Irish Cream buttercream. At the Café, I serve this dessert as a slice of rich cake topped with warm chocolate ganache and a chocolate swizzle. For parties, I cut the cake into very small pieces, slide a bamboo pick into each of the pieces, place a raspberry on top, and serve them like deliciously decadent petit fours.

Method:

Chocolate Cake Layers:

Preheat the oven to 300 degrees.

Follow the instructions on the boxes of devil's food cake mix for mixing the cake batter, making it just a bit thinner by adding 2 tablespoons of extra water for each box of mix. The extra liquid will help the cake flatten out in the pan, to create nice, even layers. The goal is to bake thin layers of cake that are as close as you can get to 3/8 inch high. (You might need to experiment with this process over time, to create the layers exactly as you want them.)

Line 2 sheet pans that are 13-by-18-inch in size with parchment paper, and spray the paper with pan release. Pour exactly 26 ounces of cake batter into each pan, spreading it evenly so it fills the pan to 1/4 inch deep. It will rise to about 3/8 inch in height when it bakes. You will have a small amount of cake batter left over, which you could bake in a small pan for one of those secret treats a cook deserves while working in the kitchen!

Bake the two cakes for about 10 minutes, until they are just cooked in the center. Because the cakes are so thin, they will bake quickly, so watch them closely, testing them periodically for doneness by sliding a toothpick in their center. If you bake them too long, they will begin to dry out around the edges, making them brittle and a little more difficult to work with. Remove the cakes from the oven when they are done, allow them to cool to room temperature, and then cover them with plastic wrap and put them in the refrigerator. (Refrigerating them will make them easier to handle later, when you assemble the dessert.)

(continued on page 262)

Ingredients:

Chocolate Cake Layers:

2	boxes	good quality devil's food cake mix (18.25 oz each)

Buttercreams:

24	oz	pâté à bombe (p. 368)
3	lb	butter (softened)
4	t	Kahlua liqueur
1	T	espresso powder
1/2	t	orange oil
1/4	t	orange blossom water
1/4	C	Bailey's Irish Cream
1	drop	almond extract
1/2	t	vanilla extract

Syrups:

2	C	granulated sugar
2	T	light corn syrup
2	C	water
1	T	Kahlua liqueur
1	t	espresso powder
2	drops	orange oil
2	drops	orange blossom water
1/2	T	Frangelico liqueur
1	drop	almond extract
2	drops	vanilla extract

Other:

1	C	chocolate ganache (p. 364)
12	each	decorative chocolate swizzles (optional)

(continued from page 261)

Buttercreams:

With an electric mixer, use a paddle attachment to whip the pâté à bombe and the softened butter together until they are smooth. Divide the mixture into 3 equal portions of 24 ounces each.

Return 1 portion to the mixer, add the Kahlua liqueur and espresso powder, and whip the ingredients to incorporate them fully. Then remove that portion from the bowl and set it aside in a separate container. Repeat this process 2 more times, whipping the second portion of the pâté à bombe and butter mixture with the orange oil and orange blossom water and the last portion with the Bailey's Irish Cream and almond and vanilla extracts.

You will now have 3 differently-flavored buttercreams. Leave them out at room temperature. (But if you will not be using the buttercreams the same day, refrigerate them, remove them from the refrigerator to let them return to room temperature when you are ready for them, and re-whip them.)

Syrups:

Combine the granulated sugar, light corn syrup, and water in a small pot, and bring the ingredients to a boil. Simmer the mixture until it has reduced by about 30 percent. Then divide the syrup evenly into 3 containers. Add the Kahlua liqueur and espresso powder to one, the orange oil and orange blossom water to another, and the Frangelico liqueur and almond and vanilla extracts to the last. Stir the individual syrups thoroughly, and allow them to sit for 20 minutes before you use them so the flavors can steep.

Assembly:

Slide the 2 cakes onto a cutting board, leaving the parchment paper on the bottoms of the cakes. Cut each cake in half to create 4 segments, each 9 inches by 13 inches. Slide your hand underneath one segment, and flip it over onto a serving platter. Peel off the parchment paper.

Use a pastry brush to apply the Frangelico syrup to the first layer. You want to soak the cake just enough to make it moist but not soggy, so add just a little of the syrup at a time—it is not essential to use it all (in fact, you will need a little extra of the syrup for the top of the cake). Then use an offset pastry spatula or a palette knife to spread an even layer of the Bailey's Irish Cream buttercream on the cake. Make the buttercream layer exactly 3/8 inch thick, to match the cake layer, taking the time to be sure the buttercream is spread all the way to the edges and is perfectly flat. (Again, you need not use it all and should reserve some of any of the buttercream flavors for the top of the cake.)

Flip another segment of cake over onto the buttercream to create the next layer, and peel off the parchment paper. This maneuver takes a bit of finesse, so be sure the edges of the cake layers are lined up, and do the flip quickly so the cake does not break. (But if it does break, you can simply put the pieces together in place, like a puzzle.)

(continued on page 263)

(continued from page 262)

Use the pastry brush to apply as much of the orange syrup as needed to the second layer of cake, and then spread a 3/8-inch layer of the orange buttercream evenly over the top.

Then flip the next segment of cake over to create a third layer, peel off the parchment paper, and add the Kahlua-espresso syrup and a 3/8-inch layer of the Kahlua-espresso buttercream. Flip the fourth segment of cake over onto the top, and soak it with the extra of any of the syrups—even mixing them, if you like.

Spread a very thin layer of any of the buttercreams across the top, just enough to coat it. Again, use any buttercream you have left, or even a blend of the extra buttercreams. The goal is simply to seal the top of the cake. Then put the cake in the refrigerator. (This cake is best served at room temperature so the buttercream is nice and soft. But until you are within a couple hours of serving, it is best stored in the refrigerator.)

If it is not still warm, reheat the chocolate ganache. You can warm the ganache in brief bursts in a microwave, stirring it frequently and checking to see if it is warm, or you can put it in a heat-proof bowl and warm it slowly over a pot of simmering water.

If you plan to present the whole, uncut cake, remove it from the refrigerator 2 to 3 hours beforehand. Spread a layer of warm chocolate ganache over the top when you are ready to show off your cake, allowing the ganache to run over the edges. At serving time, cut the cake slowly, using a knife that you have run under hot water.

If you want to cut and serve individual pieces instead, cut the cake when it is still cold, using a knife that has been run under hot water. Cut slowly, allowing the knife to melt through the buttercream without crushing it, and transfer each slice carefully to a serving plate. Then pour the warm chocolate ganache over each piece, and top it, if you like, with a decorative chocolate swizzle.

almond tea cake

yield: 4 servings

These soft, moist little cakes hang together delicately, with their eggs, butter, and generous quantity of finely-ground almonds. You can buy a blanched almond meal for this recipe or grind sliced almonds yourself, using a spice grinder. Because the tricky part is getting the cakes out of the molds when they are finished baking, I bake them in coffee cups that have rounded bottoms so there are no corners for the cake to get stuck in. Plus, I butter and flour the insides of the cups and spray them with a little pan release to help ease the process. Then I place the filled cups in a deep sheet pan and cover the pan with layers of plastic wrap and aluminum foil and bake the cakes until the egg is set and the cakes are firm but still moist. The almond tea cakes are presented with crème anglaise, sugared blueberries and cranberries, and a sprinkling of microgreens or edible flowers, adding a glow of color that is an especially nice treat when the cakes are served during the holidays.

Method:

Almond Cake:

Preheat the oven to 325 degrees. In the bowl of an electric mixer, use a paddle attachment on high speed to cream the softened butter and granulated sugar until they are light and fluffy. Reduce the mixer speed to low, and add the eggs one at a time, following each egg with about one-third of the cake flour and mixing the ingredients thoroughly between each addition.

Turn the mixer off, and use a rubber spatula to scrape the paddle and the sides of the bowl. By hand, gently stir in the ground almonds, lemon zest and juice of the whole lemon, and almond extract.

Grease the insides of 4 small (3-inch) baking cups with butter, and then dust them with flour and spray the insides with pan release. Divide the cake batter evenly among the 4 cups. Each portion will be about 4 ounces.

Place the cups in a sheet pan that is deeper than the height of the cups, such as a 9-inch-by-13-inch pan. Cover the entire pan tightly with plastic wrap, and then cover it with a layer of aluminum foil. Bake the cakes for about 35 minutes, or until a toothpick or small knife inserted in the center of each cake comes out clean.

Pull the sheet pan from the oven, and allow the cakes to rest at room temperature until they are cool enough to handle. Turn the cups over to remove the cakes, let them cool completely, and place them in the refrigerator in an airtight container. (If a cake does not fall easily out of a cup, use a thin knife to slide around the outside edges of the cake, and try again.)

Assembly:

Put each cake in a wide, shallow bowl. Warm each of them in a microwave for 10 seconds at a time, checking the cake between each 10-second segment until it is a bit warm to the touch.

Pour 2 ounces of crème anglaise around the outside of each cake. Place 4 sugared blueberries and 4 sugared cranberries on top of and next to the cake, and garnish the plate with a few microgreens or edible flowers.

Ingredients:

Almond Cake:

2/3	C	butter (softened)
1/2	C	granulated sugar
3	each	eggs
3 1/2	T	cake flour
3/4	C + 2T	ground almonds
1	each	lemon (lemon zest & juice of whole lemon)
1	t	almond extract

Other:

8	oz	crème anglaise (p. 365)
12	each	sugared blueberries (p. 370)
12	each	sugared cranberries (p. 370)
1/4	C	microgreens or edible flowers

tuxedo cake

yield: 12 servings (9" cake)

For my rendition of this classic black-and-white dessert, I bake tall chocolate cakes in springform pans and then slice them into thin layers, stacking them as high as 8 layers tall. Between each layer, I spread cardamom buttercream frosting, balancing the rich decadence of the chocolate with the creamy lightness and subtle cardamom flavor of the buttercream. Then I cover the cake with buttercream and refrigerate it. After the cake is cooled and the buttercream is firm, I pour warm chocolate ganache over the top, allowing it to drift gracefully over the cake's sides. To finish this dessert in the dramatic style of the tuxedo it imitates, I top it with fresh red roses.

Ingredients:

Chocolate Cake:

2	boxes	good quality devil's food cake mix (18.25 oz each)

Cardamom Buttercream:

2	lb	butter
3	lb	vegetable shortening
2	lb	powdered sugar
1	T	kosher salt
1/2	T	vanilla extract
1	t	ground cardamom
1	C	heavy cream

Other:

1	C	chocolate ganache (p. 364)
3	each	roses for garnish (optional)

Method:

Chocolate Cake:
Preheat the oven to 300 degrees.

Prepare one box of cake mix according to the directions on the box, and pour all of the batter into a single 9-inch springform pan. Then prepare the other box of cake mix, and fill a second springform pan. Bake both cakes for 35 to 40 minutes, or until a toothpick inserted in their centers comes out clean. (The tops of the cakes will be significantly domed, but you need not be concerned.) Allow the cakes to cool to room temperature, and then remove them from the springform pans and place them in the refrigerator to cool further.

Cardamom Buttercream:
A traditional buttercream is made primarily with butter, sugar, and eggs. This version is a bit different, in part because it includes vegetable shortening, which makes the buttercream more stable, less prone to slumping on the cake, and better able to hold up in warm settings.

Allow the butter and vegetable shortening to soften to room temperature. Then combine them in an electric mixer bowl, and whip them on medium speed, using the mixer's paddle attachment, until they are mixed evenly.

Turn the mixer off, and add the powdered sugar. Whip the mixture on low speed for 4 minutes, stop the mixer, and add the remaining ingredients, continuing to whip the mixture on low speed until the cream is incorporated. Then change the setting to high speed to continue whipping for another 2 minutes.

You can use the buttercream immediately. If you want to store it in the refrigerator, when you are ready to use it remove it from the refrigerator, allow it to return to room temperature, and re-whip it.

Assembly:
Use a long knife to cut off the domed tops of the two cakes so that the tops are completely flat. The easiest way to trim the domes is to hold the knife at a stationary angle and slice back and

(continued on page 267)

The New Scenic Café

(continued from page 266)

forth slowly while rotating the cake. You can certainly discard the cake scrap, but at the Café, we like to nibble ours when we feel in need of a kitchen treat. Or we sometimes allow cake scraps to dry and then turn them into chocolate crumbs to be sprinkled on other desserts.

Using the same technique you employed to slice off the domed top, slice each cake twice more to create three even layers apiece, placing each layer gently on a flat surface after you cut it. When you are done, you will have 6 thin layers of chocolate cake (though if you are feeling adventurous, you could cut each cake into 4 layers and produce 8 layers).

Place the first layer of cake on a serving platter, and spread a thin (approximately 3/16-inch thick) layer of cardamom buttercream over it. Then set the next layer of cake on top, and spread another 3/16-inch thick layer of buttercream over that layer. Continue alternating layers of cake and buttercream until you have used all of the cake layers.

Spread a thin "crumb coat" layer of cardamom buttercream over the top of the cake, as well as over its sides, and then put the cake in the refrigerator to set up for at least an hour. Remove the cake from the refrigerator, and spread a finish layer of buttercream on the outside. Return the cake to the refrigerator.

Just before you are ready to serve the cake, reheat the chocolate ganache if it is not still warm. (You can warm the ganache in brief bursts in a microwave, stirring it frequently and checking to see if it is warm, or you can put it in a heat-proof bowl and warm it slowly over a pot of simmering water.) Pour the ganache over the top of the cake, using a small spatula to even it out while it is still molten and pushing it far enough to the edges so that it drifts over and down the sides. The cool temperature of the cake will cause the ganache to solidify, so you will want to work quickly.

If you like, garnish the top of the cake with fresh roses or other flowers. Or simply leave it as-is. Either way, it is beautiful!

Breads

270   *The New Scenic Café*

The New Scenic Café

baguette

yield: 1 regular or 2 small loaves

The traditional French baguette is the daily bread, the bread of the moment. It has a nice narrow shape, with a chewy, crunchy crust and is baked into a portion that is easy to use for small sandwiches or to tear apart and eat with cheese. The baguette is also a great size and texture for making crostini or for creating small slices of toast to eat with pâté. This baguette recipe has only 4 ingredients: yeast, flour, salt, and water. Yet the beauty of its simplicity is what makes this such a wonderful bread.

Ingredients:

1/2	T	active dry yeast
2 1/4	C	white bread flour
2/3	T	kosher salt
1 3/4	C	water (80 degrees)

Method:

Combine the active dry yeast, white bread flour, and kosher salt in the bowl of an electric mixer. Using a dough hook, mix them together on low speed for 1 minute. Then add the 80-degree water, and continue to mix the ingredients on low speed for 2 more minutes.

Increase the mixer speed to medium, and mix the dough for another 6 to 7 minutes, until it becomes smooth and elastic. Remove the dough from the bowl, and place it on a lightly-floured work surface.

Form the dough into a ball, place it in a mixing bowl, and cover it with a towel. Let it rise for approximately 1 hour at room temperature, until it has doubled in size.

You can use the dough at this point—it will be delicious. Or you can fold it gently in on itself, reshape it into a ball, and let it rise 1 or 2 more times, repeating the process of folding the dough and reshaping it each time. An extra rising or two allows the yeast to feed a bit longer and develop more complex flavors.

Place the dough on a floured work surface, dust your hands with flour, and use the palm of one hand to flatten the dough gently and press it into a rounded rectangular shape. Press out any large air pockets.

Fold one edge of the dough over to the center of the loaf, and press it down gently to seal the fold. Fold the opposite edge over the top so that it overlaps the first fold, and press down along the seam to seal the two folds together.

Using your thumbs, make an indentation in the center of the dough, along its entire length. Then bring the top half of the dough toward you, folding along the indentation. Use the bottom of your palm to press down on the seam gently, to seal it along the length of the loaf.

(continued on page 275)

(continued from page 274)

With firm and even pressure, use both hands to roll the dough back and forth, slowly moving your hands to the outside, until the loaf is even in thickness and about 24 to 26 inches long. (If your oven will not accommodate that length, you can divide the dough in half and create 2 shorter baguettes.)

As you roll the dough, if it seems tight and resistant to stretching let it rest for a few minutes and then come back to it. When it is the size and shape you want, use the outsides of your palms to roll the ends of the loaf into sharp points.

Transfer the dough to a floured baking sheet, cover it with a towel, and allow it to rise for about 45 minutes, or until it has doubled in size.

Preheat the oven to 425 degrees. Use a sharp knife or razor blade to cut several diagonal slashes across the top of the loaf, and bake it for 20 to 25 minutes, until the crust is hard and golden and tapping the loaf produces a hollow sound. Remove the baguette from the oven, and cool it on a wire cooling rack.

---

pain d'epi

This variation on the baguette uses the same ingredients as the baguette recipe but produces a bread of a different shape, one that diners can pull individual dinner "rolls" from as they pass it around the table. To create the pain d'epi from the loaf of dough, you use a scissors, starting from one end of the loaf and cutting from the outside to the center, leaving only a bit intact. The finished pain d'epi looks like the flower of a wheat stalk ("epi" in French), with little buds that can be pulled away from the whole loaf. It is a classic yet unique and relatively easy way to bring beautiful bread to the table.

Method:

Follow the instructions in the baguette recipe to make the dough and form a loaf. Then place the loaf on a floured sheet pan.

Preheat the oven to 425 degrees.

Holding a pair of sharp scissors at a low angle (almost horizontal), start at one end of the loaf, and cut about 3/4 of the way through the dough, creating a pointed flap. Immediately use your other hand to bend the flap gently to one side. Then move about 2 inches down the loaf, make another cut, and bend that flap to the other side.

Continue in this manner, alternating sides, until you reach the other end of the loaf. Then cover it with a towel, and allow it to rise for about 45 minutes, or until it has doubled in size. Bake the bread for 20 to 25 minutes, until the crust is hard and golden and tapping the loaf produces a hollow sound. Remove the pain d'epi from the oven, and cool it on a wire cooling rack.

The New Scenic Café

Breads

bishop's hat rolls

yield: 12 rolls

These delectable little rolls are so named because the 4 sharp points that stick up from their tops after they are baked make them resemble a bishop's hat. They are a relatively easy roll to make, yet they draw more discussion and are more requested than any other breads I have served. Like the baguette, these rolls are made from only four ingredients. Still, they are such a treat, especially when they are warm and fresh.

Ingredients:

10	oz	water (80 degrees)
1 1/4	t	active dry yeast
14 1/2	oz	high-gluten flour
1/2	T	kosher salt

Method:

Note that you will need to put this bread dough in the refrigerator overnight before baking it, so you will want to plan ahead.

In the bowl of an electric mixer, combine the 80-degree water and active dry yeast, and stir them by hand to dissolve the yeast. Sift together the high-gluten flour and kosher salt, and add them to the yeast mixture.

Using a dough hook, mix the dough on low speed until it is even and smooth. Increase the speed to medium, and continue to mix the dough until it is bouncy and barely sticks to your fingertips when you gently poke it. If the dough is too sticky, add small amounts of additional flour.

Remove the dough from the mixing bowl. Put it on a floured work surface, and shape it into a ball. Then put the ball of dough in a large mixing bowl that has been sprayed lightly with pan release, cover the bowl tightly with plastic wrap, and put it in the refrigerator overnight.

Remove the dough from the refrigerator, take it out of the bowl, and place it on a floured work surface. Using a bench knife, cut a 2-ounce piece from the ball of dough. Hold the piece in your hands, pulling its sides gently to tuck them under. Work your way around its outside until you have made the piece into a well-formed ball. Pinch its underside to seal the tucked folds together. Then place the roll, seam side down, on a sheet pan that you have dusted with flour.

Continue cutting 2-ounce pieces and forming rolls until you use all the dough, leaving about 3 inches between each ball of dough as you place it on the sheet pan to allow the rolls to expand without touching. Cover the pan with a towel, and let the rolls rise for about 45 minutes, or until they have doubled in size.

Preheat the oven to 500 degrees. Just before baking the rolls, use the tip of a sharp scissors to cut a cross pattern in the top of each roll, creating 4 sharp points. Bake the rolls for 5 to 7 minutes, until they are golden brown and have a crisp crust. Pull the rolls from the oven, and allow them to cool at room temperature.

The New Scenic Café

brioche

yield: 1 loaf

Brioche is a classic, rich bread that has a slightly sweet and buttery flavor. It is a versatile bread that is delicious in a variety of foods, including French toast, sandwiches, croutons, as a component of an entrée, and as a vehicle for carrying a canapé. I first began baking brioche at the New Scenic Café to use as a bun for miniature lamb burgers, and diners loved it. As it turned out, the brioche was remarked upon even more so than the lamb! Today, I most often bake full-size "Pullman" loaves of brioche. Sometimes, I cut the center out of the loaf to create a cylindrical crouton that I toast, soak in Taleggio fondue (page 120), and serve as a starter with grilled pheasant. Other times, I cut the loaf into cubes, toast it, and serve it as a canapé with butter-poached lobster tossed in a togarashi spice mix (page 74). Brioche is a beautiful bread to work with and serve, in great part because of the golden hue the butter gives its appealing crust.

Method:

In a small pot, warm the milk gently to 80 degrees. Pour the active dry yeast into the warm milk, stir it until it dissolves, and then transfer the mixture to the bowl of an electric mixer.

Add the white bread flour, kosher salt, brown sugar, honey, egg, and egg yolks, and use a dough hook attachment to mix them on low speed until the dough is even and smooth. With the mixer running, add the softened butter in small amounts. Continue to mix the dough until the butter is incorporated fully.

Grease the inside of a bread loaf pan with butter, and set the pan aside. Place the dough on a floured work surface, dust your hands with flour, and use the palm of one hand to flatten the dough gently, pressing it into a rounded rectangular shape. Press out any large air pockets.

Fold one edge of the dough over to the center of the loaf, and press it down gently to seal the fold. Fold the opposite edge over the top so that it overlaps the first fold, and press down along the seam to seal the two folds together.

Using your thumbs, make an indentation in the center of the dough, along its entire length. Then bring the top half of the dough toward you, folding along the indentation. Use the bottom of your palm to press down on the seam gently, to seal it along the length of the loaf.

Turn the dough so that the seam side is down. With firm and even pressure, use both hands to roll the dough back and forth, moving your hands to the outside slowly, until the loaf is even in thickness and a bit longer than the length of the loaf pan. Lift the dough up, with the seam still facing down, and tuck both ends of the dough under. Then set it in the greased bread pan.

Preheat the oven to 325 degrees. Cover the bread pan with a towel, and let the dough rise for 45 minutes, until it has nearly doubled in size. Bake the brioche for 35 to 40 minutes. You will know it is done when the top is a deep golden brown and tapping the loaf with a fingertip produces a hollow sound. Take the brioche out of the oven, remove it from the bread pan immediately, and cool it on a wire cooling rack.

Ingredients:

6	oz	whole milk
1 1/2	t	active dry yeast
18	oz	white bread flour
3	t	kosher salt
1	oz	brown sugar
2	T	honey
1	each	egg
2	each	egg yolks
3	oz	butter (softened)

butter rolls

yield: 16 rolls

These are pull-apart-style dinner rolls, made with a rich, buttery dough. I form small, ball-shaped portions of dough and put them in a jelly roll pan or a deeper 9-by-13-inch pan. (You can also bake them in a springform pan, a cake pan, or just about any kind of baking pan.) They stick together when the dough rises and when the rolls are baked, but they pull apart easily when it's time to enjoy them, making them a great bread for sharing at the table. They tend to become a bit dry after a day or two, so you will want to eat these satisfying butter rolls when they are at their freshest and best.

Ingredients:

18	oz	all-purpose flour
2 1/4	t	active dry yeast
1/3	C	granulated sugar
1	t	kosher salt
1	C	whole milk
1/2	C	unsalted butter
3	each	egg yolks

Method:

In the bowl of an electric mixer, sift together the all-purpose flour, active dry yeast, granulated sugar, and kosher salt. Position the bowl in the mixer stand, and fit it with a dough hook.

In a small pot, heat the milk and unsalted butter, stirring the ingredients until the butter melts and the liquid is warm. When the mixture reaches a temperature between 115 and 125 degrees, pour it into the flour mixture, add the egg yolks, and mix the ingredients on low speed until they are combined evenly.

Increase the mixer speed to medium, and mix the dough for about 8 minutes, until it is smooth and shiny.

Remove the dough from the mixer bowl, shape it into a ball, and place it in a large mixing bowl that has been sprayed lightly with pan release. Cover the bowl tightly with plastic wrap, and let the dough rise at room temperature for 45 minutes, until it doubles in size.

Grease your baking pan lightly with butter, and set it aside. Turn the dough onto a clean work surface—you need not use flour on the surface because the dough is soft but not sticky—and press the dough gently to deflate any large air bubbles.

Divide the dough into 16 equal pieces, each weighing about 2 ounces. Set a piece of dough in your palm, again without any flour, and with the edge of your other slightly-curved palm press gently but firmly on the dough, rotating it repeatedly until it forms a smooth-skinned ball with a sealed bottom. Put the ball of dough in the baking pan, with the seam facing down. Repeat this process with the remaining dough, lining the balls up evenly, with about 1/4 inch of space between them.

Cover the baking pan with plastic wrap, and let the dough rise at room temperature for 30 minutes, until it is nearly double in size. Meanwhile, preheat the oven to 375 degrees.

Remove the plastic wrap, and bake the rolls for about 15 minutes, until they are nicely puffed and brown. Pull the baking pan out of the oven, and allow the rolls to cool in the pan.

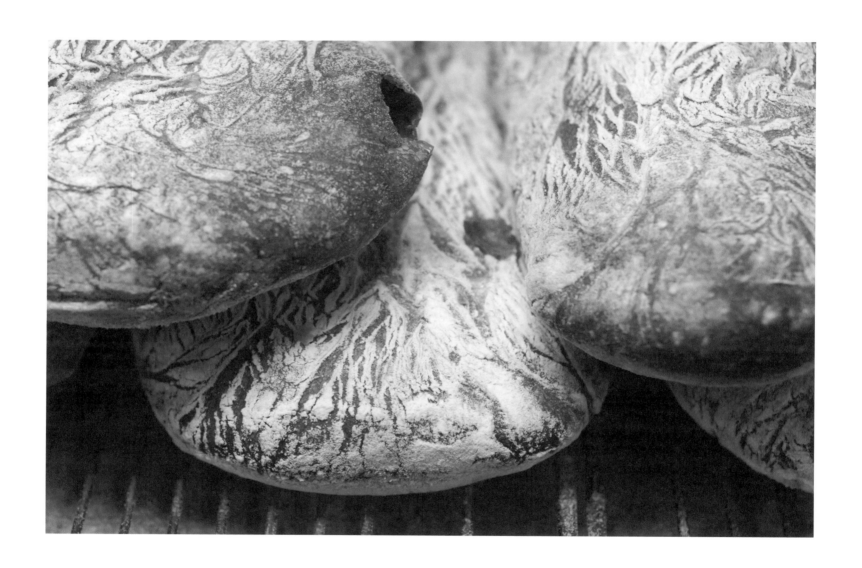

The New Scenic Café

sourdough ciabatta

yield: 2 loaves

This sourdough ciabatta is so soft on the inside and so deliciously crunchy on the outside, sometimes a batch of it scarcely emerges from the oven at the New Scenic Café before we in the kitchen find ourselves devouring a loaf. You will need a sourdough starter, which you can make yourself, beg from a friend, or even order online. One tasty variation on this recipe is an herbed sourdough, which I recommend you give a try. Adding even a small amount of dried herbs to the dough adds a lot of flavor. I use this sourdough ciabatta frequently at the Café, as our "service bread" and with salads, entrées, and soups. And because it toasts and grills so beautifully, I also use it for a wide variety of sandwiches. It is a bread that is never in danger of sitting around long!

Method:

In the bowl of an electric mixer, combine the 80-degree water and active dry yeast, and stir them by hand until the yeast is dissolved. Then add the bread flour, sourdough starter, and kosher salt (as well as the dried herbs, if desired). Using a paddle attachment, mix them on low speed until the dough is uniform and begins to "climb" up the paddle.

Let the dough rest for 10 minutes. Then scrape it out of the bowl onto a floured work surface, dust your hands with flour, and stretch the dough, folding it over on itself from each of 4 different sides. Flip the dough over, shape it into a ball, and place it in a large mixing bowl that has been sprayed lightly with pan release.

Cover the bowl with plastic wrap, and let the dough rest for 10 minutes. Repeat the process of stretching and folding it 3 more times, allowing it to rest on the work surface for 10 minutes between each time.

Return the dough to the bowl, and cover it with plastic wrap. (At this point, if you do not want to bake the dough right away you can put it in the refrigerator overnight. The next day, allow it to warm to room temperature for at least 1 hour before you continue with the rising.)

(continued on page 286)

Ingredients:

1	t	active dry yeast
11	oz	water (80 degrees)
13	oz	bread flour
11	oz	sourdough starter (room temperature)
4	t	kosher salt

Optional:

1/2	t	dried rosemary
1/2	t	dried tarragon
1/2	t	dried marjoram
1/2	t	dried thyme

(continued from page 285)

Allow the dough to rise for about 1 hour at room temperature, until it doubles in size. Preheat the oven to 425 degrees.

Coat 2 sheet pans with a generous amount of flour. It is important at this juncture that you do not "punch down" the dough or deflate its air bubbles. Instead, while the dough is still in the bowl use a dough scraper or rubber spatula to divide it into 2 equal portions.

Coat your hands well with flour, scoop half of the dough out of the bowl carefully, and place the dough on one of the sheet pans. Stretch the dough gently to form a rectangular loaf that is about 12 inches long. Dust the top of the loaf with flour, and tuck the edges under all the way around to make the sides more even and give the loaf a bit more shape.

Repeat this process of stretching and shaping the second half of the dough, and place it on the other sheet pan. Then allow the loaves to rise, uncovered, for 20 to 30 minutes, until they double in size.

Slide the sheet pans gently into the preheated oven, and bake the loaves for about 30 minutes, until their crusts are golden brown and the loaves sound hollow when you tap them on their undersides. Pull the sheet pans from the oven, remove the loaves immediately from the pans, and cool the loaves on a wire cooling rack.

focaccia

yield: two 10" to 12" round loaves

Focaccia is a wonderfully versatile savory bread. The dough itself is forgiving, and the steps to make the bread are easy and quick, making it a great way to get beginners or children involved in the kitchen. To me, focaccia is the bread equivalent of baking cookies; after you make the basic dough, you can add whatever seasonings or flavors you like, and the bread will take on a completely different character. Focaccia makes a lovely accompaniment to just about any dinner or salad when cut and toasted. It also works great when sliced in half to use for sandwiches. I have often built a "deli stacker" sandwich on focaccia that includes capicola (an Italian cold cut), turkey, ham, Gruyere cheese, whole grain mustard, shallot, and tomato. A lovely loaf of freshly-baked focaccia can also be a gratifying gift to give a loved one on a special occasion.

Method:

Note that you will need to refrigerate the focaccia dough for 12 to 24 hours prior to baking, so you will want to plan ahead.

In an electric mixer bowl, combine the all-purpose flour, kosher salt, and active dry yeast, using a dough hook attachment to mix them on low speed. Add the olive oil and 80-degree water, and continue to mix the ingredients for 7 minutes. Then scrape the dough onto a floured work surface, and let it rest, uncovered, for 5 minutes.

Stretch the dough gently until it is about double in width and length, and then fold its 4 sides into the center, like an envelope. Press the folds down a bit, rub the dough on both sides with just enough olive oil to coat it, and then dust the top with flour. Leave the dough on the work surface, cover it with a towel, and let it rise at room temperature for 30 minutes.

Repeat the process of stretching the dough, folding its 4 sides in, and oiling and flouring it. Cover the dough with a towel again, and let it rise for 1 hour.

Divide the dough in half, shape each portion into a ball, and coat the balls of dough lightly with olive oil. Place the balls on a sheet pan, cover the pan with plastic wrap or a plastic bag, and refrigerate the dough for 12 to 24 hours.

Spray two 10-inch or 12-inch round cake pans with pan release. Press 1 ball of dough onto each of the pans, leaving the indentations from your fingers in the surface of the dough to give your loaves a bit of rustic character. Cover the pans with a towel, and allow the dough to rise at room temperature for about 1 hour, until it has doubled in size.

Preheat the oven to 425 degrees. Season the tops of both loaves with kosher salt and cracked black pepper. If desired, mix together any or all of the optional dried herbs, and sprinkle them over the tops of the loaves as well.

Bake the focaccia for about 10 minutes, until the top is a golden brown. Pull the pans from the oven, remove the loaves immediately from the pans, and cool them on a wire cooling rack.

Ingredients:

2 2/3	C	all-purpose flour
1	t	kosher salt
1	t	active dry yeast
3 1/2	T	olive oil (plus more for coating)
1	C	water (80 degrees)

Optional:

1	t	dried basil
2	t	dried parsley
1	t	dried oregano
1/2	t	dried thyme
1/2	t	dried dill
1	t	dried chives
1/4	t	dried tarragon

chubble

yield: 12 - 16 rolls

"Chubble" is a condensed word for "cheesy bubble" bread. It is a rich and savory pull-apart style bread that can be baked in a loaf pan or in a smaller form like a muffin tin. Along with two kinds of tangy cheese, this chubble bread recipe includes garlic, scallions, bacon, herbs, and red pepper flakes, all of it chopped and incorporated loosely in the dough. Chubble is a great addition to a summer barbecue. And it offers an enjoyable activity in the kitchen when you want your dinner guests to get their hands in on the food-building. If you grow your own herbs or cure your own meats, chubble also offers a delicious way to highlight your homegrown products.

Ingredients:

Sponge:

1	t	active dry yeast
1/2	C	water (100 degrees)
3/4	C	all-purpose flour

Dough:

1	t	active dry yeast
1	C	water (100 degrees)
3	t	olive oil
2	t	kosher salt
3 1/2	C	all-purpose flour

Filling:

1/4	C	Pecorino Romano cheese (grated)
2	C	Gruyere cheese (shredded)
2	t	garlic (minced)
6	each	scallions (sliced thinly)
2	C	bacon (cooked & chopped)
1/4	C	parsley (chopped)
2	t	kosher salt
1 1/2	t	dried oregano
1	t	crushed red pepper flakes
3	T	olive oil

Method:

Sponge:
In a mixing bowl, sprinkle the active dry yeast over the 100-degree water, whisk in the yeast, and let the mixture stand for 10 minutes, until it appears creamy. Stir in the all-purpose flour by hand. Cover the bowl with plastic wrap, and let the sponge rise at room temperature for about 45 minutes, until it doubles in size.

Dough:
In another bowl, sprinkle the active dry yeast over the 100-degree water, whisk in the yeast, and let the mixture stand for 10 minutes, until it appears creamy.

In the bowl of an electric mixer, use a paddle attachment to combine the yeast mixture, olive oil, kosher salt, and the fully-risen sponge, until all the ingredients are blended well. Add the all-purpose flour 1/4 cup at a time. When you have added 3 of the cups, begin adding the flour more slowly, checking the dough until it changes from very sticky to only slightly sticky. Once the dough has reached the appropriate texture, stop adding flour, even if there is still a small amount left.

Switch the mixer attachment to a dough hook, and mix the dough on medium speed for 3 to 4 minutes, until it is soft, velvety, and just a bit sticky—and can be pulled up into peaks using your fingers. Flour a work surface lightly. Then scrape the dough out of the bowl and onto the work surface. Dust your hands with flour, and then knead the dough by hand for 1 minute.

Shape the dough into a ball, and transfer it to a bowl that has been sprayed lightly with pan release. Cover the bowl with plastic wrap, and allow the dough to rise at room temperature for 1 to 2 hours, until it doubles in size.

Filling:
In a large bowl, toss together all of the ingredients until they are mixed evenly and coated lightly with oil. Set the bowl of filling aside.

(continued on page 289)

(continued from page 288)

Assembly:

Pour 2 tablespoons of olive oil on a work surface, set the dough on it, and use your palms to press it flat. Using a bench knife, chop the dough into cubes that are roughly 1 inch in size. Toss the cubes on the work surface to coat them in the oil.

Transfer the dough cubes to a large mixing bowl, add the filling mixture, and toss them together until they are mixed evenly. Spray the inside of a muffin tin with pan release. Then fill the cups 2/3 full, cover them with plastic wrap, and allow the dough to rise at room temperature for about 1 hour, until it has doubled in size and has risen slightly above the height of the muffin tin. (You could also bake the dough in ring molds, as pictured here, or in other small containers. If you use ring molds, be sure to set them on a non-stick surface, such as a silicone baking mat.)

While the dough is rising, preheat the oven to 325 degrees. Brush the dough with olive oil, and bake it for 20 to 25 minutes, until the tops are browned nicely. Remove the muffin tin from the oven, set it on a wire cooling rack, and allow the chubble to cool for 10 to 15 minutes before removing it from the tin.

Breads

pizza crust

yield: 3 crusts

I enjoy working with a variety of pizza dough, including crunchy, thin cracker-crust dough or the chewy dough used to create a Chicago-style deep dish pizza. Regardless of variety, I cold-rise my pizza dough overnight to allow the flavors to develop. You can bake the dough from this recipe right away, even though that overnight rise does add extra dimension to the flavor. Keep in mind that the crust's flavor can be masked by strongly-flavored toppings such as cheese and tomato sauce. The simpler the toppings, the more the taste of a good crust will be a highlight. Doing a simple pizza margarita with olive oil, basil, tomato, and a little garlic, for example, allows the flavor of this crispy pizza crust to shine through.

Ingredients:

2 1/4	C	high-gluten flour
1	t	kosher salt
1/2	t	active dry yeast
4 - 5	T	olive oil
7/8	C	water (ice cold)
1/4	C	cornmeal for dusting

Method:

Note that these instructions include refrigerating the pizza dough overnight, but you can choose to skip that step and use the dough right away.

Combine the high-gluten flour, kosher salt, and active dry yeast in an electric mixer bowl, using a dough hook attachment to mix them. Add 1 tablespoon of the olive oil, along with the ice-cold water, and mix the ingredients on medium speed for 5 to 7 minutes, until the dough becomes uniform, sticky, and smooth.

Remove the dough from the mixer bowl, and put it on a floured work surface. Then divide it into 3 portions, each weighing about 7 ounces, and form them into balls. Rub their outsides with olive oil, and set them on a sheet pan that has been sprayed lightly with pan release. Cover the pan with plastic wrap or a plastic bag.

Refrigerate the dough overnight. Two hours before you plan to bake the dough, remove it from the refrigerator. Allow it to sit, still covered, at room temperature.

Preheat the oven to 475 degrees, and prepare a baking surface for the crusts by dusting one pan for each crust you plan to bake with cornmeal. You can use a regular pizza pan. Or, I find using the back side of a sheet pan works well.

Dust the balls of dough with flour. Then roll each ball into the shape and size you want, using a rolling pin or pizza dough roller (unless you are a skilled pizza dough tosser and prefer to shape your dough that way!). Place each crust on the prepared baking surface, brush the top of the dough lightly with olive oil, and season it lightly with salt and black pepper.

Put the crusts in the oven, and bake them for 8 to 10 minutes, until they are cooked through but browned only lightly on the outside. Remove the pans from the oven, and allow the crusts to cool on wire cooling racks.

If you plan to use the pizza crusts right away, cover them with toppings, and bake them for 5 to 8 minutes, still at 475 degrees. You can also store the crusts in the refrigerator for a day or two. Or, for longer storage, you can wrap them tightly in plastic wrap and freeze them.

lavosh crackers

yield: two 13 x 18-inch sheet pans

Not a lot of people bake their own bread today, and a household in which baking homemade crackers is the norm is even more of a rarity. But try your hand at making these delightfully thin and crisp Armenian-style crackers, and you will quickly see why it is worth the effort. You can roll out the sheets of dough for these crackers by hand. But they are best when rolled and stretched very thinly. So if you can, use a dough sheeter to do the rolling. (You can get a standalone dough sheeter, and there is also a dough sheeter attachment for an electric mixer, which can function as a pasta roller as well.) Brush the large, thin sheets of dough with olive oil, butter, or even duck fat. Then sprinkle them with any of a variety of flavors, such as sea salt, rosemary, or a grated hard cheese like Parmesan. After you bake the sheets, break them into shards, and just like that, you have crisp, tasty crackers! Like most things that are homemade, they are a superb departure from the standard store-bought version.

Method:

Note that you will need to refrigerate this dough overnight before baking it.

Combine the active dry yeast, honey, olive oil, and 80-degree water in an electric mixer bowl, and whisk them together by hand until the honey has dissolved.

Add the all-purpose flour and kosher salt to the bowl, and use a dough hook attachment to mix the ingredients on low speed until they form a stiff, smooth ball. Scrape the dough out of the bowl, form it back into a ball, and set it in a clean mixing bowl that has been sprayed lightly with pan release. Cover the bowl tightly with plastic wrap, and refrigerate it overnight.

Preheat the oven to 350 degrees, and remove the dough from the refrigerator. Divide the dough into 2 pieces, dust the outsides of both pieces with flour, and use a rolling pin to roll the pieces into 2 sheets that are each about 1/4-inch thick. Dust the outsides of the dough with additional flour, and roll each sheet of dough through a dough sheeter or pasta roller, making the sheets as thin as you can. The thinner the dough, the crisper the finished crackers will be.

Lay the sheets of dough on sheet pans that have been sprayed lightly with pan release. You can cut the sheets into smaller pieces, if needed, to make them fit on the pans. (And if you prefer more uniformly-shaped crackers, you can use a pizza wheel to cut the dough while it is on the sheet pans, before you bake it.) Brush the tops of the sheets of dough with olive oil, and season them with kosher salt and cracked black pepper. If you like, you can add other toppings and seasonings, such as cumin, thyme, garlic, poppy seeds, sesame seeds, or curry powder.

Bake the sheets of dough for 3 to 5 minutes, or until they are golden brown and crisp. Remove the pans from the oven, and place them on a wire cooling rack. After the sheets of cracker bread have cooled, you can break them into small, easy-to-eat cracker pieces.

Ingredients:

3	g	active dry yeast
1	t	honey
2	T	olive oil (plus more for brushing)
7	oz	water (80 degrees)
14	oz	all-purpose flour
2	t	kosher salt

Toppings (examples):
  sea salt
  dried rosemary
  grated Parmesan cheese
  ground cumin
  dried thyme
  garlic (minced)
  poppy seeds
  sesame seeds
  curry powder

Good Breed

Sandwiches

294

The New Scenic Café

asparagus & egg

yield: 4 servings

Eggs can be delicious any time of day, especially when they are paired with fresh asparagus, piquant cheese, and crispy sourdough ciabatta bread. When I first opened the New Scenic Café, we offered breakfast in addition to lunch and dinner. We no longer serve breakfast, but I continue to bring the taste of breakfast to our lunch menu, with such dishes as quiches and omelets as well as this egg sandwich. It showcases mildly bitter frisée, grilled asparagus, eggs, and Gruyere cheese on sourdough ciabatta bread that has been smeared with rich lemon-basil aioli sauce. This combination of flavors has captured the interest of the Scenic's diners for years. Paired with a side salad and a glass of champagne, it also works wonderfully as a light brunch item to celebrate the summer with friends.

Ingredients:

1	head	frisée
6	T	butter
8	slices	sourdough ciabatta (p. 285)
24	spears	asparagus (pencil size)
8	each	eggs
8	slices	Gruyere cheese
1/2	C	lemon-basil aioli (p. 367)

Method:

Rinse the frisée in cool water, and either spin it dry in a salad spinner or use a clean towel to gently blot it dry. Using a sharp knife, shave the frisée into thin, wispy pieces, and set it aside.

Spread butter on one side of each slice of the sourdough ciabatta. On a griddle or in a large sauté pan, grill one side of the bread on medium heat until it is golden brown and crisp, taking care that it has not been cooked so long it dries out all the way through and that it is still soft on the uncooked side. Remove the ciabatta, and set it aside.

On the same griddle or pan and still on medium heat, lay 6 spears of asparagus to cook along with about 1 teaspoon of butter placed off to one side. Next to the asparagus, crack 2 eggs into the pan side by side so they are touching, and break the yolks. Season the eggs with salt and pepper, and turn the asparagus occasionally as it cooks

Cook the eggs to medium, and then flip them over carefully, keeping the 2 eggs joined together as one piece if you can. Immediately after you flip the eggs, line up the asparagus spears in an even layer on top of the eggs. It is fine if the asparagus is not yet fully cooked. It will continue to cook a bit more as you finish constructing the sandwich.

Lay 2 slices of Gruyere cheese over the asparagus so that the slices cover the eggs completely. Put a lid over the pan for about 30 seconds, until the cheese just begins to melt. (If the cheese melts for too long, it will run off the sides of the bread and into the pan.)

Cover the uncooked side of one slice of the grilled ciabatta bread with an even layer of frisée. Then use a spatula to lift the eggs, asparagus, and cheese, and slide them carefully on top of the frisée. Smear the other slice of grilled bread with about 2 tablespoons of lemon-basil aioli, and set it on top of the sandwich.

Repeat this process for the other 3 sandwiches.

Slice the sandwiches in half, cutting perpendicular to the asparagus so that each piece of asparagus is cut in half. Serve the sandwiches immediately.

Sandwiches

The New Scenic Café

heirloom tomato

yield: 4 servings

There is no better way to enjoy a good tomato than to slice it, sprinkle it with a little salt and pepper, and eat it just as it is. And I use this sandwich as a vehicle to take that same "honest food" experience to our guests. It is only when I have access to very good tomatoes, though, that I offer dishes that highlight tomatoes, such as this heirloom tomato sandwich. I especially like using heirloom tomatoes because they are usually more flavorful than hybrid tomatoes. Heirlooms are non-hybrid varieties that are available in a multitude of rich colors and shapes and are derived from seeds that have been passed down through the generations. Heirloom varieties such as Brandywine, Green Zebra, and Black Cherry are especially nice as the centerpiece of this sandwich, but any good, fresh tomatoes will work well. I combine the tomatoes with fresh mozzarella cheese, fresh basil leaves, and fried garlic chips on grilled sourdough ciabatta bread and top it all with white truffle oil. This delicious sandwich, with its marriage of simple garden flavors, reminds me of summer, crisp white wine, and sun.

Method:

Spread butter on one side of each slice of the sourdough ciabatta. On a griddle or in a large sauté pan, grill one side of the slices on medium heat until they are golden brown and crisp yet still soft on the uncooked sides. Take the ciabatta out of the pan, and set it on a working surface.

Remove any stems from the basil. Then lay the leaves out flat over the uncooked sides of the 4 slices of grilled bread.

Slice the fresh mozzarella cheese into discs that are about 1/4 inch thick, and lay 3 or 4 slices of the cheese on top of the basil on each sandwich. Season the mozzarella with a pinch each of kosher salt and cracked black pepper.

Cut the heirloom tomatoes into slices that are also about 1/4 inch thick, and lay 3 or 4 slices of tomato over the mozzarella. Season the tomatoes with a bit more salt and pepper.

Slice the shallot into very thin slivers, and scatter them across the tomatoes, followed by 1/4 cup of elephant garlic chips per sandwich.

Drizzle 1 teaspoon of white truffle oil over each sandwich, place the other slices of grilled bread on top of each, and serve them while they are fragrant and fresh.

Ingredients:

4	T	butter
8	slices	sourdough ciabatta (p. 285)
16	each	fresh basil leaves
8	oz	fresh mozzarella cheese
2 - 3	each	heirloom tomatoes
1	each	shallot
1	C	elephant garlic chips (p. 366)
4	t	white truffle oil

roasted chicken

yield: 4 servings

I roast a whole chicken to create this rich, toasty chicken sandwich, but this is also a great recipe to pull out when you want to use up leftover chicken. I break the chicken into small, bite-size pieces and sauté it until it is browned lightly. Then I smear one side of a fresh, crusty baguette with a bit of black mission fig jam, cover the other side with Camembert cheese, and toast the bread in the oven until the cheese is deliciously gooey. After laying the chicken over the hot Camembert, I top the sandwich with slivered scallions, fresh cilantro, and a squeeze of fresh lemon juice. This is a chicken sandwich that begs to be accompanied by a glass of crisp, white wine and a sunny summer day!

Ingredients:

Black Mission Fig Jam:

1	lb	dried black mission figs
1	C	granulated sugar
1/3	C	tawny port
1	each	lemon (juiced)
3	T	kosher salt
2	C	water

Other:

20	oz	roasted chicken
4	each	scallions
1	each	24" baguette (p. 274)
6	oz	Camembert cheese
3	T	olive oil
1/2	bunch	cilantro
1	each	lemon

Method:

Black Mission Fig Jam:

Put all of the ingredients in a large pot, place a lid on the pot, and simmer the mixture gently over low heat for 2 hours. Check the jam frequently, to be sure it is not boiling or drying out. The figs will soak up a lot of the water, so if too much evaporates, add just enough water to keep them moist. When it is finished cooking, transfer the mixture to a blender, and purée it until it is smooth.

Assembly:

Pull the chicken apart into small, bite-size pieces (but without shredding it). If you are using a whole roasted chicken, mix the dark and white meats together. The variety will add a nice bit of complexity to the flavor of the sandwich.

Cut the scallions into long, thin slivers, and soak them for a few minutes in a bowl of ice water. Soaking the scallions gives them a little extra crunch and causes them to curl so they have more texture.

Preheat the oven to 400 degrees.

Cut the baguette into 4 equal pieces, each about 6 inches long. Then slice the 4 pieces open lengthwise, leaving the back edge of each connected like a hinge, and fold them open. Spread 4 tablespoons of black mission fig jam on the cut side of the top half of each of the baguette pieces. Slice the Camembert cheese into small pieces, and lay them across the cut side of the bottom halves of the baguette.

(continued on page 301)

(continued from page 300)

Heat the olive oil in a large sauté pan, and add the chicken pieces. Toss the chicken in the oil for a minute or two, until the pieces are hot and slightly browned, and remove the pan from the heat.

Set the sections of baguette on a sheet pan, put them in the oven, and toast them for about 5 minutes. The cheese should be just melted, and the bread should be hot but not dried out. Remove the baguette sections from the oven, and set them on serving plates.

Divide the sautéed chicken pieces among the 4 sandwiches, laying the chicken on top of the melted Camembert. Remove the scallions from the ice water, let them drain on a paper towel for a minute, and then shake them to remove any excess water. Scatter the scallions evenly across the chicken, followed by a few sprigs of cilantro and a few drops of freshly-squeezed lemon juice. Fold the tops over to close the sandwiches, and serve them right away, while they are crispy and hot.

pistachio-crusted walleye

yield: 4 servings

I began offering this sandwich when the New Scenic Café first opened, and it has remained a flagship sandwich ever since. I bring it back as a summer special every year. This is a simple pan-seared fish that is taken to another level of nutty, rich flavor with its crust of freshly-ground pistachios. I serve the walleye on thin, crisp slices of sweet cranberry pecan bread, along with a bit of mixed field greens tossed in roasted garlic vinaigrette and a touch of tangy lemon-basil aioli.

Ingredients:

4	each	walleye fillets (6 oz each)
2	T	olive oil
1/2	C	pistachios (finely ground)
8	slices	cranberry pecan bread
4	oz	mixed field greens
2	T	roasted garlic vinaigrette (p. 370)
1/2	C	lemon-basil aioli (p. 367)

Method:

If the walleye fillets still have their skins, remove and discard them. Preheat the broiler in the oven.

Heat a large sauté pan over medium heat, and add the olive oil. Season the walleye fillets on both sides with salt and pepper, and lay them in the sauté pan. Allow the fillets to cook for 5 minutes or until they are cooked about halfway through. Do not turn the fillets over. They will be cooked all the way without flipping them.

Sprinkle 2 tablespoons of ground pistachios across the top of each fillet, and continue cooking the fish on the same side until it is fully cooked. When it is done, the meat will be solid white and opaque all the way through to the center.

While the walleye fillets are cooking, lightly toast one side of all of the slices of bread on a sheet pan under the broiler. Place 1 piece of the bread on each of 4 serving plates, toasted side down.

In a small mixing bowl, toss the mixed field greens with the roasted garlic vinaigrette. Divide the greens evenly, placing a bed of them on each of the 4 slices of bread. Use a spatula to move 1 walleye fillet onto each bed of greens. Then spread 2 tablespoons of lemon-basil aioli on each of the other 4 slices of bread, place a slice on top of each sandwich, and serve them while the fish is crispy and hot.

pistachio-crusted goat cheese

yield: 4 servings

This sandwich dates back to the earliest New Scenic Café menus, and it has been a favorite ever since. It uses the same grilled pistachio-crusted goat cheese coins that we serve on our salad of the same name (page 130), which has also been a Café favorite. I serve the nut-crusted and warmed goat cheese on toasted cranberry pecan bread, along with mixed field greens and crisp, cold cucumber slices. It is a wonderful vegetarian dish, with the warm, molten goat cheese serving as the "sauce."

Method:

You will want to prepare the goat cheese coins ahead of time and then keep them in the refrigerator for at least 30 minutes, until just before you use them.

To make the coins, allow the goat cheese to soften to room temperature, and then use a melon baller to scoop out eight 1 1/2-ounce balls.

Put the ground pistachios on a plate or other flat surface, and press the softened goat cheese balls into the pistachios, coating each one completely. Shape the balls into slightly-flattened coins that are roughly 2 inches wide and 1/2 inch thick. Refrigerate them for at least 30 minutes or until they are cold and firm all the way through.

Preheat the broiler in the oven. In a mixing bowl, gently toss the mixed field greens with the roasted garlic vinaigrette. Lightly toast one side of each of the slices of cranberry pecan bread on a baking sheet under the broiler. Then place one slice of the bread on each of 4 serving plates, toasted side down, and add a bed of the dressed mixed field greens atop each slice.

Heat a sauté pan on medium-high heat, and add the olive oil. Place the pistachio-crusted goat cheese coins carefully in the hot oil, making sure the pan is not crowded and the coins are not touching. (You can sauté them in 2 or 3 batches if necessary.)

Sauté the coins for 1 to 2 minutes, until they are golden brown, and then flip them over. Cook them for another minute, and remove them from the pan, placing 2 coins on top of each bed of mixed greens.

Slice the chilled cucumber thinly on a diagonal, creating long, oval-shaped slices. Lay 2 or 3 slices on top of each pair of goat cheese coins, season the slices with salt and pepper, and place the other slices of toasted bread over each sandwich. Serve the sandwiches immediately, while the goat cheese is warm and creamy.

Ingredients:

12	oz	goat cheese (chevre, soft)
1	C	pistachios (finely ground)
4	oz	mixed field greens
2	T	roasted garlic vinaigrette (p. 370)
8	slices	cranberry pecan bread
2	T	olive oil
1	each	cucumber (small)

banh mi

yield: 4 servings

"Banh mi" is a Vietnamese term that refers to a style of bread similar to the baguette, but it is a bit softer and has a thinner crust. The term has also become associated with a Vietnamese-style sandwich made with many different combinations of ingredients. In this version, I use a fresh baguette, pork terrine, chicken liver pate, pickled carrot, pickled daikon radish, cucumber, and fresh cilantro. I also add some creamy Kewpie mayonnaise blended with Sriracha hot sauce. Kewpie is a Japanese brand of mayonnaise that, instead of being made with whole eggs, is made with rice vinegar and egg yolks. Its rich flavor and bright acidity brings all the flavors of this sandwich together nicely.

Ingredients:

Sriracha Kewpie Mayonnaise:

8	oz	Kewpie mayonnaise
1	T	Sriracha hot sauce
1/2	t	fish sauce
1/2	T	rice vinegar
1	T	lemon juice
1/4	t	sesame oil
1/2	T	brown sugar

Other:

1	each	24" baguette (p. 274)
8	oz	pork terrine (p. 369)
8	oz	chicken liver paté (p. 363)
4	oz	pickled carrot (p. 368)
4	oz	pickled daikon radish (p. 368)
1	each	cucumber (small)
20	sprigs	fresh cilantro

Method:

Preparing the pork terrine takes 2 or 3 days of lead time, and the chicken liver paté requires several hours, so plan accordingly when you want to prepare this sandwich. But you will find the effort and time well worth it!

Sriracha Kewpie Mayonnaise:
Combine all of the ingredients in a mixing bowl, and use a whisk to stir the mixture until it is blended evenly. Transfer the Sriracha Kewpie Mayonnaise to a squeeze bottle, if you have one, and store it in the refrigerator. (A squeeze bottle will work well for applying the mayonnaise to your sandwiches, but you can use any tightly-covered container for storage.)

Assembly:
Preheat the oven to 400 degrees.

Strain the pickled carrot and pickled daikon radish from their brine, and shake off any excess moisture. Slice the cucumber thinly and on a steep angle, creating long, thin oval shapes.

Cut the baguette into 4 equal pieces. A standard size baguette is just over 24 inches long, so you will have 4 sandwiches that are each about 6 inches long. Next, slice each section of baguette lengthwise across the middle, without cutting all the way through it. Leave one side attached as a "hinge" so that it opens like a hot dog bun. Spread the 4 baguette sections open, with the cut sides facing up, and place them on a sheet pan.

Slice the pork terrine into thin, 1/4-inch slices, and lay about 2 ounces of it on one side of each section of baguette. Next, smear about 2 ounces of chicken liver pate on the other side of each baguette. Place the sheet pan in the oven, and bake the sandwiches for 6 to 7 minutes. The terrine and pate should be hot, and the bread should be toasted and warm but not dried out. Remove the pan from the oven, and set each sandwich on a plate.

Lay about 1 ounce of each pickled vegetable over the top of the pork terrine on each sandwich. Lay 3 slices of cucumber across the pickled vegetables, and drizzle 1 to 2 tablespoons of Sriracha Kewpie Mayonnaise over the cucumber. Then add a few sprigs of fresh cilantro to each sandwich, close them, and serve the banh mi while they are deliciously warm.

The New Scenic Café

seared halloumi

yield: 4 servings

Halloumi is a cheese made from goat and sheep milk. It originated in the island of Cyprus but is also produced in Greece and throughout the Middle East and has made its way to the U.S. as well. One of the most enticing characteristics of halloumi is its salty, briny flavor. It is also great to cook with because it sears to a crust without melting, while still softening nicely in the center. I combine the seared halloumi with a kalamata olive tapenade, cucumber, tomato, fresh mint, fresh dill, and a little lemon juice, all on a grilled torpedo roll, which is a soft-style bread. (The torpedo roll works particularly well, but any long, soft roll will do nicely.) I have often thought this is the tastiest vegetarian sandwich I have ever made. With its fresh vegetables and tangy Mediterranean flavors, it is the kind of sandwich that celebrates summer yet tempts the palate in any season.

Method:

Kalamata Tapenade:

Drain the kalamata olives, and rinse them thoroughly in cold water. Then lay them on paper towels or on a clean kitchen towel, and allow them to dry well before you use them. Chop the Italian parsley finely, drain the brine from the capers, and mince the garlic.

Combine the olives, parsley, capers, garlic, cracked black pepper, lemon juice, and olive oil in a food processor, and pulse it until the mixture is smooth and paste-like in consistency. Put the mixture in the refrigerator, and allow it to rest for at least an hour before you use it, to help it stiffen and give the flavors time to meld.

Assembly:

Slice the halloumi cheese into roughly 2-ounce pieces, each about 3/8 inch thick, for a total of 8 slices. Cut the cucumber on a diagonal, into long, oval-shaped slices that are about 1/8 inch thick. And slice the tomato into thin slices that are about 1/8 inch thick. Lay the 4 mint leaves on top of each other, roll them up, and slice them into a thin chiffonade (thinly sliced little ribbons).

Cut each torpedo roll into 2 pieces of 6 inches each. Next, slice each of the 4 pieces lengthwise across the middle, all the way through. Spread butter on the cut sides of the rolls, and grill them in a large sauté pan or on a griddle. Remove the torpedo rolls from the pan, and place them on 4 serving plates. In the same pan, heat the olive oil over medium-high heat until it is hot.

Add the slices of halloumi to the pan, leaving a little space between each slice. (You can cook the halloumi in multiple batches, if necessary.) Sear the first sides for about 2 minutes, until they are golden brown. Flip them over, and sear the second sides for another 2 minutes. Then transfer 2 slices of seared halloumi to the bottom half of each grilled torpedo roll.

Lay 2 or 3 slices of tomato on top of the halloumi, followed by 2 or 3 slices of cucumber. Scatter the chiffonade mint across the cucumber, and then lay 2 sprigs of fresh dill over the mint. Cut the lemon in half, and squeeze a couple of teaspoons of lemon juice over each sandwich. Then, spread 4 tablespoons of kalamata tapenade on the cut side of the other halves of the torpedo rolls, and place them on top. Serve the sandwiches while they are soft and warm.

Ingredients:

Kalamata Tapenade:

1	C	kalamata olives
1	T	Italian parsley
1	T	capers
1	T	garlic
1/4	t	cracked black pepper
1	T	lemon juice
1	T	olive oil

Other:

16	oz	halloumi cheese
1	each	cucumber (small)
1	each	ripe tomato (medium size)
4	leaves	fresh mint
2	each	12" torpedo rolls
4	T	butter
2	T	olive oil
8	sprigs	fresh dill
1	each	lemon

jalapeño bacon & avocado

yield: 4 servings

I love a good Bacon Lettuce and Tomato sandwich, and this version of the B.L.T. is like its older, more mature cousin. I start with jalapeño-cured smoked bacon, with its nice bit of warm zing, which you can find if you do a bit of searching at grocery stores or markets, or online. I pile it on toasted slices of six-seed sourdough, which brings an alluring complexity to the sandwich. Then, I add ripe, creamy avocado, fresh tomato, and mache greens, which are very soft and supple greens that are similar to baby spinach (baby spinach leaves make a wonderful substitution). I finish the sandwich with lemon-basil aioli, to bring a bit more depth of flavor than regular mayonnaise can offer. For bacon lovers, this sandwich is the pinnacle of delight!

Ingredients:

12	strips	jalapeño-cured smoked bacon
8	slices	six-seed sourdough
2	each	ripe avocados
2	each	ripe tomatoes (medium size)
4	oz	mache greens (or baby spinach)
1/2	C	lemon-basil aioli (p. 367)

Method:

Cook the strips of jalapeño-cured smoked bacon to your favorite level of crispness, drain them, and set them aside.

On a sheet pan under the broiler, toast one side of the slices of six-seed sourdough lightly.

Cut the ripe avocados in half lengthwise around the pits, remove and discard the pits, and scoop out the avocado as intact halves. Set the avocado halves flat-side-down on a cutting board, and slice them lengthwise into thin slices.

For each sandwich, pick up a sliced avocado half, and spread its slices out across the untoasted side of one slice of bread. Next, lay 3 strips of warm bacon on top of the avocado on each of the sandwiches. Slice the tomatoes into 1/4-inch slices, and lay 3 slices across the bacon. Season the tomatoes with kosher salt and fresh cracked black pepper.

Top the tomatoes with the mache greens (or baby spinach leaves), leaving the mache in the nice, fluffy "heads" that it comes in.

Spread 2 tablespoons of lemon-basil aioli on the untoasted sides of the other slices of bread, place those slices on top, and serve the sandwiches while the bacon is still fragrant and warm.

grilled chicken breast

yield: 4 servings

Over the years, this sandwich has been a regular and favored entry on the New Scenic Cafe menu, especially in the spring and summer. That's when its combination of lemon-basil aioli, creamy Brie cheese, and grilled asparagus seem to suit the season particularly well. The grilled chicken breast is a great "bridging" sandwich as well, enabling me to introduce less familiar sandwich components, such as the Brie and asparagus, in combination with the more familiar ingredient of grilled chicken. Whatever the season, I think you will enjoy this melding of flavors and textures.

Ingredients:

4	each	chicken breasts (6 oz ea, boneless/skinless)
1	T	olive oil (if cooking in pan)
8	slices	cranberry pecan bread
24	spears	asparagus (pencil size)
6	oz	Brie cheese
1/2	C	lemon-basil aioli (p. 367)

Method:

Preheat the broiler in the oven.

Season the chicken breasts with salt and pepper, and cook them all the way through, either on a grill or in a sauté pan with the olive oil, about 6 to 8 minutes on each side.

While the chicken is cooking, place the slices of cranberry pecan bread on a sheet pan and under the broiler. Toast the slices on one side lightly, taking care they do not dry out, remove them from the broiler, and put them on serving plates.

When the chicken is nearly done, add the asparagus to the grill or sauté pan, and cook it for about 2 minutes, turning it occasionally, until it is tender but still bright green.

Cut the Brie cheese into thin slices, leaving the rind on, and lay the cheese across 4 of the slices of toasted bread, dividing the cheese evenly among the sandwiches. Lay the chicken breasts on top of the Brie slices, and then lay the asparagus on top of the chicken, with 6 spears of asparagus on each sandwich.

Spread 2 tablespoons of lemon-basil aioli on the untoasted side of each of the other slices of bread, and place them on top. Serve the sandwiches while the chicken is hot and the brie is warm and creamy.

bison pastrami

yield: 4 servings

Bison is a softer, leaner meat than beef, and bison pastrami is especially tender. It makes a delicious sandwich that our diners at the New Scenic Café have raved about for years. The trick is, acquiring the bison pastrami, which has not always been easy. (I have tried making this same sandwich with beef pastrami. Although it is tasty and you could use beef pastrami as a substitute in this recipe, it isn't quite as good.) If you can't locate any bison pastrami, you can order it from various sources online, or you could consider getting a bison brisket and making your own pastrami at home. I serve the bison pastrami hot, on grilled sourdough ciabatta, and top it with sautéed poblano pepper, sautéed red onion, and melted Gruyere cheese. Then I finish it with a roasted red pepper and horseradish sauce. You won't find a more hearty and satisfying sandwich than this one!

Method:

Roasted Red Pepper & Horseradish Sauce:

Put the roasted red bell peppers in a food processor, and pulse them until they are just barely puréed but not completely smooth. Then move the puréed peppers to a mixing bowl, add the remaining ingredients, and stir them with a whisk until the mixture is combined evenly. Pour the finished sauce into a covered container, and store it in the refrigerator.

Assembly:

Slice the red onion and poblano pepper into short, thin (1/8 inch) julienne strips.

Spread butter on one side of the slices of sourdough ciabatta, grill them in a large sauté pan or on a griddle, and then remove them from the pan and set them aside somewhere warm.

Pour the olive oil into the same sauté pan, and heat it over medium heat. When the oil is hot, add the sliced onions and peppers, sautéing them until they are soft and beginning to caramelize. Remove the onions and peppers from the pan, and set them aside.

Return the same pan to the medium heat, and spread the bison pastrami evenly in the pan. Heat the pastrami for about 2 minutes, flipping it to be sure it is warmed through and taking care because bison is very lean and tends to dry out if cooked too long. Remove the pan from the heat. With the pastrami still in the pan, divide it into 4 equal portions.

Place an even amount of the grilled onion and pepper mixture on top of each portion of pastrami, and then lay 2 slices of Gruyere cheese over the top of each one. Return the pan to the heat for just a minute. The steam from the pastrami will rise and melt the Gruyere. Put one slice of grilled ciabatta on each of 4 serving plates.

When the cheese has just melted (but has not run down through the vegetables and pastrami), move each portion onto one slice of the bread. Spread 2 tablespoons of roasted red pepper and horseradish sauce on the cut side of each of the remaining slices of bread, and place them on top. Serve the sandwiches while they are nice and hot!

Ingredients:

Roasted Red Pepper & Horseradish Sauce:

4	oz	roasted red bell pepper (p. 370)
1	C	sour cream
1	C	mayonnaise
1/4	C	prepared horseradish
2	t	lemon juice
1	t	crushed red pepper flakes
1	t	kosher salt
1	pinch	dried thyme

Other:

1	each	red onion (medium size)
1	each	poblano pepper
4	T	butter
8	slices	sourdough ciabatta (p. 285)
2	T	olive oil
1	lb	bison pastrami (sliced thinly)
8	slices	Gruyere cheese

pork pibil

yield: 6 servings

Ingredients:

Marinade:

2	T	annatto seeds
1/2	T	black peppercorns
1	t	allspice berries
1/2	T	cumin seeds
2	each	whole cloves
1	each	habanero pepper
1	T	garlic (minced)
1	T	orange juice concentrate
1/4	C	white wine vinegar
1	T	lemon juice
1	T	lime juice
1	T	tequila
1	T	kosher salt

Pork Pibil:

2	lb	pork shoulder or butt
2	each	banana leaves

Other:

6	each	stirato rolls
6	T	butter
1	each	shallot (sliced thinly)
1/2	bunch	cilantro
3/4	C	sour cream

This recipe takes you on a delicious adventure into the world of traditional Mexican cooking. Pork pibil, also called "cochinita pibil," starts with annatto seeds. They are the seeds of the tropical achiote tree and have a soft flavor similar to paprika. I grind the annatto seeds, along with other spices and ingredients, to create a marinade for the pork, which I cut into cubes and marinate overnight, the pigment in the annatto giving a pink hue to the meat. The next day, I wrap the pork in banana leaves (which you can find at some gourmet food stores, Asian grocery stores, or online) and slow-roast the meat in the oven. Traditionally, the banana leaves are used to keep the pork moist and protect it from direct heat. Although there are certainly more modern ways to achieve that effect, I find that the banana leaves also add their own unique flavor to the meat and bring a bit of fun and international flair to the cooking. And if you have a fire pit and want to try the traditional underground-cooking route, all the better! I serve the pork with sour cream and a bit of fresh cilantro, all stacked in a stirato roll, which is a square-shaped roll with a thin crust and a light, tender texture. (Slices of ripe avocado make a nice addition to the sandwich as well.) The pork has a distinct, earthy flavor that is so good you will soon forget the bit of extra time it takes to create this memorable sandwich.

Method:

Note that you will need to marinate the pork overnight and then cook it for several hours the following day, so you will want to plan ahead when you make this dish. That said, be prepared to love it!

Marinade:

Combine the annatto seeds, black peppercorns, allspice berries, cumin seeds, and whole cloves in a spice grinder, and grind them to a fine powder. Put the ground spices, along with the remaining ingredients, in a blender, and blend the mixture to a smooth purée.

Pork Pibil:

Cut the pork shoulder or butt into 2-inch cubes, place it in a mixing bowl, and pour the marinade over the top. Mix it until all of the cubes of meat are coated evenly, cover the bowl, and refrigerate it overnight.

The next day, preheat the oven to 300 degrees. Line a baking pan with the banana leaves, laying the leaves perpendicular to each other and being sure to use a pan that is large enough to hold all the pork. Put the marinated pork in the pan, and then wrap the ends of the banana leaves over the top of the pork to create a bundle, as if you were wrapping a gift.

(continued on page 313)

(continued from page 312)

Cover the pan tightly with a layer of plastic wrap and then with a layer of aluminum foil, and place the pan in the oven. Bake the pork for 2 to 4 hours, until it is cooked fully. Check for doneness by pulling out a piece of pork and squeezing it. The meat should break apart easily if it is ready.

Pull the pan from the oven, and remove the pork from the banana leaves. While the pork is still warm, either shred it using 2 forks or crumble it by hand. You can use the meat immediately, or you can put it in the refrigerator to cool and then reheat it later before you serve it.

Assembly:
Slice the stirato rolls in half, butter them, and grill them on medium heat in a sauté pan or on a griddle. Put the grilled rolls on serving plates, and place about 5 ounces of warm roasted pork pibil on the bottom half of each roll, topping the pork with thin slices of shallot and a few sprigs of fresh cilantro. Spread about 2 tablespoons of sour cream on the cut side of the other half of each roll, place it on top, and serve the sandwiches immediately.

314

tempeh reuben

yield: 4 servings

Before it became the New Scenic Café, the original Scenic featured a vegetarian reuben sandwich a bit like this one, and I've carried the tradition forward, building on that great foundation. I mix the tempeh, which is made from fermented soybeans and other grains, together with onion, garlic, soy sauce, and white pepper. Then I bring the tempeh together with the deep flavor of dark raisin rye bread, the sour taste of sauerkraut, the earthy tang of Gruyere cheese, and the zest of Russian dressing. The slices of ripe tomato I layer on as well bring in a flavor that helps merge the concept of a reuben with the fresh flavors of vegetarian cuisine.

Method:

Russian Dressing:
Dice the red onion and the tomato finely. Combine them with the other ingredients in a mixing bowl, and whisk the mixture until it is combined evenly. Store the dressing in the refrigerator.

Tempeh:
Unwrap the five-grain tempeh, and crumble it loosely into an electric mixer bowl. Dice the white onion finely (with pieces no larger than 1/4 inch), and add it to the bowl, along with the minced garlic, soy sauce, and white pepper. Using a paddle attachment, mix the ingredients on low speed until the mixture just begins to stick together slightly, taking care not to mix it so long that the tempeh becomes pasty.

Assembly:
Place all of the slices of dark raisin rye bread on a sheet pan, and lightly toast them on one side under the broiler. Set them aside somewhere warm.

In a large sauté pan or on a griddle, heat the olive oil over medium heat. When the oil is hot, add the tempeh mixture to the pan in 4 separate, loose portions. Cook the tempeh for about 3 minutes on that side, or until it begins to brown. Flip each portion over, using the spatula afterwards to gather and shape the tempeh into the general shape of your sandwich, and brown that second side for another couple of minutes.

While the tempeh is browning on the second side, place 1/2 cup of sauerkraut in the pan next to each portion. By the time the tempeh is finished browning, the moisture from the bottom of the sauerkraut will have turned to steam and heated the sauerkraut all the way through. Turn the heat under the pan off, put one slice of the toasted bread on each of 4 serving plates, toasted side down, and slice the tomato into 1/4-inch slices.

Move one portion of sauerkraut on top of each portion of tempeh, and then lay 2 slices of Gruyere cheese across the tops. Let the cheese melt, and then lift each portion carefully, setting each on one slice of toasted bread. Lay 2 or 3 tomato slices on each sandwich, and season the tomato with salt and pepper. Spread about 2 tablespoons of the Russian dressing on the other slices of bread, and place them on top. Serve the sandwiches while they are hot.

Ingredients:

Russian Dressing:

2	T	red onion (diced)
3	T	tomato (diced)
1	C	mayonnaise
1	T	Dijon mustard
1	pinch	cayenne pepper
1	T	prepared horseradish

Tempeh:

16	oz	five-grain tempeh
8	oz	white onion (diced)
1	T	garlic (minced)
1	T	soy sauce
1	pinch	white pepper

Other:

8	slices	dark raisin rye bread
4	T	olive oil
2	C	sauerkraut
8	slices	Gruyere cheese
1	each	ripe tomato (medium)

prosciutto, medjool date, & arugula
yield: 4 servings

Loving the taste of dates as I do, I found myself searching for a way to use them in a sandwich and eventually created this one, which is based on a salad I have featured on our menu at the Café. It brings together the rich, caramel-sweet flavor of Medjool dates, the smokiness and delicate texture of prosciutto, and the spiciness of arugula, to form a fantastic taste merger. I added flavorful Gruyere cheese, put it all on grilled sourdough ciabatta, and voila! A delicious sandwich that gives date lovers an opportunity to indulge.

Ingredients:

8	each	Medjool dates
4	T	butter
8	slices	sourdough ciabatta (p. 285)
8	slices	Gruyere cheese
20	slices	prosciutto
4	oz	baby arugula
2	T	cream sherry vinaigrette (p. 365)
4	t	white truffle oil

Method:

Slice the dates lengthwise into 1/8-inch slices. They are very sticky, so take your time, and pause to clean your knife as needed so your slices are clean and neat.

Spread butter on one side of all of the slices of sourdough ciabatta, and grill that side in a large sauté pan or on a griddle, on low heat. While the bread is grilling, lay 1 even layer of sliced dates (2 dates per sandwich) on each of 4 of the slices of bread, and lay 2 slices of Gruyere cheese across each of the other 4 slices of bread. As the bread cooks, the cheese will begin to melt and the dates will warm, making the dates nicely soft.

When the bread is grilled to a golden brown, remove the slices from the pan, and put them on 4 serving plates. Place 5 slices of prosciutto on top of the dates on each sandwich, peeling up each slice of prosciutto, gathering it into a loose bundle, and putting it on the sandwich. The prosciutto should cover the sandwich's entire surface.

In a mixing bowl, toss the baby arugula lightly with the cream sherry vinaigrette, until the arugula is coated. You can use larger-size arugula, if you like, but the leaves are not quite as tender and might require slicing. Baby arugula is beautifully tender and is also usually a bit curly, which helps give the sandwich body.

Divide the dressed arugula evenly among the sandwiches, arranging it over the prosciutto. Then cover the tops of the sandwiches with the slices of grilled bread on which you have melted the Gruyere cheese, and drizzle 1 teaspoon of white truffle oil across the top of each. Using a sharp knife, slice each sandwich in half, and serve the sandwiches while they are hot and crisp.

fresh herring & prosciutto
yield: 4 servings

The Knife River flows into Lake Superior 5 miles northeast of the New Scenic Café, and about 1/2 mile out from the mouth of the river local fisherman Steve Dahl catches fresh herring every year, from April to December. I have had a long-standing agreement with Steve to bring as much herring as he can, whenever he can, no need to call ahead. As soon as he drops off a fresh catch, we cook it and serve it to our guests. There are always more mouths watering for Steve's fresh herring than he can accommodate!

Using the bounty right outside our door, we combine the fresh herring with a bit of white wine and butter, layer it with a slice of prosciutto, and bake it. Then we put the baked herring on grilled ciabatta bread, along with shaved frisée that has been dressed with fennel mustard vinaigrette and a small slather of lemon-basil aioli, for a light and delicious meal fresh from the Lake Superior waters.

Ingredients:

2	heads	frisée
6	T	butter
4	each	fresh herring fillets (4 - 5 oz each)
1/4	C	white wine
4	slices	prosciutto
8	slices	sourdough ciabatta (p. 285)
2	T	fennel mustard vinaigrette (p. 366)
1/2	C	lemon-basil aioli (p. 367)

Method:

Rinse the frisée in cool water, and either spin it dry in a salad spinner or use a clean towel to gently blot it dry. Using a sharp knife, shave the frisée into thin, wispy pieces, and set it aside.

Preheat the oven to 400 degrees.

Place 2 tablespoons of the butter in a large, oven-proof sauté pan, and heat it gently over low heat, just long enough to melt the butter. Lay the herring fillets in the pan, making sure they are not touching, and pour the white wine over them.

Season the fillets with cracked black pepper, and then lay one slice of prosciutto across each of them, crumpling the prosciutto slightly to give the fish additional crispness when it is finished cooking.

Place the pan in the oven, and roast the fillets for 7 to 10 minutes, until they are just cooked all the way through. While the fillets are baking, spread butter on one side of all the slices of sourdough ciabatta, and grill them on medium heat in a large sauté pan or on a griddle, until they are golden brown on that side. Remove the bread slices from the pan, and place them on 4 serving plates.

In a small mixing bowl, toss the frisée with the fennel mustard vinaigrette, until the frisée is coated evenly. Divide the dressed greens equally among 4 of the slices of bread, and then lay one herring fillet on top of each bed of greens. Spread 1 or 2 tablespoons of lemon-basil aioli on the un-grilled side of the other slices of bread, place them on top, and serve the sandwiches immediately, while the herring is nice and hot.

herring fishcakes

yield: 4 servings

If you would like to experiment with an alternative to the "fresh herring & prosciutto" sandwich recipe on the preceding page (page 318), or if you find yourself with extra fresh herring, you might enjoy making Scandinavian-style herring fishcakes for your herring sandwich, rather than using herring fillets. The same basic sandwich composition works wonderfully. And you can easily freeze the fishcake batter in freezer-proof bags, for a delicious jump-start to a future meal.

Method:

Fishcake Batter:

In a food processor, chop the fresh herring fillets until they are minced finely, and then transfer the herring to a large mixing bowl. In a small bowl, whisk together the cornstarch and milk, and then add that mixture to the minced herring. Add the minced white onion, egg yolk or egg white, nutmeg, kosher salt, and white pepper as well, and mix all the ingredients by hand until they are incorporated evenly.

Put the fishcake batter in a covered container, and refrigerate it until you are ready to use it. (If you are freezing the batter, put it in freezer-proof ziplock bags, and squeeze out as much air as possible before you seal the bags.)

Assembly:

To cook the fishcakes, heat the olive oil in a large sauté pan over medium heat. Use a spoon or a small ice cream or cookie scoop to make eight 2-ounce balls of fishcake batter, and set them in the hot oil. Then, using a lightly-greased flat spatula, press the balls of batter flat, into disks that are about 1/2 inch thick.

Cook the first side of the fishcakes for about 2 minutes, until they have seared to a golden brown. Then, flip the fishcakes over, and cook them for another 2 minutes, to sear the second side. Prepare the frisée and bread as explained in the preceding "fresh herring & prosciutto" sandwich recipe, and put the 4 sandwiches together, substituting 2 fish cakes for the prosciutto-covered fillet on each sandwich.

Ingredients:

Fishcake Batter:

1	lb	fresh herring fillets
1	T	cornstarch
1/4	C	milk
2	T	white onion (minced)
1	each	egg yolk or egg white
1/2	t	nutmeg
1	t	kosher salt
1	t	white pepper

Other:

1/4	C	olive oil
2	heads	frisée
6	T	butter
8	slices	sourdough ciabatta (p. 285)
2	T	fennel mustard vinaigrette (p. 366)
1/2	C	lemon-basil aioli (p. 367)

grilled cheese with brie

yield: 4 servings

Nothing says "comfort food" quite like a grilled cheese sandwich. And this version, with its sweet Honeycrisp apple flavor and rich fig molasses, says "comfort" in a particularly singular and satisfying way. I grill our homemade ciabatta bread, melt Gruyere cheese on it, add some Brie cheese and very thin slices of apple, and then drizzle fig molasses and a touch of white truffle oil over the top. Although I enjoy this sandwich any time of year, it is particularly appealing on an early autumn day, served with hot apple cider or a nice glass of pinot noir.

Ingredients:

1	each	Honeycrisp apple
4	T	butter
8	slices	sourdough ciabatta (p. 285)
16	slices	Gruyere cheese
8	oz	Brie cheese
4	T	fig molasses
4	t	white truffle oil

Method:

Using a very sharp mandoline slicer, cut wafer-thin, 1/16-inch cross-section slices of Honeycrisp apple, cutting across the core and pulling off any remaining pieces of seed. You need not worry about removing the core. The slices are so thin that the core of the apple will be easily edible. Plus, the cross-section star pattern that results is lovely. You will need to cut 5 slices of apple for each sandwich.

Spread butter on one side of each of the slices of sourdough ciabatta, and lay them buttered-side-down in a large sauté pan or on a griddle, over low heat. While the bread is toasting, lay 2 slices of Gruyere cheese across each slice of bread.

Using a sharp knife, cut the Brie cheese into thin slices that are about as long as the width of the bread. Lay the Brie on the untoasted side of 4 of the bread slices, dividing it evenly, and spread the apple slices evenly over the other 4 slices of bread. Season the apple with a bit of kosher salt and cracked black pepper.

After the bread is toasted to a golden brown and the cheese has begun to melt, put the two halves of each sandwich together, and place the sandwiches on serving plates. Drizzle 1 tablespoon of fig molasses over the top of each sandwich, followed by 1 teaspoon of white truffle oil, and cut each sandwich in half. Serve the sandwiches immediately, while the cheese is delectably soft and melting and the bread is warm.

The New Scenic Café

croque provençal
yield: 4 servings

In French cuisine, there is a group of sandwiches based on the croque monsieur, which is a grilled ham and cheese sandwich with béchamel sauce that is typically topped with Emmental or Gruyere cheese. Two of the most common variations of these sandwiches are the croque madame, which includes a fried or poached egg, and the croque provençal, which incorporates tomato slices. This sandwich is deliciously messy and intended to be eaten with a knife and fork. To build my croque provençal, I put thick slices of smoked ham on grilled sourdough ciabatta bread and then add fresh tomato, rich béchamel sauce, and a dash of black truffle oil. Over the top, I lay slices of Gruyere cheese and broil the sandwich until the cheese is melted and hot. You will need a napkin when you sit down to enjoy this sandwich… or, likely, 2 or 3 napkins! But you will find this classic French food well worth the effort. One day, a gentleman visiting from France took a photo of our croque provençal at the Café and sent the picture back to his family with the note, "There is good French cuisine in America!"

Method:

Preheat the broiler to 400 degrees. Cut the tomatoes into slices that are about 1/4-inch thick.

Spread butter on one side of each slice of the sourdough ciabatta, and grill that side of the bread in a large sauté pan or on a griddle, on medium heat. Remove the grilled bread, and place it on a sheet pan, grilled side down.

Lay the slices of ham in the same pan, still on medium heat, and warm them for about 30 seconds. Flip the ham slices over, warm them for another 30 seconds, and then remove them from the pan and divide them evenly among 4 of the slices of bread.

Lay 2 or 3 slices of tomato over the ham on each sandwich, and season the tomato with salt and pepper. Spread 2 tablespoons of béchamel sauce on the non-toasted side of each of the other slices of bread, and lay them on top of the sandwiches, toasted side up.

Drizzle 1 teaspoon of truffle oil over each sandwich, and then lay 3 slices of Gruyere cheese across the tops, so that each sandwich is covered completely with the cheese.

Put the pan of sandwiches under the broiler for about 2 minutes, until the cheese is melted and just beginning to brown. Remove your croque provençal from the oven, transfer them to serving plates, and enjoy!

Ingredients:

4	T	butter
8	slices	sourdough ciabatta (p. 285)
20	oz	smoked ham (sliced thickly)
2 - 3	each	ripe tomatoes (medium)
1/2	C	béchamel sauce (p. 362)
4	t	white truffle oil
12	slices	Gruyere cheese

prime rib dip
yield: 4 servings

A French dip sandwich is a simple dish, yet it is a solid and sumptuous item to include on a menu. I wanted to offer one at the Café, but I felt I needed a French dip that could make its own mark, something a bit more special. So I settled on the delicious decadence of prime rib for the meat. I roast a whole prime rib to medium-rare, allow it to cool, and then shave it thinly. To the warm shaved meat, I add caramelized slices of red onion and poblano pepper and then melt Gruyere cheese over the top. I serve it on a grilled torpedo roll, which is a soft bread that works particularly well for this sandwich (although any long, soft roll will do). To give the meal an extra-hearty flair, I serve the sandwich with an embellished version of au jus: a bowl of freshly-made French onion soup.

Ingredients:

Prime Rib:

2 - 3	lb	prime rib roast
1/4	C	olive oil
2	T	kosher salt
1	T	cracked black pepper
1	T	dried thyme
4	C	rock salt

Other:

1	each	red onion
1	each	poblano pepper
2	each	12" torpedo rolls
4	T	butter
2	T	olive oil
8	slices	Gruyere cheese
4	bowls	French onion soup (p. 360)

Method:

Prime Rib:

Because it is difficult to roast a smaller quantity of meat properly, I recommend a prime rib that is 2 or 3 pounds, even though it will provide more meat than you will need for 4 sandwiches.

Preheat the oven to 425 degrees.

Rub the entire prime rib roast with the olive oil, kosher salt, cracked black pepper, and dried thyme. Then, on a sheet pan, create a bed of rock salt that is roughly the size and shape of the prime rib. Place the prime rib on top of the salt, leaving the meat uncovered, and put the pan in the oven.

Roast the prime rib for 15 minutes, turn the oven temperature down to 225 degrees, and continue to roast it for about 30 minutes more, until an instant-read digital thermometer inserted in the center reads 130 degrees. Remove the prime rib from the oven, allow it to cool at room temperature for 15 minutes, and then place it in the refrigerator for about 1 hour to cool completely. Then, shave the meat into very thin slices, like deli meat, and divide it into 5-ounce portions.

Assembly:

Warm the French onion soup on low heat while you assemble the sandwiches.

Slice the red onion and poblano pepper into thin strips that are about 1/8 inch wide.

Cut each torpedo roll into 2 equal pieces of 6 inches each. Then slice the 4 pieces open lengthwise, leaving the back edge of each connected like a hinge. Spread butter on the cut sides of the rolls, grill them in a large sauté pan or on a griddle, and then place them on 4 serving plates and set them someplace warm.

(continued on page 325)

(continued from page 324)

In the same pan, heat the olive oil over medium heat and sauté the onions and peppers together until they are soft and caramelized. Set them aside, and add the individual portions of sliced prime rib to the pan, tossing the meat for 1 or 2 minutes until it is warm and keeping the portions separate. Season the prime rib slices with salt and pepper, and turn the heat under the pan down to low.

Gather each portion of prime rib into a tight pile in the pan, and add a share of the sautéed onions and peppers to each of the 4 portions of meat. Lay 2 slices of Gruyere cheese across each portion, and set a lid over the pan for 1 minute, until the cheese melts. Transfer each portion to the bottom side of a grilled torpedo roll, close the top side of the roll, and serve the sandwiches next to bowls of the hot French onion soup.

Sandwiches

Soups

The New Scenic Café

sweet corn with chipotle

yield: 3 quarts

Based on a classic tortilla soup, this dish is a nod to the Oaxacan heritage and cuisine I grew to love in my earliest years working with food. A centerpiece of the flavor in this recipe is chipotle peppers, which are jalapeño peppers that have been smoke-dried and, in the canned varieties, marinated in the Mexican sauce called adobo. I roast the sweet corn that I use in this soup. Roasting it softens and enhances the corn's flavor and brings a sweeter, smokier taste to the soup's flavor background. To the mix, I also add cilantro, poblano pepper, tomato, onion, celery, garlic, and herbs. This soup makes a nice, slightly spicy summer dish that pairs well with meat or veggies off the grill and a light, fruity rosé wine.

Ingredients:

3	C	sweet corn kernels
4	T	olive oil
3	C	onion (chopped)
1	C	celery (chopped)
2	T	garlic (minced)
8	C	water
2	each	canned chipotle peppers (whole)
1	each	poblano pepper (minced)
15	oz	canned tomatoes (diced)
1	t	cumin seeds (toasted & ground)
1	T	Mexican oregano
1	t	dried thyme
1	each	bay leaf
2	T	cilantro (chopped)

Method:

Preheat the oven to 350 degrees.

In a mixing bowl, toss the sweet corn kernels with 2 tablespoons of the olive oil, and then spread the corn on a sheet pan. Roast it until the kernels begin to brown slightly. Remove the sheet pan from the oven, and set the corn aside.

In a large pot, heat the other 2 tablespoons of olive oil over high heat, and add the chopped onion, chopped celery, and minced garlic. Sauté them for about 5 minutes, until they soften.

Stir in the water, whole chipotle peppers, minced poblano pepper, and canned tomatoes. Add the ground cumin, Mexican oregano, dried thyme, and bay leaf. (Mexican oregano is stronger and less sweet than standard Mediterranean oregano and also has notes of citrus and licorice. It is available in dried form at many gourmet food stores.)

Heat the soup, stirring frequently, until it comes to a low boil. Add the roasted corn, and season the soup to taste with kosher salt. Reduce the heat to low, and allow the soup to simmer for 15 minutes. Continue to stir it occasionally.

Add the chopped cilantro to the pot just before you serve the soup, so that the cilantro still looks green and fresh when you deliver the soup to the table. Be sure not to serve the whole chipotle peppers. They are best left sitting in the pot, where they will continue to add flavor to your soup.

The New Scenic Café

cream of asparagus with blue cheese & cherries

yield: 3 1/2 quarts

Because asparagus is one of my favorites, making a creamed soup with it seemed natural, and it's a great way as well to use asparagus ends left from another recipe. But I also wanted to blend in some special flavors, to create an asparagus soup that would be distinctive and memorable. Because I'm drawn to fruit and to pungent tastes, I looked for some fruity and prominent flavors to include and settled on dried tart Michigan cherries and Danish blue cheese for my soup recipe. Both have strong flavors, but those flavors become much more subtle when combined in this soup. This is a hearty, "stick-to-your-ribs" soup that, when chicken is added, becomes even heartier. You can also make this soup using broccoli instead of asparagus.

Method:

Heat the olive oil in a large pot, over high heat, and then add the chopped onion, chopped celery, chopped carrots, and minced garlic. Put a lid on the pot, and "sweat" the vegetables for about 5 minutes, stirring them frequently, until they soften. Add the butter, and stir it until it melts.

Reduce the heat to medium, and stir in the all-purpose flour, to create a roux with the butter. Combined with the vegetables, the mixture will look like chunky cookie dough.

Add the milk, heavy cream, and water, stirring after you add each one, to blend the ingredients with the roux. Add the bay leaf, dried cherries, and chopped asparagus, and heat the soup to a simmer. Reduce the heat to low, cover the pot again, and allow the soup to simmer for about 10 minutes, until the asparagus just becomes tender.

Crumble the Danish blue cheese into the soup, stirring it until the cheese is combined evenly, and then season the soup to taste with kosher salt and pepper.

Ingredients:

2	T	olive oil
1 1/2	C	onion (chopped)
1 1/2	C	celery (chopped)
1 1/2	C	carrots (chopped)
1	T	garlic (minced)
1/4	C	butter
1/2	C	all-purpose flour
2	C	milk
2	C	heavy cream
4	C	water
1	each	bay leaf
1/2	C	dried cherries
3	C	asparagus (chopped)
4	oz	Danish blue cheese

tomato with red beet & cumin

yield: 3 quarts

This unassuming yet delicious puréed soup is based on the concept of borscht, which is a Ukrainian beet soup. Traditional borscht is served hot or cold, but the flavors are at their best in this soup when it is served hot. I start by making a simple tomato soup and then add cooked beets and toasted cumin. The combination of the sweetness of the beets and the earthiness of the cumin creates a harmonious flavor blend that I have used in a variety of foods. That combination melds wonderfully in this soup with the rich acidity of the tomato, the fresh cilantro, and the touch of crème fraîche added at the end.

Ingredients:

2	T	olive oil
1 1/2	C	onion (chopped)
1	T	garlic (minced)
1 1/2	C	celery (chopped)
1 1/2	C	carrots (chopped)
4	C	water
1	each	bay leaf
15	oz	tomato sauce
1	t	kosher salt
3	C	cooked beets (diced)
1 1/2	T	cumin seeds (toasted & ground)
2	T	cilantro (chopped)
2	C	crème fraîche (p. 365) (or sour cream)

Method:

In a large pot, heat the olive oil over high heat. Add the chopped onion, and sauté it for 1 minute. Then add the minced garlic, and sauté the mixture for 1 minute more.

Add the chopped celery and carrots. Stirring frequently, continue to sauté the vegetables on high heat for another few minutes, until they are tender.

Add the water, bay leaf, tomato sauce, and kosher salt, and bring the mixture to a low boil. Add the cooked, diced beets and the toasted, ground cumin seeds, reduce the heat to low, and simmer the soup for 30 minutes, uncovered. Then mix in the chopped cilantro.

Using a countertop blender or an immersion stick blender, purée the soup until it is smooth. Season it to taste with salt and cracked black pepper.

When you serve the soup, spoon a bit of crème fraîche (or sour cream) in the center of each bowl, for a little cool creaminess to round out all the flavors.

The New Scenic Café

gazpacho

yield: 2 quarts

This traditional Spanish soup is built on a base of fresh tomatoes and served chilled. The added cucumber, red onion, celery, red bell pepper, and poblano pepper make this dish a wonderful showcase of fresh garden vegetables, accented with balsamic and sherry vinegars, herbs, and extra virgin olive oil. To add even more personality to your gazpacho, you could incorporate roasted corn or Spanish chorizo. This gazpacho can also serve as the foundation for a number of other dishes. For example, it works wonderfully in a panzanella salad, mixed together with roughly-torn chunks of toasted bread.

Method:

Gazpacho:

Note that you will want to prepare this recipe a day ahead and place it in the refrigerator overnight, to allow the flavors to meld and the raw vegetables to soften slightly.

Cut the fresh tomatoes, cucumber, red onion, celery, red bell pepper, and poblano pepper all to the same size, in a dice that is about 1/4 inch on all sides.

Chop the fresh basil finely.

Put the canned crushed tomatoes in a food processor, and pulse them a few times until they are chopped finely.

In a large mixing bowl or other container, combine the chopped vegetables with the remaining soup ingredients, stir them together well, and season the gazpacho to taste with salt and pepper.

Cover the bowl, put it in the refrigerator, and allow the gazpacho to sit overnight. The flavors will meld nicely, and the raw vegetables will soften slightly.

Assembly:

Put the gazpacho in serving bowls, drizzle 2 tablespoons of extra virgin olive oil over each portion, and top each bowl with a couple sprigs of a fresh herb. If you like, serve the soup with a side of toasted fresh bread.

Ingredients:

Gazpacho:

2	lb	fresh tomatoes
1/2	C	cucumber
1/2	each	red onion
1/2	C	celery
1/2	each	red bell pepper
1/2	each	poblano pepper
1/4	C	fresh basil
1	C	canned crushed tomatoes
1	T	garlic (minced)
2	T	balsamic vinegar
1	T	sherry vinegar
1/2	T	celery seed
1	T	vegetable base
1/2	t	dried thyme
1/2	t	dried oregano

Other:

1/2	C	extra virgin olive oil
20	sprigs	fresh herbs (cilantro, parsley, basil, etc.)

cucumber & avocado purée
yield: 4 servings

This refreshing puréed soup makes a great summer dish and also works beautifully as a sauce, to spread on a plate and serve with grilled chicken and vegetables. I make it in two steps, first creating a curry-cumin spice mix in the form of a paste and then combining the paste in a blender with fresh cucumber and ripe avocado. You can also store the curry paste in the refrigerator and use it to make more soup anytime you have a ripe avocado and fresh cucumber on hand. When I want to turn this chilled soup into a more substantial meal, I top it with shrimp or seared sea scallops.

Ingredients:

Spice Mix:

1/4	C	fresh ginger root
1/2	bunch	cilantro
1/4	C	garlic (minced)
1	T	ground cumin
1/2	t	ground thyme
1	t	chili garlic sauce
1/2	T	white truffle oil
2	T	olive oil
1	t	sesame oil
1/4	C	brown rice vinegar
1	t	soy sauce
1/4	C	vegetable base

Soup:

4	C	cucumber (chopped)
4	each	avocados (peeled & chopped)
1/2	C	spice mix (above)

Method:

Spice Mix:

Peel and mince the fresh ginger root, and chop the cilantro.

In a blender, combine the ginger and cilantro with all of the remaining spice mix ingredients. Pulse the blender a few times to combine the ingredients, switch the blender to high speed, and puree the mixture for about 30 seconds, until it is smooth.

Pour the spice mix into a storage container, cover it with a lid, and refrigerate it. The spice mix will last for several weeks.

Soup:

I recommend preparing this soup 1 serving at a time because it can be difficult for a blender to effectively purée more than a single portion.

To make a serving, combine 1 cup of chopped cucumber, 1 chopped avocado, and 2 tablespoons of spice mix in a blender. Pulse the blender a few times to combine the ingredients, switch the blender to high speed, and purée the soup until it is smooth. Pour that serving into a bowl, and repeat this process for the remaining 3 servings. This soup is best when served immediately. Top each serving with a sprig of fresh cilantro, if you like, or some shrimp or seared sea scallops.

green split pea with potato & ham hock

yield: 3 quarts

This classic green split pea soup brings together a rich variety of spices with the smoky flavor of ham hock and the hearty texture of potato. Split peas have a kind of dusty sweetness that blends well with the other ingredients, especially the savory pork. As an alternative, rutabaga makes a great substitute for potato in this soup, adding a sweet component and a deeper, earthier taste. I think of split pea soup as a late fall flavor. It's always comforting to envision coming inside to a bowl of hot pea soup and a crusty dinner roll. On a chilly day, what could be better?

Method:

Combine the water, vegetable base, whole smoked ham hock, herbs, and spices in a large pot. Cover the pot with a lid, bring the mixture to a low boil, and allow it to simmer for 1 1/2 hours, to create a broth.

In a separate pot, heat the olive oil. Add the chopped onion, carrot, and celery and the minced garlic, sauté ("sweat") them until they are soft and translucent, and then stir them into the broth.

Add the dried green split peas and the diced potatoes to the broth mixture, return it to a simmer, and cook it for 30 to 40 minutes, stirring occasionally, until the peas have just become tender.

Then add the diced ham, stir the soup thoroughly, and season it to taste with kosher salt.

Ingredients:

6	C	water
1/2	C	vegetable base
1	each	smoked ham hock (whole)
1	t	dried thyme
1	t	rubbed sage
1	each	bay leaf
1/2	t	dried oregano
2	T	parsley flakes
1/4	t	dill
1	t	white pepper
1/4	C	olive oil
2	C	onion (chopped)
2	C	carrot (chopped)
2	C	celery (chopped)
1/4	C	garlic (minced)
12	oz	dried green split peas
2	C	potatoes (diced)
12	oz	ham (diced)

oaxacan pork picadillo stew

yield: 3 quarts

One of my first passions as a new chef was to carry the distinctive flavors of Mexico's Oaxacan region into my cooking, and this pork picadillo stew is one of my favorites. Pork picadillo is an Oaxacan entrée of stewed pork sweetened with raisins and almonds. Working from the deep, rich flavors of that classic dish, I created a softened version, adding more tomato and stock. This soup draws more comment than any other I offer, perhaps in part because people don't know quite what to expect. They sometimes are not familiar with Oaxacan cuisine or with the term 'picadillo." Rather than describing the soup on the menu, I rely on my staff to explain it to our guests, which leads to enjoyable conversations about its origins and flavors and creates the expectation of a piquant treat.

Ingredients:

2	T	olive oil
2	C	onions (chopped)
1	C	celery (chopped)
1	T	garlic (minced)
3	C	water
28	oz	canned crushed tomatoes
1	each	canned chipotle pepper (whole)
1	t	dill
1/4	t	white pepper
1	pinch	ground clove
1	t	ground cumin
1	t	dried thyme
1	t	ground cinnamon
1	each	bay leaf
1	t	Mexican oregano
1	lb	pork tenderloin (cooked)
1/2	C	slivered almonds (toasted)
1	oz	raisins
1	oz	golden raisins
1/4	oz	cilantro (chopped)

Method:

Heat the olive oil in a large stock pot over medium heat. Add the chopped onions, sauté them for 2 minutes, and then add the chopped celery and minced garlic. Continue to sauté (or "sweat") the vegetables until they soften all the way through, stirring them frequently.

Add the water, canned crushed tomatoes, and chipotle pepper, and continue to cook the mixture. Add the dill, white pepper, ground clove, ground cumin, dried thyme, ground cinnamon, bay leaf, and Mexican oregano. (Mexican oregano is stronger and less sweet than standard Mediterranean oregano and also has notes of citrus and licorice. It is available in dried form at many gourmet food stores.)

Bring the soup to a low boil, reduce the heat, and allow the soup to simmer for 15 minutes, uncovered.

Cut the cooked pork tenderloin into 1/2-inch cubes, and add it to the soup, along with the slivered almonds, raisins, and golden raisins. Return the soup to a simmer, and cook it for another 15 minutes.

Season the soup to taste with kosher salt. Just before you serve it, add the chopped fresh cilantro, and stir the soup thoroughly.

thai peanut curry with chicken

yield: 4 quarts

This Thai-inspired soup is just a bit spicy, with a warm, nutty flavor that rounds out the spice. The chicken stock in this recipe gives the soup body, and the peanut butter adds a savory, umami flavor. You could substitute tahini or sesame oil in place of the peanut butter, for a taste change. And you could also turn this recipe into a wonderful entrée by preparing it with less stock, so that it is thicker, and serving it over a plate of steamed basmati rice.

Ingredients:

2	T	olive oil
1	C	celery (chopped)
2	C	onion (chopped)
1 1/2	C	carrots (chopped)
1	T	garlic (minced)
2	T	ginger root (peeled & minced)
13.5	oz	canned coconut milk
1	C	peanut butter
6	C	chicken stock
1	T	Thai red curry powder
1	T	cumin seeds (toasted & ground)
1	pinch	crushed red pepper flakes
2	T	cilantro (chopped)
2	T	cornstarch
1/4	C	cold water
3	C	chicken (cooked & chopped)
30	oz	canned garbanzo beans (rinsed & drained)
1	each	ripe tomato (medium size, chopped)

Method:

In a large pot, heat the olive oil over high heat. Add the chopped celery, onion, and carrots, and sauté them for about 5 minutes, stirring often, until the vegetables are tender. Add the minced garlic and ginger, and sauté the vegetables on high heat for 1 more minute.

Add the coconut milk, peanut butter, and chicken stock. Continue heating the mixture, stirring to dissolve the peanut butter, and then turn the heat down to low.

Add the Thai red curry powder, ground cumin, crushed red pepper flakes, and chopped cilantro. Continue to heat the soup, stirring occasionally, and allow it to come to a simmer.

In a small bowl, combine the cornstarch and cold water, to make a slurry. Stir it into the simmering soup, and then add the cooked chicken, garbanzo beans, and chopped tomato.

Allow the soup to return to a simmer, cook it for another 5 minutes, and season it to taste with kosher salt.

curried carrot ginger purée

yield: 3 quarts

This full-flavored soup combines the sweetness of carrots and the spice of ginger, in a distinctly rich and smooth purée. I begin with a large quantity of chopped carrots and onions, "sweating" them in the sauté pan so that their outsides do not brown and the soup retains a bright orange color. I add fresh ginger root, water, coconut milk, turmeric, curry powder, cilantro, and kosher salt and cook the mixture. Then I purée it until it is smooth and melt in a little butter as it purées, to enhance the soup's silky texture. This is one of the richest soups I make and one of the more earthy combinations of flavors. The ginger adds a bit of warmth and spice, playing a surprising note on the tongue with its striking flavor. For an even richer soup, substitute chicken or vegetable stock for the water.

Method:

In a large pot, heat the olive oil over medium heat. Add the chopped onion and carrots, place a lid on the pot, and "sweat" the vegetables for about 5 minutes, stirring them frequently so they do not brown, until the carrots are softened all the way through.

Add the minced garlic and the peeled, chopped ginger root, replace the lid, and continue to sweat the vegetables for another 3 minutes, still stirring the mixture often. Stir in the water, canned coconut milk, turmeric, curry powder, chopped cilantro, and kosher salt. Heat the soup to a boil, stirring occasionally, and then reduce the heat to low.

In small batches, use a blender to purée the soup until it is smooth. Add a portion of the softened butter to each batch as it purées, allowing the butter to melt and blend completely into the mixture.

If needed, season the soup to taste with additional kosher salt. Then serve this distinctive soup and enjoy!

Ingredients:

2	T	olive oil
3	C	onion (chopped)
6	C	carrots (chopped)
2	T	garlic (minced)
1/3	C	ginger root (peeled & chopped)
6	C	water
13.5	oz	canned coconut milk
1	t	turmeric
1	T	curry powder
2	T	cilantro (chopped)
1	T	kosher salt
1	C	butter (softened)

The New Scenic Café

cream of roasted red bell pepper

yield: 3 quarts

Nothing quite rivals roasted peppers for delivering delicious, distinctive flavor to a dish, and this creamy red bell pepper soup is no exception. Before I opened the New Scenic Café, I worked in several restaurants at which we used roasted poblano peppers and roasted red bell peppers in Mexican cuisine. Since those days, I've looked for ways to make use of that experience and also take a chance on something new—and this recipe is the result. I roast the red bell peppers over an open flame, purée them, make a tasty cream soup, and then stir in the roasted red bell peppers. What results is a soup that, based on the comments and recipe requests I've received, is one of the Café's top ten. This is a versatile recipe. Small additions to it can create dramatically different and enticing results. I have added such embellishments to it as wild rice, smoked salmon, beets, asparagus, broccoli, or chicken, all with delightful results. This soup also works well as a sauce, served over a breakfast frittata, for instance, or a bowl of hot steamed rice.

Method:

Using a food processor or a blender, pulse the roasted red bell peppers into a coarse purée, and set them aside. (It is not necessary to blend the peppers until they are completely smooth. Small bits of pepper give the soup an appetizing texture and appearance.)

In a large pot, heat the olive oil over high heat. Add the chopped onion, chopped celery, chopped carrot, and minced garlic, and cover the pot with a lid. "Sweat" the vegetables for about 5 minutes, stirring them frequently, until they are tender.

Reduce the heat to medium. Then add the butter, stir it until it melts completely, and mix in the all-purpose flour, creating a roux right inside the pot along with the vegetables.

Add the milk, and stir it until it has mixed evenly with the roux. Add the heavy cream and the puréed red bell peppers, and stir the mixture thoroughly.

Add the dried thyme, white pepper, bay leaf, parsley flakes, kosher salt, dill, celery seed, and nutmeg. Heat the soup to a simmer, stirring it frequently. (Cream-based soups tend to scorch easily on the bottom, so be sure to stir the soup thoroughly.)

Reduce the heat to low, and add the cream cheese in small pieces so it melts easily, stirring the soup until the cheese has been combined evenly. Leave the pot uncovered, and allow the soup to simmer for 20 minutes, continuing to stir it frequently.

Season the soup to taste with additional pepper and kosher salt.

Ingredients:

17	oz	roasted red bell peppers (p. 370)
2	T	olive oil
1 1/2	C	onion (chopped)
1 1/2	C	celery (chopped)
1	C	carrot (chopped)
1	t	garlic (minced)
4	oz	butter
1/2	C	all-purpose flour
2	C	milk
2	C	heavy cream
1	t	dried thyme
1/2	t	white pepper
1	each	bay leaf
2	T	parsley flakes
3	t	kosher salt
1/2	t	dill
1/2	t	celery seed
1	pinch	nutmeg
8	oz	cream cheese (softened)

black bean & butternut squash
yield: 3 quarts

A typical Mexican or Southwest-inspired black bean soup includes "mirepoix" (onion, celery, and carrot), a bit of tomato, and some kind of spice, perhaps in the form of chipotle pepper or chili powder. In fact, you will find a tasty Spicy Black Bean soup recipe in this chapter (page 329). I also wanted to find a different avenue for using black beans in a soup, one that brought in some uncommon elements and created a diverse flavor combination. I settled on using roasted butternut squash, which brings a harvest flavor to the bowl as well as beautiful color. The deep, dark black beans next to the light and vibrant orange of the butternut squash offer an enticing visual contrast as well as great flavors. If you have a garden and want to use your extra squash in a meal, this soup is quick, easy, and delicious. Add chicken when you want to give the soup another dimension and a bit more bounty and substance.

Ingredients:

2	T	olive oil
1 1/2	C	onion (chopped)
1	C	celery (chopped)
1	C	carrot (chopped)
1	T	garlic (minced)
6	C	water
30	oz	canned black beans (drained & rinsed)
1	lb	butternut squash (roasted & diced)
1	each	bay leaf
1	T	parsley flakes
1	T	cumin seeds (toasted & ground)
1	t	crushed red pepper flakes
2	each	large, ripe tomatoes (diced)
2	T	kosher salt
2	T	cornstarch
1/4	C	cold water
2	T	cilantro (chopped)

Method:

In a large pot, heat the olive oil over high heat. Add the chopped onion, chopped celery, chopped carrot, and minced garlic, cover the pot with a lid, and "sweat" the mixture for about 5 minutes, until the mirepoix vegetables are tender, stirring them frequently.

Reduce the heat to medium, and add the water, canned black beans, and roasted and diced butternut squash. Continue to heat the soup for another few minutes, still stirring it frequently. Stir in the bay leaf, parsley flakes, toasted and ground cumin seeds, crushed red pepper flakes, diced tomatoes, and kosher salt. Bring the soup to a simmer, stirring it occasionally, and then reduce the heat to low.

Combine the cornstarch and cold water in a small mixing bowl, to create a slurry. Stir the slurry into the simmering soup to thicken it just a bit. Cover the pot with a lid again, and allow the soup to simmer for another 20 minutes, giving it an occasional stir.

Season the soup to taste with kosher salt and pepper. Just before you serve the soup, stir in the fresh, chopped cilantro so that it will be a nice, bright green when you deliver the soup to the table.

cream of potato with tarragon

yield: 3 quarts

I began this soup as a creamed leek soup with potatoes and tarragon. But I found that rather than highlighting the onion-like flavor of leeks, I wanted the flavor of the potatoes and tarragon to shine through. This recipe works wonderfully with any kind of potato. Early on, I used a mélange of potatoes, including fingerlings, sweet potatoes, red potatoes, Yukon golds, and russets and eventually settled on the rich, creamy taste of Yukons. I start by cooking a cream soup from mirepoix (onion, celery, and carrot), a roux, cream, and milk and then add the cooked potatoes, spices, and herbs. A great alternative is to purée some of the potato to add creaminess to the soup, using the starch in the potato to create the body rather than thickening the soup with flour. You can also roast the potatoes rather than boiling them, to bring a slightly different flavor to this hearty, rustic soup.

Method:

In a large pot, heat the olive oil over high heat. Add the chopped onion, chopped carrots, chopped celery, and minced garlic. Cover the pot with a lid, and "sweat" the vegetables for about 5 minutes, stirring them frequently, until they are tender.

Add the butter, and stir it until it melts. Reduce the heat to medium, and add the all-purpose flour, stirring it well, to create a roux with the butter, which will thicken the soup later on. The mixture will look a bit like thick cookie dough.

Add the milk, stirring it thoroughly to dissolve the roux. Then stir in the heavy cream and water. Add the kosher salt, dried thyme, bay leaf, white pepper, dried chives, and dried tarragon, and stir the mixture thoroughly.

Bring the soup to a simmer, reduce the heat to low, and add the cooked and diced Yukon gold potatoes. Return the soup to a simmer, and allow it to simmer uncovered for another 10 minutes, stirring it thoroughly to avoid scorching. Season it to taste with pepper and kosher salt.

Wait to stir in the sliced scallions until just before you serve the soup, so the scallions will still be crisp and freshly green when you deliver the soup to the table.

Ingredients:

2	T	olive oil
1 1/2	C	onion (chopped)
1 1/2	C	carrot (chopped)
1	C	celery (chopped)
1	T	garlic (minced)
4	oz	butter
1/2	C	all-purpose flour
2	C	milk
2	C	heavy cream
4	C	water
1	T	kosher salt
1	t	dried thyme
1	each	bay leaf
1/2	t	white pepper
2	T	dried chives
2	T	dried tarragon
2	lb	Yukon gold potatoes (boiled, peeled, & diced)
2	each	scallions (sliced finely)

cream of tomato
yield: 2 quarts

I stumbled unsuspectedly on food ecstasy when I created this soup! Certainly, I intended for it to be good. But I had no idea how popular it would become and how continually it would be requested by diners at the New Scenic Cafe. It is a simply-constructed soup, made with a few chopped vegetables, a roux of butter and flour, cream, milk, spices, herbs, vegetable base, and tomatoes. Diced canned tomatoes work well in this dish, although you might enjoy intensifying the soup's flavor by using fresh tomatoes roasted in a low-temperature oven (essentially dehydrating them). I often serve this soup with a satisfyingly large grilled cheese sandwich, made with sourdough ciabatta and Gruyere and Cheddar cheeses.

Ingredients:

2	T	olive oil
1	C	onion (chopped)
1	C	celery (chopped)
1	C	carrots (chopped)
1	T	garlic (minced)
1/4	C	butter
1/2	C	all-purpose flour
1	C	milk
2	C	heavy cream
2	C	water
1/4	C	vegetable base
28	oz	diced canned tomatoes
1	each	bay leaf
1/4	t	white pepper
1	t	dill
2	T	parsley flakes
1	t	dried thyme
1	T	dried chives

Method:

Heat the olive oil in a large pot, over high heat. Add the chopped onion, chopped celery, chopped carrots, and minced garlic. Cover the pot with a lid, and "sweat" the vegetables for about 5 minutes, until they are tender, stirring them often.

Add the butter to the mixture, and stir it until the butter melts. Then stir in the all-purpose flour, creating a roux right inside the pot along with the vegetables.

Add the milk, heavy cream, water, vegetable base, and canned diced tomatoes, and stir to incorporate them fully. Stir in the bay leaf, white pepper, dill, parsley flakes, dried thyme, and dried chives. Continue to heat the soup, stirring it frequently, until it comes to a simmer and begins to thicken.

Reduce the heat to low, and allow the soup to simmer for 30 minutes, continuing to stir it frequently and making sure to stir the bottom thoroughly to prevent the soup from scorching. Season the soup to taste with kosher salt and pepper. Then get ready for the compliments to begin as you serve it!

tomato, orange, & ginger

yield: 3 quarts

I did, indeed, create this soup intentionally! Although I have heard speculation more than once that this unconventional combination of flavors must have come about accidentally. The tomato and the ginger make sense to many people's palates, just as the orange and ginger make sense. The combination of all 3, however, can be a bit of a reach for some folks, until they try it. Then they like it. This soup is warm and bright, capturing the essence of fresh tomato, the bright flavor of orange, and the spicy, fresh taste of ginger. Though I think of this as a summery soup, I do make it in the winter, as a way to bring warm, summer freshness to a cold winter day. Wonderful by itself, this soup also serves as a great base to which a variety of vegetables can be added. And it works nicely as an entrée. Served over lentils or rice, it captures a bit of the essence of East Indian cuisine.

Ingredients:

2	T	olive oil
2	C	onion (chopped)
1	C	celery (chopped)
1	C	carrot (chopped)
1	t	garlic (minced)
3	C	water
28	oz	canned crushed tomatoes
15	oz	tomato sauce
2	T	ginger root (peeled & minced)
1/4	t	cayenne pepper
1	t	dried thyme
1	each	bay leaf
1	t	kosher salt
1/2	t	cracked black pepper
1/3	C	orange juice concentrate
3	each	oranges (zested & juiced)

Method:

In a large pot, heat the olive oil over high heat. Add the chopped onion, chopped celery, chopped carrot, and minced garlic. Stirring frequently, sauté them for about 5 minutes, until they soften.

Add the water, canned crushed tomatoes, tomato sauce, and minced ginger, and continue to cook the mixture on high heat, still stirring it frequently. Then add the cayenne pepper, dried thyme, bay leaf, kosher salt, and cracked black pepper.

Stir in the orange juice concentrate, along with the zest and juice from the oranges, and bring the soup to a simmer. Reduce the heat to low, and allow the soup to simmer for 30 minutes, uncovered. Serve it while it is deliciously hot and steaming.

spicy black bean

yield: 4 quarts

The cuisine of the southern region of Mexico called Oaxaca is the inspiration for this soup. Early in my career, I gained experience cooking foods steeped in this Mexican heritage when I helped create the menu for a new restaurant in Duluth, Minnesota that focused on foods from the Oaxacan area. You'll taste the flavors I fell in love with back then, in the combination of the tomato base, the rich black beans, and the chipotle peppers, sweet corn, cilantro, Mexican oregano, cinnamon, and dark chili powder. For this soup, I prefer using good-quality canned tomatoes rather than fresh tomatoes because canned tomatoes offer a deeper, more intense tomato flavor. I add tomato sauce and tomato paste as well, to make this spicy black bean soup an even heartier and more flavorful dish.

Method:

In a large pot, heat the olive oil over medium heat. Add the chopped onion, celery, and carrots, and sauté ("sweat") them for about 5 minutes, until they are tender, stirring them frequently.

Add the black beans, tomatoes, tomato sauce, tomato paste, and water, and stir them well. Continue heating the mixture for another few minutes. Then stir in the whole chipotle peppers, sweet corn kernels, chopped cilantro, Mexican oregano, ground cinnamon, and dark chili powder.

Continue heating the soup, stirring it occasionally, until it comes to a boil. Reduce the heat to low, and allow the soup to simmer for another 15 minutes. Season it to taste with kosher salt.

When you serve this tasty black bean soup, be careful not to serve the whole chipotle peppers. They are best left sitting in the soup, where they will continue to add flavor to every bowl.

Ingredients:

2	T	olive oil
1 1/2	C	onion (chopped)
1 1/2	C	celery (chopped)
1 1/2	C	carrots (chopped)
30	oz	canned black beans (rinsed & drained)
15	oz	canned diced tomatoes
15	oz	tomato sauce
6	oz	tomato paste
5	C	water
2	each	canned chipotle peppers (whole)
3	C	sweet corn kernels
2	T	chopped cilantro
1	t	Mexican oregano
1	pinch	ground cinnamon
2	T	dark chili powder

The New Scenic Café

white bean & kielbasa

yield: 3 quarts

Kielbasa is a kind of Polish sausage that is soft and evenly textured. It caramelizes nicely when it is cut and cooked, making it a flavorful ingredient for a soup. I start by creating a simple soup of sautéed vegetables, chicken stock, and herbs and add white beans, such as great northern, cannellini, or navy beans. I finish the dish by cutting the kielbasa into bite-size pieces, cooking it in a skillet or in the oven, and adding it to the soup. This dish has an old Eastern European flavor and hue. It makes a fine match with crusty bread and will warm you nicely in any season, particularly on a brisk fall day.

Method:

In a large pot, heat the olive oil over high heat until wisps of smoke form. Add the chopped onion, and cook it for 1 minute, stirring constantly.

Add the minced garlic, cook the mixture for another minute, still stirring, and then add the chopped celery and carrots. Continue cooking the vegetables over high heat for another 2 or 3 minutes, stirring frequently, until they soften.

Add the chicken stock, along with the kosher salt, dried thyme, rubbed sage, dried chives, and bay leaves. Add the white beans, turn the heat down to medium, and bring the soup to a simmer. Leave the pot uncovered.

While the soup is simmering, cut the kielbasa lengthwise twice into 4 long quarters. Then cross-cut it into bite-size pieces. Cook the kielbasa in a lightly-oiled sauté pan on medium heat for about 2 minutes, or spread it on a sheet pan and bake it in a 400-degree oven for about 5 minutes.

Add the cooked kielbasa to the soup, and simmer it for another 15 minutes. Season the soup to taste with kosher salt and cracked black pepper.

Ingredients:

2	T	olive oil
1	C	onion (chopped)
1	T	garlic (minced)
1	C	celery (chopped)
3	C	carrots (chopped)
6	C	chicken stock
1	t	kosher salt
1	t	dried thyme
1	T	rubbed sage
2	T	dried chives
2	each	bay leaves
30	oz	canned white beans (rinsed & drained)
1	lb	kielbasa sausage

potato & sage purée

yield: 4 quarts

I've always thought this soup was perfect for autumn, although it will warm and satisfy you in any season. It uses potatoes as the main body, along with the sweet, earthy flavor of sage. I chose Yukon gold potatoes for their golden yellow color, creamy consistency, and buttery flavor, but you could substitute any other kind of potato that you like and still have a great soup. By boiling the potatoes and then puréeing them with the water they were cooked in, no starch is lost, resulting in a soup that is smooth and creamy from the potatoes themselves. I do add a touch of butter for extra body and an even more velvety texture. And I add spinach at the end, just before I purée the mixture, which turns the soup a fresh green color and blends in the delicious flavor of the greens.

Ingredients:

2 1/2	lb	Yukon gold potatoes (diced)
2	T	olive oil
3	C	onion (chopped)
2	C	celery (chopped)
2	T	garlic (minced)
10	C	water
2	T	rubbed sage
1/4	C	chives
1/2	t	white pepper
9	oz	spinach leaves (rinsed well)
8	oz	butter
2	T	kosher salt

Method:

Cut the Yukon gold potatoes into a medium dice, creating cubes that are about 1/2 inch, and set them aside.

In a large pot, heat the olive oil over high heat. Add the chopped onion, chopped celery, and minced garlic. Cover the pot with a lid, and "sweat" the vegetables for about 5 minutes, stirring them frequently, until they are tender.

Add the water, rubbed sage, chives, white pepper, and diced Yukon gold potatoes, and bring them to a boil. Reduce the heat to medium, and boil the mixture for about 20 minutes, until the potatoes are soft, leaving the pot uncovered and stirring occasionally.

Fill a separate, small pot with water, and heat it to boiling (and also make up a bowl of ice water). Blanch the spinach leaves quickly in the boiling water, for about 10 seconds. Then strain them out of the boiling water, and plunge them into the bowl of ice water for another few seconds. Strain the spinach leaves out of the ice water, squeeze as much excess water out of them as you can, and chop them finely.

Add the chopped spinach, butter, and kosher salt to the soup pot, and stir the ingredients to combine them in the soup.

In small batches, purée the soup in a blender until it is completely smooth. Season your potato and sage purée to taste with additional kosher salt.

cream of wild rice

yield: 3 quarts

Wild rice soup is an often-requested staple in northern Minnesota, capturing the essence of the northern Minnesota experience, where wild rice is abundant in the state's cold rivers and lakes. Variations in ingredients abound in wild rice soups and can include chicken, Canadian bacon, ham, mushrooms, garden greens, or just about any elements you like. Using this soup as a base, you can build in many different directions. You can use it as a small soup course, perhaps alongside a bit of foie gras, or as a vehicle for making good use of leftover chicken stock or roasted chicken. And it is delicious just as it is, as a vegetarian soup that highlights the wild rice. I prefer to use hand-harvested, wood-parched wild rice, which is produced using a traditional metal basin and canoe paddle to parch the rice over an open fire. It is light in color and is more rich, nutty, and toasty in flavor than commercially-produced wild rice. I buy my wild rice from several local sources, including local harvester, Sherry Rovig. Good-quality wild rice is also easy to buy online.

Method:

Heat the olive oil in a large stock pot over high heat. Add the chopped onion, chopped celery, chopped carrots, and minced garlic. Cover the pot with a lid, and "sweat" the vegetables for about 5 minutes, stirring them frequently, until they are tender.

Add the butter, and stir it until it melts. Reduce the heat to medium, and add the all-purpose flour, creating a roux with the butter. Combined with the vegetables, the mixture will look like thick cookie dough.

Stir in the milk, heavy cream, water, and vegetable base. Add the cooked wild rice, bay leaf, rubbed sage, dried chives, crushed red pepper flakes, and kosher salt. Continue heating the soup, stirring it frequently, until it begins to simmer. Then reduce the heat to low, and simmer the soup for 30 minutes, leaving it uncovered and stirring it frequently. (Cream-based soups tend to scorch easily on the bottom of the pot, so be sure to stir the soup thoroughly.)

Season the soup to taste with kosher salt and black pepper. Then enjoy the looks of appreciation you get when you serve this creamy, satisfying wild rice soup!

Ingredients:

2	T	olive oil
1 1/2	C	onion (chopped)
1 1/2	C	celery (chopped)
1 1/2	C	carrot (chopped)
1	T	garlic (minced)
4	oz	butter
1/2	C	all-purpose flour
2	C	milk
2	C	heavy cream
3	C	water
1/4	C	vegetable base
4	C	cooked wild rice (p. 190)
1	each	bay leaf
1	T	rubbed sage
1	T	dried chives
1	pinch	crushed red pepper flakes
1	T	kosher salt

toasted barley & mushroom

yield: 3 quarts

When bread is toasted, it darkens and roasts, becoming crisp and taking on deeper and more complex flavors. The same is true of many foods, including the barley I use in this soup. I begin by toasting it on a sheet pan in the oven. Toasting gives this highly nutritious and earthy grain an accentuated hue and a nuttier flavor, bringing what I think of as the essence of autumn scents and tastes to the soup. And the mushrooms deliver even more body and flavor. I have made this soup using many varieties of mushrooms, including crimini, shiitake, oyster, and button mushrooms. Feel free to use any mushrooms you enjoy and can get your hands on—each variety brings its own distinctive taste to the soup. I add a bit of sesame oil as well, to enhance the toasted flavor of the barley. And just before serving, I finish the soup with a touch of bright, fresh cilantro.

Ingredients:

3/4	C	pearl barley grains (whole)
2	T	olive oil
1	T	garlic (minced)
1	C	onion (chopped)
1	C	celery (chopped)
1	C	carrot (chopped)
1	t	kosher salt
1/2	t	dried thyme
1/4	t	white pepper
1	each	bay leaf
1	T	dried chives
1/2	t	crushed red pepper flakes
1/2	t	rubbed sage
6	C	water
1/4	C	vegetable base
1	t	sesame oil
1 1/2	C	mushrooms (sautéed)
1/4	C	cilantro (chopped)

Method:

Preheat the oven to 425 degrees.

Spread the pearl barley grains on a sheet pan, and place them in the oven for 7 minutes. Open the oven door, and shake the sheet pan to move and turn the barley grains. Then toast the barley for another 7 minutes, remove the sheet pan from the oven, and set it aside.

Heat the olive oil in a large stock pot over high heat. Add the minced garlic, chopped onion, chopped celery, and chopped carrots. Cover the pot with a lid, and "sweat" the vegetables for about 5 minutes, stirring them frequently, until they are tender.

Reduce the heat to medium, and stir in the kosher salt, dried thyme, white pepper, bay leaf, dried chives, crushed red pepper flakes, and rubbed sage. Then add the toasted barley, water, vegetable base, sesame oil, and sautéed mushrooms, and stir them thoroughly. Bring the soup to a simmer.

Reduce the heat to low, and allow the soup to simmer for about 35 minutes, stirring it occasionally, until the barley is tender. Season it to taste with kosher salt and black pepper.

When you are ready to serve the soup, stir in the chopped cilantro, for a bright, fresh look and taste in every bowl.

The New Scenic Café

cream of roasted brussels sprouts

yield: 3 quarts

As a Brussels sprouts enthusiast, over the years I've looked for a variety of ways to use them at the New Scenic Café. I found that simply tossing Brussels sprouts with olive oil, salt, and pepper and roasting them produced delicious results. And their green, soft, and supple outer leaves were great in salads. But using them in salads left an abundance of cores remaining, for which I wanted to find a tasty use. So I roasted them until they were browned and added them to a creamy base, to build this roasted Brussels sprouts soup. I use thyme and bay leaf in this recipe, but you can add any extra herbs you like, such as tarragon or basil. Or for a slightly lighter and brighter taste, you could add fresh thyme. This soup is delightful in vegetarian form, and it is also great with the addition of smoky bacon. With or without the bacon, this soup and its caramelized Brussels sprouts flavor pair wonderfully with a French chardonnay.

Method:

Preheat the oven to 350 degrees.

Trim the stems from the Brussels sprouts, and remove any outer leaves that are brown. Slice them in half (or in quarters if they are large), toss them in a mixing bowl with 1 tablespoon of the olive oil, and season them with kosher salt and cracked black pepper.

Spread the Brussels sprouts on a sheet pan, and roast them in the oven for about 8 minutes, until they begin to turn a light golden brown. Remove them from oven, and set them aside.

In a large pot, heat 2 tablespoons of the olive oil over high heat. Add the chopped onion, chopped carrots, chopped celery, and minced garlic. Cover the pot with a lid, and "sweat" the vegetables for about 5 minutes, stirring them frequently, until they are tender.

Add the butter, and stir it until it melts. Reduce the heat to medium, and add the all-purpose flour, stirring it well, to create a roux with the butter. The mixture will have a texture like thick cookie dough.

Add the milk, stirring it thoroughly to dissolve the roux, and stir in the heavy cream and water. Then add the roasted Brussels sprouts, along with the kosher salt, dried thyme, bay leaf, white pepper, crushed red pepper flakes, and chopped ripe tomato. (If you are using bacon, add it also.) Stir the mixture well.

Bring the soup slowly to a simmer, reduce the heat to low, and allow the soup to simmer uncovered for about 15 minutes, stirring it thoroughly to avoid scorching. Season it to taste with cracked black pepper and kosher salt.

Ingredients:

2	lb	Brussels sprouts
3	T	olive oil
1 1/2	C	onion (chopped)
1 1/2	C	carrot (chopped)
1	C	celery (chopped)
1	T	garlic (minced)
4	oz	butter
1/2	C	all-purpose flour
2	C	milk
1	C	heavy cream
4	C	water
1	T	kosher salt
1	t	dried thyme
1	each	bay leaf
1/2	t	white pepper
1	pinch	crushed red pepper flakes
1	each	ripe tomato (chopped)

Optional:

1	C	bacon (cooked & chopped)

french onion

yield: 2 1/2 quarts

For this distinctive version of the French classic, I give credit to a good friend and former sous chef at the New Scenic Café, Eric Sturtz. The recipe builds on French cooking tradition, with Eric's touch and sense of taste transforming this standard into an outstanding soup that has been a unique addition to the Café's cuisine. Eric cuts the onions a little thicker than is usual, but not too thick, which allows them to caramelize as they cook for several hours and still remain intact. The recipe also includes cream sherry that has been reduced until the alcohol has evaporated. Its rich caramel and molasses flavors and smooth texture, more typically enjoyed as a dessert wine, bring an unexpected and welcome taste to this classic soup. We top each bowl with a large, freshly-made garlic crouton, cover it with slices of Gruyere cheese, and melt and brown them under the broiler. Many guests at the New Scenic Café have remarked that this is the best French onion soup they have ever had—including many of our French guests! For that, we thank Eric for the gift of his inspired palate and talent.

Ingredients:

French Onion Soup:

2 1/2	lb	white or yellow onion
2	T	olive oil
1	T	garlic (minced)
1/2	t	cracked black pepper
1	t	dried thyme
1	each	bay leaf
1/2	C	red wine
2	qt	beef stock (p. 363)
1/2	C	cream sherry

Croutons:

1/2	C	olive oil
2	T	garlic (minced)
1	t	cracked black pepper
1	T	kosher salt
20	slices	bread (such as ciabatta or baguette, cut 3/8 inch thick)

Other:

16	oz	Gruyere cheese (sliced)

Method:

French Onion Soup:

Trim both ends off all the white or yellow onions, split each onion in half, and remove the skins. Lay the halves down flat on a cutting board, with the cut sides down, and slice the onions into 1/4-inch thick strips. (Looking at the outside of an onion, you will see that the onion's natural lines run in one direction. Cut in the same direction, parallel to those lines, to create slices that remain intact while the onions are cooking. Cutting in the opposite direction often results in slices that break apart into short pieces.)

Heat the olive oil in a large, wide pot over medium heat. Add the sliced onions, place a lid on the pot, and "sweat" the onions for about 5 minutes, stirring them often, until they are soft. Remove the lid, reduce the heat to low, and cook the onions slowly (for as long as 1 or 2 hours), stirring them frequently. When they are done, the moisture will have evaporated and the onions will have turned a deep caramel color.

(The caramelization does take time, but it is important to allow the process to happen slowly. Slow caramelization results in onions that just about melt in your mouth, while onions that are cooked too quickly will still caramelize on the outside but will not be completely soft and sweet all the way through.)

When the onions are finished cooking, add the minced garlic to the pot, and cook the onions and garlic for another 5 minutes, stirring them occasionally. Then add the cracked black pepper, dried thyme, bay leaf, red wine, and beef stock. Stir the mixture thoroughly, and allow it to continue simmering.

In a separate, large sauté pan, add the cream sherry. Heat it slowly over low heat, to bring it to a simmer. (It is possible that the alcohol fumes will catch fire, which is okay as long as you make sure nothing else is within range of the flames. The flames will extinguish on their own.)

(continued on page 361)

(continued from page 360)

Allow the cream sherry to simmer for about 5 minutes, until the majority of the alcohol has evaporated. (You can tell by smelling it.) Then pour the reduced cream sherry into the soup. Increase the heat to high, until the soup reaches a low boil, and then return the heat to low and let it simmer uncovered for 30 minutes. Season the soup to taste with kosher salt.

Croutons:
Preheat the oven to 300 degrees. Combine the olive oil, minced garlic, cracked black pepper, and kosher salt in a small mixing bowl. Stir the mixture well, and allow it to rest for about 15 minutes, to give the garlic flavor time to meld with the oil.

Lay the slices of bread on a sheet pan. Use a pastry brush or basting brush to apply the oil mixture to the slices of bread, stirring the oil frequently. Use just enough to coat the tops of the slices. Bake the croutons for 5 to 10 minutes, checking them periodically, until they are crisp and just beginning to turn a light golden brown. Remove them from the oven, and allow them to cool. (If needed, they can be stored in an airtight container at room temperature for several days.)

Assembly:
Preheat the broiler. If the soup has been allowed to cool, reheat it in a pot. Fill heat-proof bowls to within 1/2 inch of the rims of the bowls.

Create a single crouton layer across the surface of each bowl of soup, breaking the croutons into "puzzle" pieces, if necessary, to form a full layer. Lay slices of Gruyere cheese over the croutons so that the tops are covered completely and the slices of cheese hang just a bit over the sides of the bowls. You will need about 3 slices of cheese per bowl.

Set the bowls of soup on a sheet pan. Place the pan under the broiler for about 3 minutes, until the cheese melts, begins to bubble, and just starts to brown and become crisp around the edges and on the sides of the bowls.

Serve the soup immediately, while the cheese is still bubbling hot. And if you'd like something to accompany it, this soup goes wonderfully with our Prime Rib Dip sandwich (page 324).

Sub-Recipes

apple cider gastrique

1/2	C	granulated sugar
1	T	water
1	C	apple cider
1/2	C	apple cider vinegar
1	t	cornstarch
1	T	cold water
1	t	lemon zest

In a medium sauce pan on medium heat, combine the granulated sugar and water. Tilt the pan gently from side to side as the sugar melts, to distribute the water evenly and prevent any hot spots. Cook the mixture for about 5 minutes, stirring it frequently, until the sugar caramelizes to a medium-brown color. Stir in the apple cider and apple cider vinegar. (The caramel will harden, but it will melt again.) Reduce the heat to low, and simmer the mixture for another 10 minutes, stirring it occasionally, until it is reduced by about half. In a small bowl, make a slurry by mixing together the cornstarch and cold water. Stir the slurry into the hot liquid, raise the heat to medium, and allow the mixture to reach a boil. Allow it to continue to boil for another couple of minutes, until it has the consistency of thick syrup. Remove the pan from the heat, and add the lemon zest, stirring it in thoroughly. Allow the apple cider gastrique to cool, pour it into a covered container, and store it at room temperature. Keep it covered, and it will stay fresh for several weeks or even several months.

apricot saffron sauce

1 1/2	C	dried apricots (1/4-inch dice)
2 1/2	C	water
1/4	C	cream sherry
1/2	t	saffron threads
1 1/2	T	brown sugar
1	t	ginger root (peeled & minced)
1	each	whole clove
1/2	T	cornstarch
2	T	cold water

Combine the diced apricots, water, cream sherry, saffron threads, brown sugar, minced ginger, and whole clove in a small sauce pot over low heat. Bring it to a boil slowly, stirring it frequently. In a small bowl, mix the cornstarch and cold water together, to make a slurry. Stir it into the hot liquid, and let the sauce simmer on low heat for 15 minutes, continuing to stir it frequently, and then remove and discard the whole clove. Refrigerate the sauce if you are not using it immediately.

avocado mousse

1	each	avocado
2	t	kosher salt
2	t	lime zest

Cut the avocado in half, remove the pit, and scoop out the flesh. Place the avocado in a food processor, along with the kosher salt and lime zest, and purée the mixture until it is smooth. (You might need to pause once or twice and use a rubber spatula to scrape down the sides of the processor.) Transfer the avocado mousse immediately to a ziplock bag, squeeze out as much air as possible, seal the bag, and store the mousse in the refrigerator.

bacon lardons

8	oz	slab bacon (unsliced)
1	T	olive oil

Lardons are small, crisp pieces of bacon used as flavor accents in salads and other dishes, often about 1/4 by 1/4 inch thick and 1 to 1 1/2 inches long. They are crisp on the outside but chewy through the center and are easiest to make from a slab of unsliced bacon. If you cannot get a slab, buy the thickest, best-quality sliced bacon you can. (At the Café, we buy whole slabs of applewood-smoked bacon from a company called Nueske's in Wisconsin.) Cut the pieces 3/8 by 3/8 inch thick and 1 1/2 inches long, to allow for shrinkage during cooking. Put the olive oil in a medium sauté pan (the bacon has plenty of fat, but the oil helps get the cooking started), and place it over high heat until it shows a few wisps of smoke. Add the bacon to the hot pan, and cook it for about 1 minute, moving the pan around quickly and tossing the pieces so they sear on all sides. (It is important to cook the bacon quickly in a hot pan so it gets crisp on the outside but is still chewy on the inside.) When they are browned all the way around, remove the lardons from the pan, and place them on a paper towel to drain. Store any unused lardons in a covered container in the refrigerator.

balsamic reduction

1	C	balsamic vinegar
3	T	granulated sugar

Combine the balsamic vinegar and granulated sugar in a small pot, and place it over low heat. Cook the mixture gently, uncovered, for about 15 minutes, allowing it to evaporate until it is approximately half the original volume (about 1/2 cup) and stirring it frequently. Be careful not to reduce it too far or heat it too quickly because the sugar can burn easily. When the reduction is finished, it will coat the back of a spoon and look like syrup when dripped on a plate. And it will thicken more as it cools. Store it at room temperature in a small squeeze bottle.

basil pesto

1	lb	basil
6	cloves	garlic (whole)
1	t	kosher salt
1	t	cracked black pepper
3/4	C	olive oil

Remove the basil leaves from the stems (you will use only the leaves). Put the garlic cloves, kosher salt, cracked black pepper, and one small handful of basil leaves into a food processor. Turn the processor on, and alternate between adding the oil and adding the rest of the basil leaves, keeping the mixture thick in consistency yet just thin enough for the food processor to continue moving. Transfer the finished pesto to an airtight container, and store it in the refrigerator if you are not using it immediately. (Note that unlike many pesto recipes, this recipe does not contain dairy or nuts, allowing it to be used when allergies to those substances might be a concern.)

béchamel sauce

3	C	heavy cream
1/2	t	kosher salt
1/2	t	grated nutmeg
1	pinch	white pepper
2 1/4	oz	cream cheese

This non-traditional version of a classic béchamel sauce maintains the standard flavor but is made without flour as a thickener, which allows it to be used in gluten-free recipes. It stiffens to a spreadable, semi-solid consistency when cooled and reheats to a smooth sauce. In a medium pot, combine the heavy cream, kosher salt, grated nutmeg, and white pepper over medium heat. Bring the mixture to a boil, and then reduce the heat to low. Simmer the cream until it reduces by approximately 20 percent (down to about 2 1/2 cups). Add the cream cheese in small pieces, stirring the mixture until the cheese is melted completely. Use the sauce immediately, or transfer it to a storage container, and put it in the refrigerator to cool completely.

beef stock

5	lb	beef bones
2	T	olive oil
1	C	carrots (chopped)
1	C	onions (chopped)
1	C	celery (chopped)
6	cloves	garlic (whole)
1/4	bunch	Italian parsley
1	each	medium ripe tomato (chopped)
1	T	dried thyme
1	each	bay leaves
3/4	C	red wine
		cold water

Preheat the oven to 350 degrees. Place the beef bones on a sheet pan, and roast them for 45 minutes. Heat the olive oil in a large stock pot over high heat, and then add the chopped carrots, chopped onions, and chopped celery, and cook them for about 5 minutes, stirring them frequently, until they caramelize. Add the whole garlic cloves, and cook the mixture for another 2 minutes. Then add the roasted beef bones and the other remaining ingredients, including enough cold water to cover all the ingredients in the pot. Put a lid on the pot, and with the heat still on high bring the mixture to a simmer. Then reduce the heat to low, and simmer the stock for at least 4 to 5 hours (or for a richer stock, simmer it for as long as 8 to 10 hours). Strain the stock through a fine mesh strainer. Use the stock immediately, or transfer it to a storage container, and allow it to cool to room temperature before placing it in the refrigerator to cool completely. After it has cooled, remove any fat that has solidified on the top.

---

beet purée

1/2	C	cooked red beets (peeled & chopped)
1/2	t	kosher salt
1	pinch	ground cumin
1/4	C	water

Combine all of the ingredients in a blender, and purée the mixture until it is smooth. Add small amounts of additional water, if necessary, to keep the purée moving in the blender. If you are not using the purée immediately, store it in the refrigerator. It will store well for up to 2 days.

---

blue cheese & goat cheese mousse

8	oz	goat cheese (chevre)
4	oz	cream cheese
3	oz	Danish blue cheese
1	t	garlic (minced)
1/2	t	dried thyme
1	t	dried chives
1	t	white truffle oil
1/2	t	granulated sugar

Allow the goat cheese, cream cheese, and Danish blue cheese to soften to room temperature (which requires about 1 hour). Place all of the ingredients in an electric mixer bowl, and, using the paddle attachment, mix them on low speed for 1 minute. Increase the speed to high, and whip the mixture for 1 minute more. If you are not using the mousse immediately, store it in a covered container in the refrigerator.

---

browned butter

1	C	butter

In a small pot, warm the butter over medium heat, stirring it frequently and watching it carefully after it begins to foam to be sure it does not burn. When the butter is a medium-brown color, remove the pot from the heat, and pour the butter immediately into a heat-proof container. Allow it to cool to room temperature, stirring it with a whisk periodically until it is an even brown color and smooth in texture. The browned butter can be used immediately.

---

browned butter caramel

1/2	C	butter
3/4	C	granulated sugar
3	T	water
1	C	heavy cream
1/8	t	vanilla extract

In a medium pot, cook the butter over medium heat, stirring it frequently, until the milk solids turn brown. Add the granulated sugar and water, stir the mixture well, and continue to cook it over medium heat until the sugar caramelizes to a medium-brown color. Pour the heavy cream in quickly, and remove the pot from the heat. The caramel will bubble up, but the cream's cold temperature will stop the bubbling as long as you add the cream all at once. Stir in the vanilla extract. Then return the pot to the medium heat, bring the caramel to a boil once more, and remove it from the heat and let it cool. Use the browned butter caramel immediately, or put it in a container and refrigerate it.

---

candied kumquats

1 1/2	C	granulated sugar
2	C	water
1	lb	kumquats (whole)

In a medium pot, combine the granulated sugar and water over medium heat. Stir them until the sugar has dissolved. Reduce the heat to low, add the whole kumquats, and put a plate or lid on top of them to keep them submerged. Cook the kumquats gently over low heat for 30 minutes, stirring them occasionally, until they are tender and translucent. Strain the kumquats from the syrup (be sure to keep the syrup), and set them aside in a heat-resistant storage container. Pour the syrup back into the pot, and stir it periodically as you simmer it over medium heat for about 15 minutes, until it reduces by about half. Pour the reduced syrup over the kumquats, and if you are not using them immediately, cool and store them in the refrigerator.

---

candied pepitas

1/4	C	granulated sugar
1	T	water
3/4	C	pepitas (pumpkin seeds)

In a small pot, combine the granulated sugar and water over medium heat, and cook it until it reaches 240 degrees. Add the pepitas, and stir them slowly using a heat-proof spoon or spatula, while continuing to heat the mixture. The sugar will form crystals on the pepitas, but as you continue heating them, the sugar will melt again and eventually begin to caramelize. Keep stirring slowly until the mixture reaches a medium-caramel color, and then remove the pepitas from the pot, and spread them out in a thin layer on a sheet pan lined with a silicone baking mat or parchment paper. Cool the pepitas, and if you are not using them immediately, store them at room temperature in an airtight container.

---

chicken liver pâté

2	T	olive oil
1	T	garlic (minced)
2	T	shallot (minced)
1	lb	chicken livers
1/4	t	ground clove
1/4	t	fennel seed (toasted & ground)
1/2	t	ground cumin
1/2	T	dried chives
1	t	dried thyme
1	t	Chinese Five Spice
1/2	T	kosher salt
1	t	granulated sugar
1	T	cream sherry
2	T	butter
2	T	heavy cream

Preheat the oven to 350 degrees. In a large pot, heat the olive oil over high heat. Add the minced garlic and shallot, and reduce the heat to medium. Sweat the garlic and shallot, uncovered, for 2 minutes, stirring them frequently, until they are soft and translucent. Add the chicken livers, and stir them periodically as you sauté them for about 5 minutes, until they are cooked to medium. Remove the pot from the heat, and stir in the spices, herbs, kosher salt, and granulated sugar. Add the cream sherry, butter, and heavy cream, stirring them to combine them thoroughly. Pour the mixture into a blender, and purée it until it is completely smooth. Then pour the puréed mixture into an ungreased baking dish that fits inside another, larger baking pan. Put the filled baking dish inside the larger pan. Then create a water bath by adding water to the larger pan until it is filled to the same depth as the pâté inside the baking dish. Using aluminum foil, put a single cover over both pans, and poke a few vent holes in the foil. Bake the pâté mixture for about 30 minutes, until an instant-read digital thermometer inserted in the center reads 145 degrees. Remove the smaller baking dish from the water bath, and put it in the refrigerator to cool. After it has cooled fully, keep the pâté covered.

---

chicken stock

1	C	olive oil
3	C	celery (chopped)
3	C	carrot (chopped)
3	C	onion (chopped)
2	T	garlic (minced)
1/2	T	herbs de Provence
2	T	dried chives
1/4	t	celery seed
1/4	t	dill weed
1/4	t	white pepper
1	each	bay leaf
1/2	t	rubbed sage
1	T	kosher salt
5	each	black peppercorns
1	pinch	saffron threads
8	oz	chicken bones, skin, & fat
3	qt	water

Optional:

1	T	corn starch
1/4	C	cold water

Heat the olive oil in a large stock pot over high heat. Add the chopped celery, carrot, and onion, cover the pot, turn the heat down to medium, and sweat the vegetables for about 5 minutes, stirring them frequently, until they begin to soften. Add the minced garlic, and cook the ingredients for another 1 to 2 minutes, still stirring them regularly. Add the remaining ingredients (except for the optional cornstarch and the 1/4 cup of cold water). Increase the heat to high until the stock begins to boil, reduce the heat to low, and simmer the mixture for 2 hours (or for up to 3 hours for a richer stock). Check the stock frequently to be sure it is cooking at a gentle simmer. Boiling the stock too hard will result in a "muddy" stock, and simmering it too lightly will yield a weak stock. Strain the stock through a fine mesh strainer. The stock is now finished if you intend to use it in a soup or as a base for a sauce or other such recipe. (If you are not using it immediately, allow the stock to cool to room temperature, and store it in the refrigerator.)

Optional: To make a rich chicken stock sauce like the one used in the Grilled Quail recipe in this book (page 187), return the stock to a clean pot, and simmer it slowly until it reduces to about half (to approximately 4 cups), using a ladle periodically to skim off any fat that accumulates on the surface. Then mix the cornstarch and cold water together in a small bowl to create a slurry, and stir it into the simmering stock. Bring the stock to a boil once more, stir it well, and then turn off the heat. Use the stock sauce immediately, or store it in the refrigerator.

chocolate ganache

30	oz	semi-sweet chocolate
4	C	heavy cream

Put the semi-sweet chocolate in a large, heat-resistant bowl. (If the chocolate is in bar form, first shave it or cut it into small pieces.) In a large pot over medium heat, bring the heavy cream to a boil. Immediately pour the hot cream over the chocolate, and allow the mixture to sit for a few minutes, until the chocolate has melted. Stir the ganache with a whisk until it is smooth and glossy. Use it right away, or it can be refrigerated and rewarmed later.

chocolate mole

1/4	C	pasilla chiles (puréed)
1/4	C	guajillo chiles (puréed)
1/4	C	ancho chiles (puréed)
2	T	olive oil
1	C	white onion (diced)
1	T	garlic (minced)
1	each	canned chipotle pepper
3	C	water
1	t	kosher salt
1 1/2	T	brown sugar
2	T	honey
1	pinch	dried thyme
1	pinch	cinnamon
1	t	oregano
1/2	T	balsamic vinegar
1/2	each	bay leaf (crushed)
1/2	C	pistachios (ground)
3	T	masa harina
2	T	vegetable base
1	C	water
4	oz	Belgian chocolate (chopped)
1/4	C	cilantro (chopped)

Dried pasilla, guajillo, and ancho chile peppers are available in Mexican markets or online. To make the chile purées, you will need to roast the chiles, remove their seeds and stems, soak them, and then purée them. You will find more information on this process in books on traditional Mexican cooking or by searching for a reputable source online.

In a large pot, heat the olive oil on high heat. Add the chopped white onion, turn the heat down to medium, and cook the onion for about 5 minutes, stirring it frequently, until it is caramelized. Add the minced garlic, puréed chiles, and chipotle pepper, and sauté the ingredients for another 2 minutes. Then stir in the 3 cups of water, along with the kosher salt, brown sugar, honey, dried thyme, cinnamon, oregano, balsamic vinegar, and crushed bay leaf. Allow the mixture to simmer, covered, over low heat for 2 hours, stirring it occasionally. In another pot of medium size, combine the ground pistachios, masa harina, vegetable base, and 1 cup of water. Cook them over medium heat for about 10 minutes, stirring the ingredients constantly, until they thicken. After the 2-hour simmer is complete, add this pistachio mixture to the simmering contents of the large pot, increase the heat to medium, and bring it to a boil. Add the Belgian chocolate, return the heat to low, and simmer the mixture for another 30 minutes, stirring it periodically. Then stir in the chopped cilantro, pour the sauce into a blender, and purée it until it is smooth. If you are not using the mole immediately, allow it to cool to room temperature, and store it in the refrigerator. When you are ready to use the mole, reheat it gently in a pot over low heat.

cilantro beurre monté

8	oz	butter
4	T	water
2	bunches	cilantro
1	pinch	kosher salt
1/2	t	vegetable base
1	pinch	ground cumin

Melt the butter in a small pot on the stove or in a small dish in the microwave. Pour the melted butter and water into a blender, and allow them to cool to room temperature. Meanwhile, fill a large bowl with ice water to create an ice-water bath. Also fill a medium pot with water, and bring it to a boil. Blanch the cilantro in the boiling water for about 5 seconds, and then plunge it into the ice-water bath for another couple of seconds. Squeeze as much water out of the cilantro as possible, and chop it finely. In the blender, purée the butter and water for a few seconds. Then add the chopped cilantro, kosher salt, vegetable base, and ground cumin. Pulse the blender a few times to mix the ingredients together. Then purée the mixture until it is smooth, watching carefully until it turns from pale green to bright green and avoiding blending it too long, which will heat it up and "break" the butter (cause it to separate). Use the cilantro beurre monté immediately.

cipollini onion confit

1/4	C	kosher salt
1/4	C	granulated sugar
1/2	C	apple cider
1/2	C	apple cider vinegar
1	T	black peppercorns
2	each	bay leaves
4	C	water
2	lb	cipollini onions
8	C	olive oil

Note that this recipe requires 2 days of preparation time, to allow for brining the onions.

In a large pot or bowl, combine the kosher salt, granulated sugar, apple cider, apple cider vinegar, black peppercorns, bay leaves, and 4 cups of water, to create a brine, stirring it until the salt and sugar have dissolved. Slice off the root ends of the onions, soak the onions in a separate container of warm water for 15 minutes, and peel off their skins. Then submerge the whole onions in the brine, cover the container, put it in the refrigerator, and soak the onions for at least 48 hours. Preheat the oven to 250 degrees. Remove the onions from the brine, and put them in a baking pan that is deep enough so that all of the onions fit below the pan's rim by at least 1 inch. Pour the olive oil over the onions, making sure the onions are covered in oil completely. Cover the pan with aluminum foil, and bake the onions for 2 hours, until they are translucent but still intact. Pull the pan from the oven, remove the onions carefully from the oil, and place them to cool on a sheet pan. After both the onions and oil are cool, put the onions in a covered storage container, and pour enough oil over them to cover them completely. The onion confit can be used immediately, and you can also store it in the refrigerator. Any remaining oil can be used to make more onion confit or in other cooking endeavors.

creamed leeks

1	lb	leeks
2	t	olive oil
2	C	heavy cream
2	t	kosher salt
1	pinch	white pepper

Trim the green tops off of the leeks, and discard them. Cut the leeks in half lengthwise, and then cross-cut them into thin slices that are about 1/8 inch thick. Heat the olive oil in a wide, shallow pot over high heat. Then add the leeks, put a lid on the pot, reduce the heat to medium, and sweat the leeks for 5 minutes, stirring them frequently, until they are soft and translucent. Add the heavy cream, kosher salt, and white pepper. Turn the heat down to low, and simmer the mixture for about 15 minutes, stirring it frequently, until it thickens and reduces in volume by approximately half. Serve the creamed leeks immediately, or store them in the refrigerator.

cream sherry & foie gras sauce

2	T	olive oil
1/2	C	shallot (sliced)
1	T	garlic (minced)
1/4	C	cream sherry
2	C	heavy cream
4	oz	foie gras
1	t	kosher salt
1/2	t	black truffle oil

In a medium pot, heat the olive oil over high heat. Add the sliced shallot and minced garlic, reduce the heat to medium, and sweat the shallot and garlic, uncovered, for about 2 minutes, stirring them frequently, until they are soft and translucent. Add the cream sherry, and cook the mixture for approximately 2 minutes, to allow the alcohol to evaporate. (You can tell by smelling it.) Add the heavy cream, turn the heat down to low, and simmer the mixture until it has reduced by about 20 percent, continuing to stir it frequently. Dice the foie gras, and stir it into the pot, along with the kosher salt and black truffle oil. Continue to simmer and stir the mixture for another 10 minutes, until the foie gras has melted. Then purée it in a blender until it is smooth. Use the sauce immediately, or store it in the refrigerator.

cream sherry vinaigrette

3/4	C	walnut oil
3	T	brown rice vinegar
1/4	C	cream sherry
1/2	t	granulated sugar
1/2	t	garlic (minced)
1/2	t	shallot (minced)
1/2	t	kosher salt
1	pinch	cracked black pepper
2	drops	vanilla extract

Combine all of the ingredients in a blender, and purée them well. Use the vinaigrette immediately, or store it in a covered container in the refrigerator.

crème anglaise

1	C	heavy cream
1	C	milk
7	T	granulated sugar
1/2	each	vanilla bean
3	each	egg yolks

Combine the heavy cream, milk, and 4 tablespoons of the granulated sugar in a small pot. Using the tip of a sharp knife, scrape the seeds from the 1/2 vanilla bean, and then add both the seeds and the pod to the cream mixture. Place the pot over medium heat, and simmer the ingredients for about 10 minutes, stirring them frequently to dissolve the sugar. Remove the pot from the heat, and let it sit for 30 minutes, stirring it occasionally, to allow the vanilla to infuse its flavor. Meanwhile, fill a large bowl with ice water, to create an ice-water bath. In another, smaller bowl, use an electric mixer on high speed to whip the egg yolks and the other 3 tablespoons of sugar, until the yolks thicken and lighten in color. Add the whipped egg yolks to the cream mixture, and return the pot to low heat. Cook the mixture gently for another 5 minutes, whisking it constantly until it thickens. Then pour it into a metal bowl, and set the bowl in the ice-water bath. Stir the crème anglaise until it is cool, and then pour it through a fine mesh strainer. You can use the crème anglaise immediately or store it in the refrigerator.

crème fraîche

| 4 | C | heavy cream |
| 1/4 | C | buttermilk |

Note that you will need to prepare the crème fraîche 2 to 3 days before you plan to use it.

Heat the heavy cream in a pot over low heat, to precisely 100 degrees, stirring it regularly. Pour the hot cream into a mixing bowl, add the buttermilk, and stir the mixture. Cover the bowl with plastic wrap, and allow it to sit at room temperature for 2 to 3 days, until it thickens and develops a sour flavor. Then put the crème fraîche in the refrigerator to cool completely. Use the crème fraîche as-is, or whip it to the thick consistency of whipped cream. Store it in the refrigerator.

cucumber linguini

1/2	C	rice vinegar
1/4	C	granulated sugar
2	drops	sesame oil
1	pinch	crushed red pepper flakes
1	each	cucumber

Combine the rice vinegar, granulated sugar, sesame oil, and crushed red pepper flakes in a mixing bowl, whisk them until the sugar dissolves, and set the marinade aside. Using a mandoline slicer with a julienne blade attachment, slice the peeled cucumber lengthwise, creating long, linguini-like strands. When you reach the seeds, stop slicing, rotate the cucumber 90 degrees, and continue slicing. Rotate the cucumber 2 more times, so that just the core of seeds remains. (You do not need the core for this recipe.) Add the cucumber strands to the marinade, and refrigerate the cucumber linguini for at least 15 minutes before serving it.

cucumber pearls

4	C	canola oil (chilled)
3	each	cucumbers (chopped)
2	t	kosher salt
1	t	granulated sugar
2	T	rice vinegar
8	sheets	silver gelatin
2	C	cold water

Pour the chilled canola oil into a shallow dish that has a flat bottom and is about 2 inches deep, and put the dish in the refrigerator. Purée the chopped cucumbers in a blender until they are smooth. Then strain the purée through a fine mesh strainer that is lined with cheesecloth. Allow the purée to drip slowly on its own; do not push any of the cucumber solids through the strainer. Measure 2 cups of the cucumber juice, and combine it in a bowl with the kosher salt, granulated sugar, and rice vinegar.

Cut the sheets of silver gelatin into small pieces, pour the cold water into a separate small bowl, and add the gelatin to the water 1 piece at a time so that the pieces do not stick together. Allow the gelatin to "bloom," or soften, until it is supple and has absorbed almost all of the water. Remove the gelatin from the water, and place it in a metal bowl over a pot of simmering water, until the gelatin just melts. Take care not to overheat the gelatin. (Too much heat will destroy its gelling properties.) Stir the melted gelatin into the cucumber juice, and remove the dish of canola oil from the refrigerator. Then, using an eyedropper or syringe, drip droplets of the cucumber mixture into the cold oil. Allow each grouping of droplets to solidify before you add more, putting the oil back into the refrigerator between uses, to keep it cold. If the oil is allowed to warm too much, the pearls will soften and congeal into a single mass, so after you have made all of your pearls, keep them refrigerated in the oil at all times until you use them. Use the cucumber pearls within 2 days, before they begin to stick together and while they still have their bright green color.

elephant garlic chips

1	lb	elephant garlic cloves
1/2	gal	milk
4	C	canola oil
1	T	kosher salt

Peel the elephant garlic cloves, and using a mandoline slicer, cut the garlic into thin, 1/16-inch slices. Put the garlic slices in a medium pot, pour in half (1 quart) of the milk, and place the pot over medium heat. Bring the mixture slowly to a boil, stirring the garlic slices gently so they heat evenly, and allow the boil to continue for 1 minute. Remove the pot from the heat, strain the garlic out, and rinse it thoroughly with cold water. Remove the used milk from the pot (you do not need it again for this recipe), and return the garlic to the pot. Add the other half (1 quart) of the milk, and again bring it slowly to a boil, stirring the garlic carefully and allowing the boil to continue for 1 minute. Once more, remove the pot from the heat, strain the garlic slices, and rinse them well with cold water. Then let them drain well on paper towels or on a clean cloth.

Place the garlic slices in a clean pot that is medium size, pour the canola oil over them, and stir the garlic slices so they separate and float freely in the oil. Heat the oil slowly over medium heat so that the moisture begins to boil out of the garlic slices. Stir the garlic frequently, and watch it carefully to avoid overcooking it. When all of the moisture has evaporated, the garlic chips will begin to turn light brown. After they are light to medium brown and no more moisture is boiling out, use a strainer to remove the garlic chips, and put them on paper towels or on a clean cloth to drain. Season the chips with kosher salt immediately, and allow them to cool. They will become crisp as they cool to room temperature and, after they have cooled completely, can be stored in an airtight container.

---

fennel & coriander honey glaze

4	T	fennel seeds
2	T	coriander seeds
1	C	honey
2	T	fresh ginger root (peeled & grated)
1/2	C	vegetable base
1	T	truffle oil

In a small sauté pan over low heat, toast the fennel and coriander seeds lightly. Remove the pan from the heat, and allow the seeds to cool for a few minutes. Then pulse the seeds several times in a spice grinder, to grind them coarsely. In a small pot over low heat, combine the ground seeds with the remaining ingredients, and simmer the mixture for 10 minutes, stirring it frequently. Allow the glaze to cool, and either use it immediately or store it in a covered container at room temperature.

---

fennel mustard vinaigrette

1	T	fennel seeds
1/2	C	rice wine vinegar
2	T	lemon juice
2	T	mustard seed mix (p. 368)
1	T	garlic (minced)
1/2	t	kosher salt
1/2	t	cracked black pepper
1	T	honey
1/2	C	olive oil
1	C	canola oil

In a small sauté pan over low heat, toast the fennel seeds lightly. Remove the pan from the heat, allow the seeds to cool, and pulse them a few times in a spice grinder, to grind them coarsely. In a blender, combine the ground fennel seeds with the rice wine vinegar, lemon juice, mustard seed mix, minced garlic, kosher salt, cracked black pepper, and honey, and purée them. Then with the blender running on low speed, pour the olive oil and canola oil in slowly, continuing to blend the mixture until the oils have emulsified. Store the vinaigrette in a covered container in the refrigerator.

---

garam masala

1/2	C	cumin seeds
1/4	C	black peppercorns
2	T	ground cardamom
2	T	ground cinnamon
1	T	ground clove
1	T	ground mace

In a small sauté pan over low heat, toast the cumin seeds lightly. Remove the pan from the heat, allow the seeds to cool, and grind them finely in a spice grinder, along with the black peppercorns. Put the ground cumin seeds and ground peppercorns in a small bowl, add all of the other ingredients, and mix them until they are combined evenly. Store the garam masala in a covered container.

---

green oil

1/2	lb	Italian parsley
1/2	C	olive oil
1/2	t	kosher salt

Bring a small pot of water to a boil, and fill a large bowl with ice water to prepare an ice-water bath. Hold the Italian parsley by the stems, dip the leaves into the boiling water for 2 seconds, and then plunge the parsley immediately into the ice water for another 2 seconds. Squeeze as much water as possible out of the parsley, cut the stems off, and then roughly chop the leaves. Put the chopped leaves, olive oil, and kosher salt in a blender, and purée them on high speed until the mixture is smooth and dark green. Pour the purée into a strainer that has been lined with damp cheesecloth and placed over a bowl or pitcher. Let it stand for 1 hour. It will drip very slowly. Discard the solids that are in the cheesecloth, pour the green oil into a small squeeze bottle, and store it at room temperature.

---

hazelnut tuile

5	T	honey
6	T	butter
1/3	C	granulated sugar
1/2	C	all-purpose flour
1/2	C	ground hazelnuts

Using an electric mixer and paddle attachment, cream together the honey, butter, and granulated sugar on high speed, until the mixture is smooth and light in texture. Mix the all-purpose flour and ground hazelnuts together by hand in a small mixing bowl, and then add them to the butter and sugar. Mix the ingredients on low speed until they are combined evenly. Then refrigerate the batter for 10 minutes, and preheat the oven to 300 degrees. On a sheet pan lined with a silicone baking mat, spread the tuile batter in thin shapes. Or you can use a stencil. A clean sheet of thin cardboard works for a one-time use. Plastic works great if you want to reuse the stencil, and plastic that is 1 millimeter thick works best. To make a stencil, cut out as many shapes as will fit on your sheet. Then place the stencil on your baking mat. Using a small, thin offset metal spatula, spread the tuile batter into the stencil's cut-outs, scraping the batter so it is even and the same thickness as the stencil sheet. Then peel the stencil up carefully.

Bake the tuiles for about 5 minutes, watching them closely, until they are a uniform golden brown. Remove the pan from the oven immediately, and use a spatula to lift each tuile carefully. While the tuiles are still hot, you can mold them around any shape or form you like. You can also score them with a knife or pizza wheel, and then after they are cool, you can break the tuiles cleanly at the score lines to create your chosen shapes. If you have leftover batter, store it in the refrigerator, and then allow it to warm to room temperature when you want to make more tuiles.

---

herbed goat cheese mousse

8	oz	goat cheese (chevre)
4	oz	cream cheese
1	t	garlic (minced)
1/2	t	dried thyme
1	t	dried chives
1	t	white truffle oil
1/2	t	granulated sugar

Before you begin, allow the goat cheese and cream cheese to soften at room temperature for 1 hour. Then place all of the ingredients in the bowl of an electric mixer, and using the paddle attachment, mix them on low speed for 1 minute. Increase the speed to high, and whip the mixture for another minute. Use the mousse immediately, or store it in an airtight container in the refrigerator.

The New Scenic Café

lamb meatloaf mix

12	oz	lamb stew meat (or 16 oz ground lamb)
4	oz	beef fat trimmings (omit if using ground lamb)
1	T	olive oil
1	C	onion (small-diced)
1	T	garlic (minced)
1	each	whole egg
1	each	egg yolk
2/3	C	milk
1	T	parsley flakes
1	t	paprika
1/2	t	cracked black pepper
1	T	kosher salt
1	pinch	dried oregano
1	pinch	dried thyme
1	pinch	dill weed
1	t	white truffle oil
1 1/3	C	white bread (small-diced)
1/3	C	panko bread crumbs

Using a meat grinder, grind the lamb stew meat and beef fat trimmings together. (Or, if you are using ground lamb, skip this step and exclude the beef fat.) Heat the olive oil on high heat in a small sauté pan. Then add the diced onion and minced garlic, and sauté them for about 5 minutes, stirring them frequently, until they have caramelized. Remove the pan from the heat. In a large mixing bowl, whisk the whole egg and egg yolk. Add the milk, herbs and spices, and white truffle oil, and mix them until they are combined evenly. Add the diced white bread and panko bread crumbs, mix the ingredients together, and allow them to sit at room temperature for about 10 minutes, until the bread has soaked up all of the liquid. Then mix the ground meat in gently by hand, until all the ingredients are blended thoroughly but without over-mixing. (Mixing gently ensures that the meatloaf will be tender rather than tough.) Cover the bowl, and put the meatloaf mix in the refrigerator to rest for about 30 minutes before you form the meatloaf.

---

lemon aioli

1	each	egg yolk
1	t	garlic (minced)
1	pinch	cayenne pepper
1	t	kosher salt
1	T	lemon juice
1	t	lemon zest
2	t	Dijon mustard
1	C	canola oil
1/4	C	water

In a food processor, blend the egg yolk, minced garlic, cayenne pepper, kosher salt, lemon juice and zest, and Dijon mustard for about 15 seconds. Then with the food processor running on low, add the canola oil slowly in a thin stream, and then add the water slowly as well. Use the lemon aioli immediately, or store it in a covered container in the refrigerator.

---

lemon-basil aioli

1	C	mayonnaise
1	T	basil pesto (p. 362)
1	T	lemon juice
1	t	lemon zest
1/2	t	garlic (minced)
1/2	t	kosher salt
1	t	honey
2	T	white wine
1/8	t	white pepper

Combine all of the ingredients in a large mixing bowl, and whisk them until they are combined evenly and the aioli is smooth. Use the aioli immediately, or store it in a covered container in the refrigerator.

---

lemon curd

3	each	lemons (juice & zest)
3	each	egg yolks
3	each	whole eggs
1/2	lb	butter
2	T	all-purpose flour
1/2	C	granulated sugar

Zest the lemons, and then squeeze the juice from the lemons through a strainer and into a bowl or small pitcher. Set the lemon zest and juice aside. Separate 3 eggs, and put the yolks in a small mixing bowl (you will not need these egg whites for this recipe). Crack the other 3 eggs, add them whole to the yolks, and beat the eggs together lightly, using a whisk or fork. In a medium pot over low heat, melt the butter. Add the all-purpose flour to the butter, and cook the mixture for 3 minutes, stirring it constantly. Then add the granulated sugar to the pot, and continue to cook the mixture for another 3 minutes, stirring it constantly until the sugar has dissolved. Remove the pot from the heat, add the lemon juice, and stir the ingredients. Then stir in the beaten eggs. Return the pot to low heat, and cook the mixture for about 2 minutes more, whisking it constantly until it thickens. Remove the pot from the heat, stir in the lemon zest, and pour the lemon curd into a wide, shallow container. Place it in the refrigerator to cool, and then cover it with an airtight lid.

---

lemon tiramisu soaking liquid

1/4	C	sparkling white wine
2	T	rum
3	T	granulated sugar
2	drops	orange oil
1/2	t	vanilla extract
1/2	C	apple cider
1/4	C	water
3	T	key lime juice
3	T	lemon juice

In a medium bowl, combine all of the ingredients, stirring them until the granulated sugar has dissolved fully. Use the soaking liquid immediately, or store it in a covered container in the refrigerator.

---

marinated hon shimeji mushrooms

3	C	water
1	t	sesame oil
1/4	C	vegetable base
1	t	Sriracha hot sauce
1	T	soy sauce
1/4	C	rice vinegar
1	T	garlic (minced)
1	T	fresh ginger root (peeled & minced)
12	oz	hon shimeji (beech) mushrooms

Note that you can find hon shimeji mushrooms at some gourmet food stores, Asian grocery stores, and online.

In a large mixing bowl, whisk together all of the ingredients except the hon shimeji mushrooms, to combine them thoroughly. Add the mushrooms to the mixture, and allow them to marinate at room temperature for at least 2 hours or in the refrigerator for up to 2 days.

---

medjool date & cumin purée

8	oz	Medjool dates (pitted)
1	C	water
1/2	T	cumin seeds
1/2	T	garlic (minced)
1	pinch	curry powder
1	T	vegetable base
1/2	t	kosher salt
1/4	C	cilantro (chopped)

Put the pitted Medjool dates and water in a medium pot, cover the pot with a lid, and simmer the dates over low heat for 20 minutes, stirring them periodically. In a small sauté pan, toast the cumin seeds lightly, and then grind them finely in a spice grinder. Add the ground cumin seeds, minced garlic, curry powder, vegetable base, and kosher salt to the dates. Cover the pot, and simmer the mixture for another 5 minutes, stirring it occasionally. Transfer the mixture to a blender, add the chopped cilantro, and purée the ingredients until they are smooth. Use the purée immediately, or store it in a covered container in the refrigerator.

---

merguez sausage

1	lb	lean lamb meat
3	oz	lamb or beef fat
1	t	cumin seeds
1	T	coriander seeds
3	T	sweet harissa (p. 370)
1	t	Indian fennel (ground)
1	T	garlic (minced)
1/2	t	ground cinnamon
1/2	t	cracked black pepper
2	t	kosher salt

Preheat the oven to 350 degrees. Using a meat grinder, grind the lean lamb meat and the lamb or beef fat together. Toast the cumin and coriander seeds in a small sauté pan, and then grind them finely in a spice grinder. Combine all ingredients in a medium mixing bowl, blending them gently by hand until they are mixed thoroughly. Spread the mixture in a 1/2-inch layer on a sheet pan, and bake it for 8 to 10 minutes, until it is just cooked. Allow the sausage to cool, and then crumble it into small pieces. You can use it immediately or store it in a covered container in the refrigerator.

---

miso marinade

1/2	C	sake
1/2	C	sweet rice cooking wine (mirin)
5	T	white miso paste
3	T	red miso paste
1/3	C	brown sugar
1/4	C	soy sauce
1	t	cilantro (chopped)
3	drops	sesame oil
1 1/2	T	white rum

Combine all of the ingredients in a blender, and purée them until they are mixed evenly and the marinade is smooth. You can use the marinade immediately or refrigerate it in a covered container.

---

mustard seed mix

1	C	black mustard seeds
1 1/2	C	yellow mustard seeds
1/2	C	red wine vinegar
1/3	C	Dijon mustard
1/2	C	yellow mustard
1/2	C	maple syrup
1/2	C	apple cider vinegar
1	C	apple cider
1	t	dillweed
1	T	garlic (minced)
1	T	kosher salt

Note that you will need to prepare this mix 24 hours before you plan to use it.

Place all of the ingredients in a mixing bowl, and stir them to combine them evenly. In small batches, purée the mixture for a few seconds in a food processor to break up some of the whole mustard seeds. Allow the seed mix to sit for at least 24 hours before you use it, to soften the seeds and allow the mixture to thicken. It can be used in many applications and can be stored for an extended period of time in a covered container in the refrigerator.

---

pastry cream

1/2	C	granulated sugar
1/4	C	cornstarch
1	pinch	kosher salt
2	C	milk
3	T	heavy cream
4	each	egg yolks
1 1/2	T	butter
1/2	T	vanilla extract

Combine the granulated sugar, cornstarch, and kosher salt in a large pot, and then whisk in half of the milk and half of the heavy cream gradually. In a small mixing bowl, beat the egg yolks lightly, using a whisk or fork, until they are mixed evenly. Add the egg yolks to the cream mixture, and whisk them vigorously until they are well incorporated. Then stir in the remaining milk and heavy cream. Place the pot over low heat, and bring the mixture to a simmer, whisking it constantly until it is smooth. While continuing to whisk, increase the heat to medium, and allow the mixture to come to a boil. Continue cooking and stirring it for 1 minute. Remove it from the heat, whisk in the butter and vanilla extract, and then pour it into a broad, shallow container. Cover the container with plastic wrap, pressing the plastic wrap directly onto the surface of the pastry cream. Put it in the refrigerator to cool completely before you use it.

---

pâté à bombe

1 3/4	C	granulated sugar
6	T	water
12	each	egg yolks

Combine the granulated sugar and water in a small pot over medium heat, and bring the mixture to a boil. Continue to boil the syrup until it reaches 248 degrees (using an instant-read digital thermometer for best accuracy). Whip the egg yolks with an electric mixer until they thicken to the consistency of mousse and grow lighter in color. Then transfer the hot syrup into a glass measuring cup or other small heatproof pitcher, and, with the mixer turned off, pour 1 tablespoon of syrup in a thin stream into the egg yolks. Immediately turn the mixer on high speed for 10 seconds to incorporate the syrup in the egg yolks. Repeat this process until you have used all of the syrup. Then continue to whip the mixture on high speed for 10 minutes, until the pâté à bombe has doubled in volume and the mixing bowl has cooled to the touch.

---

pear cider gastrique

1/2	C	granulated sugar
1	T	water
1	C	pear juice
1/2	C	apple cider vinegar
1	t	cornstarch
1	T	cold water
1	t	lemon zest

Combine the granulated sugar and water in a medium pot, and heat it over medium heat. Without stirring the mixture, tilt the pot from side to side gently as the sugar melts, to distribute the water evenly and prevent hot spots. Continue cooking the sugar for about another 5 minutes, stirring it frequently, until it caramelizes to a medium-brown color. Stir in the pear juice and apple cider vinegar. The caramel will harden, but it will melt again. Bring it to a boil, reduce the heat to low, and simmer the mixture for another few minutes, continuing to stir it frequently, until it reduces by about half. In a small bowl, mix together the cornstarch and water to make a slurry. Add the slurry slowly to the pot while stirring the hot liquid, and return the mixture to a boil for about 1 minute, until it has the consistency of thick syrup. Remove it from the heat, stir in the lemon zest, and then allow the gastrique to cool. You can use it immediately or store it in a covered container at room temperature.

---

pickled carrot & daikon radish

1/2	lb	carrot
1/2	lb	daikon radish
2	C	water
1	C	rice vinegar
1 1/2	C	granulated sugar
1	T	kosher salt

Note that you will need to prepare these vegetables the day before you plan to serve them, to allow for overnight brining.

Using a mandoline slicer with a julienne blade (or by hand if you want to practice your knife skills!), cut the carrot and the daikon radish into long, thin 1/8-inch strips, and separate the vegetable strips into 2 different storage containers. Combine the water, rice vinegar, granulated sugar, and kosher salt in a pot over medium heat, and bring the mixture to a boil to make a brine, stirring it until the sugar and salt have dissolved. Pour half of the hot brine over each of the 2 groups of sliced vegetables, making sure they are submerged completely. Cover the containers, put them in the refrigerator, and let the vegetables sit in the brine overnight. They can continue to be stored in the refrigerator, in the brine.

---

pork terrine

1	lb	pork butt or shoulder
2	T	kosher salt
1/2	T	cracked black pepper
1	T	garlic (minced)
1	T	shallot (minced)
1	T	crushed red pepper flakes
6	C	rendered duck fat
1/4	C	chicken stock (p. 364)
3	sheets	silver gelatin
1/2	T	dried thyme
1/2	T	dried rosemary
1/2	T	dried parsley flakes
1/2	T	dried chives
1/2	t	cracked black pepper
6	T	rendered duck fat

Note that you will need to start this dish 2 to 3 days before you plan to serve it, to allow time for marinating and pressing it.

Cut the pork butt or shoulder into 2-inch cubes. Rub it with the kosher salt, cracked black pepper, minced garlic, minced shallot, and crushed red pepper flakes. Put the meat in a covered container, and refrigerate it for 24 to 48 hours (longer marination time allows the meat to absorb more flavor). Preheat the oven to 300 degrees. Heat the 6 cups of rendered duck fat in a pot on low heat until the fat melts but is not hot. Spread the cubed pork in an oven-proof baking pan, and pour the duck fat over it. Cover the pan with a layer of plastic wrap and then a layer of aluminum foil, and put the pan in the oven. Bake it for 2 hours, and then begin checking the pork for doneness every 15 minutes. When it is done, it will break apart easily when squeezed with tongs. (Cooking the meat too long can make it less moist and flavorful.) Remove the meat from the oven, and let it cool for 20 minutes. Then strain the pork from the fat, making sure to save the fat, if you like. (It has many great uses in cooking.) When the pork has cooled enough to handle but is still warm, shred it into small pieces, and set it aside. Warm the chicken stock gently. Cut the sheets of silver gelatin into small pieces, and add the gelatin to the chicken stock 1 piece at a time so that the pieces do not stick together. Allow the gelatin to "bloom," or soften, until it is supple and has absorbed almost all of the stock.

In a large mixing bowl, combine the shredded meat, softened gelatin and chicken stock, and the rest of the ingredients. Mix them well, using your hands to squeeze the mixture through your fingers, which will shred the pork a bit more and ensure that all the ingredients are combined well. With a layer of plastic wrap that is long enough to also fold over the top of the pork terrine, line an 8- or 9-inch square pan that is at least 2 inches deep. Put the pork mixture in the pan, pressing it into place in an even layer. Then fold the plastic wrap over the top of the pork terrine to cover its surface. Put a second pan of identical size on top, and then set an even layer of heavy items (filled metal cans work great) on top of that pan, to press the mixture down. Refrigerate the terrine overnight.

---

pumpkin pie spice

2	T	ground cinnamon
1 1/2	T	ground nutmeg
1 1/2	T	ground ginger
1/2	T	ground allspice
1	t	ground cloves
1	t	ground cardamom

Mix all of the spices together thoroughly so they are distributed evenly throughout the mixture. Store the pumpkin pie spice in an airtight container.

---

quinoa

2	C	water
1/2	T	kosher salt
1/2	t	turmeric
1	C	whole quinoa

Bring the water, kosher salt, and turmeric to a boil in a small pot on high heat. Add the whole quinoa, and return it to a boil. Reduce the heat to low, set a lid on the pot, and simmer the mixture for about 10 minutes, stirring it occasionally, until the water is mostly absorbed and the quinoa grains begin to open. Remove the pot from the heat, fluff the quinoa with a fork, and then replace the lid and let the quinoa sit for 15 minutes.

---

red chile adobo

1 1/4	lb	garlic cloves (peeled)
1	C	red wine vinegar
1/2	C	balsamic vinegar
2 1/2	C	cider vinegar
6	each	whole cloves
1/2	T	black peppercorns
1	each	bay leaf
1/2	t	cumin seeds
1	t	dried oregano
1	t	dried thyme
1/2	T	ground cinnamon
2	T	kosher salt
1 1/2	C	granulated sugar
1/4	C	white wine
2	T	water
3/4	C	olive oil
1/4	C	honey
1	t	vanilla extract
1/2	C	ancho chile purée
1/4	C	guajillo chile purée
4	T	melted butter

Dried ancho and guajillo chile peppers are available in Mexican markets or online. To make the chile purées, you will need to roast the chiles, remove their seeds and stems, soak them, and then purée them. You will find more information on this process in books on traditional Mexican cooking or by searching for a reputable source online.

Preheat the oven to 350 degrees. Place the peeled garlic cloves on a sheet pan (no oil is needed), and roast them for about 20 minutes, until they are a medium-brown color. Remove the pan from the oven, and allow the garlic to cool. Combine the red wine vinegar and balsamic vinegar. Then put the roasted garlic cloves in a food processor, add about 1/2 cup of the vinegar mixture (or just enough vinegar to allow the garlic to move in the processor), and purée the garlic until it is smooth, which will take about 10 minutes of constant puréeing. Combine the whole cloves, black peppercorns, bay leaf, cumin seeds, dried oregano, and dried thyme in a small bowl, and grind them finely in a spice grinder. In a large mixing bowl, whisk together the puréed garlic, remaining vinegar, ground spices, and all the other ingredients, until the mixture is combined thoroughly. Then move the mixture to a blender, and purée it in batches until it is smooth. Use the adobo immediately, or store it in a covered container in the refrigerator.

---

red wine vinaigrette

1 1/2	C	red wine
2	T	granulated sugar
1/2	C	red wine vinegar
2	T	Dijon mustard
1/2	T	garlic (minced)
1	T	shallot (minced)
1/2	t	kosher salt
1 1/2	C	olive oil
1/4	C	water

In a small pot over low heat, combine the red wine and granulated sugar. Cook it for about 20 minutes, stirring it occasionally, to reduce it slowly to 1/4 cup. Remove it from the heat, and allow it to cool. Then combine the reduced red wine, red wine vinegar, Dijon mustard, minced garlic, minced shallot, and kosher salt in a blender, and purée the mixture until it is smooth. With the blender running at low speed, pour the olive oil in slowly until it has emulsified. Whisk the water in by hand. Store the vinaigrette in the refrigerator.

---

roasted beets

whole beets (with skins)
olive oil

Preheat the oven to 375 degrees. Rub the outsides of the whole beets with just enough olive oil to coat their skins. Set the beets on a piece of aluminum foil that is large enough to fold over the top. Then fold the foil over, and crimp the sides, sealing the beets inside the pouch. Set the pouch on a sheet pan, and place it in the oven. The cooking time will vary considerably, depending on the size and quantity of the beets you are roasting. For baby beets, for example, begin checking for tenderness at 20 minutes. They are finished cooking when you can pierce them through the center easily using a small knife. (For large beets, begin checking them at 30 minutes.) Remove the beets from the oven, and open the foil pouch to allow them to cool. When they are cool enough to handle but still warm, use your hands to rub the skins off gently—they should slip off easily. Then hold the beets under warm running water, and rub them to rinse off any small pieces of skin. Store any unused beets in the refrigerator.

---

roasted garlic vinaigrette

5	oz	garlic cloves (peeled)
1	C	balsamic vinegar
1	t	cracked black pepper
1/2	T	kosher salt
1	each	canned chipotle pepper (whole)
2	C	olive oil

Preheat the oven to 350 degrees. Place the peeled garlic cloves on a sheet pan (no oil is needed), and roast them for about 25 minutes, until they are dark brown. Remove the pan from the oven, and allow the garlic to cool. Then put the roasted garlic cloves in a blender, add about 1/4 cup of the balsamic vinegar (or just enough vinegar to allow the garlic to move in the processor), and purée the garlic until it is smooth, which will take about 10 minutes of constant puréeing. Add the remaining vinegar, cracked black pepper, kosher salt, and chipotle peppers, and purée the mixture until it is smooth. With the blender running at low speed, pour the olive oil in slowly until it has emulsified. Store the vinaigrette in the refrigerator.

---

roasted red bell peppers

red bell peppers

Turn a gas stove burner on high. (Or you can use a gas cooktop grill or a barbeque grill.) Using metal tongs, set a red bell pepper on the burner, directly in the flames. Roast the pepper for about 3 minutes, turning it frequently, until the skin blackens and blisters all the way around. Remove the pepper from the flames, put it in a large bowl, and roast the rest of the peppers. Then cover the bowl tightly with plastic wrap, and allow the peppers to sit for 15 minutes. The charred skin will soften from the steam. Use your fingers to peel away the skin, and then rinse the peppers under cold water to remove most of the remaining black flecks. Cut the roasted peppers in half, and remove their cores and seeds.

---

sesame soy sauce

1/4	C	sesame seeds
1	T	fresh ginger root (peeled & grated)
2	C	soy sauce
1	T	sesame oil
1/4	C	fish sauce
1/4	T	crushed red pepper flakes
2	T	honey
1/2	C	water

Toast the sesame seeds lightly in a small sauté pan over low heat, and remove them from the heat to cool. Then put the toasted seeds and all of the other ingredients in a large mixing bowl, and whisk them together thoroughly. Store any unused sauce in a covered container in the refrigerator.

---

soft-center eggs

eggs (chilled)

Keeping the eggs refrigerated until you are ready to put them in the water, bring a large pot of salted water to a boil. Also fill a medium bowl with water and ice to prepare an ice-water bath, and set a timer for 6 1/2 minutes. Then use a spoon to lower each of the cold eggs gently into the boiling water, and start the timer immediately. When the timer is finished, use a spoon or strainer to transfer the eggs to the ice-water bath, and cool the eggs in the ice water for 1 minute. Then peel them carefully. Use the eggs immediately, or store them in the refrigerator in a cold-water bath. To reheat the eggs, submerge them in a pot of simmering water for 2 minutes.

---

spun sugar "glass"

2 1/2	C	granulated sugar
1/2	C	light corn syrup
1/2	C	water

Cover a work area with newspaper or brown paper bags (to catch any stray strands of sugar). Spray the inside of a large, heat-proof bowl lightly with pan release. Then fill another large bowl with ice water, and set it aside. Heat the granulated sugar, light corn syrup, and water in a medium pot over high heat, stirring the mixture frequently, until the sugar dissolves. Continue to cook the syrup until it reaches a temperature of 300 to 310 degrees (using an instant-read digital thermometer for best accuracy). Remove the pot from the heat, plunge the bottom of the pot immediately into the ice water, and keep stirring the syrup until it cools to 275 degrees.

Remove the pot from the ice water, and then dip a fork into the syrup, hold it about 8 inches above the bowl, and flick it back and forth quickly, allowing the syrup to come off the tines of the fork in fine strands. The strands will drape over the edges of the bowl, as well as down inside it. As the sugar strands collect, set them aside carefully, and make more. (If the syrup cools too much and does not form strands properly, reheat it gradually to just above 275 degrees.) When finished, the "glass" can be molded gently by hand into just about any light, airy shape. It is best to make the spun sugar relatively shortly before you plan to use it because humidity in the air will soon begin to damage it. You can store the spun sugar "glass" for short periods of time in an airtight container, at room temperature.

---

sugared blueberries (or cranberries)

1	C	fresh blueberries (or frozen cranberries)
1	each	egg white
1/2	C	granulated sugar

(If you are making sugared cranberries, thaw them before you begin.)

Sprinkle a thin layer of sugar on a sheet pan, and set it aside. Crack and separate the egg, placing the white in a large mixing bowl (and refrigerating the yolk for another cooking venture—you will not need it for this recipe). Use a whisk to whip the egg white until it becomes frothy. Then stir it around the bowl to form a thin layer of coating inside the bowl, and pour out any excess egg white. Add the berries to the bowl, swirl them to coat them lightly with the egg white, and then pour the berries onto the sugared sheet pan. Sprinkle more sugar over the berries, and move the pan back and forth on the counter to roll the berries and coat them with the sugar. Add small amounts of additional sugar, as needed, so that a solid layer of sugar coats each berry completely. Set the pan of coated berries aside in a warm, dry location for at least 2 hours, to allow the coating of egg whites and sugar that encapsulates the berries to dry to a firm crust.

---

sweet harissa

1	T	cumin seeds
1	T	coriander seeds
1	each	red bell pepper
14	oz	roasted red bell peppers (p. 370)
1/2	each	poblano pepper
2	each	dried Thai red chili peppers
1/4	C	Italian parsley
1/4	C	cilantro
10	each	mint leaves
1	T	paprika
1	T	garlic (minced)
1/3	C	olive oil
1	T	brown sugar
1/2	T	kosher salt

You can find dried Thai red chili peppers at some gourmet food stores, Asian grocery stores, or online.

Toast the cumin and coriander seeds in a small sauté pan over medium heat, and then grind them finely in a spice grinder. Dice the red bell pepper, roasted red bell peppers, and poblano pepper finely. Mince the dried Thai red chili peppers, and chop the Italian parsley, cilantro, and mint leaves finely. Whisk together all of the ingredients in a large mixing bowl, until they are combined thoroughly. Store the sweet harissa in a covered container in the refrigerator.

---

tartlet shells

3	T	butter (cold)
1/2	C	all-purpose flour
1	pinch	kosher salt
1	pinch	baking powder
2	T	cream cheese (cold)
1/2	T	cold water
1/2	t	apple cider vinegar

Cut the cold butter into small cubes, and put it in the freezer for 10 minutes. In a food processor, add the all-purpose flour, kosher salt, and baking powder, and pulse them a few times to combine them. Cut the cold cream cheese into small pieces, add it to the flour mixture in the food processor, and pulse the processor a few times again, until the mixture resembles coarse meal. Add the frozen butter cubes, and continue to pulse the ingredients for another few seconds until the pieces of butter are smaller than peas. Mix the cold water and apple cider vinegar together, and add them to the flour mixture. Pulse the processor 4 more times to incorporate the water and vinegar. (The mixture will still be in particles and will not yet hold together.)

Pour the mixture onto a clean work surface, and, using your hands, gather and press it together. Continue to press and knead the mixture for about 2 minutes more, until it holds together in one piece and feels slightly stretchy when pulled. Wrap the dough in plastic wrap, and refrigerate it for 45 minutes. Preheat the oven to 375 degrees. Remove the dough from the refrigerator, and on a floured work surface, use a rolling pin to roll the dough to a thickness of 1/8 inch. Use a 3-inch ring cutter to cut circles out of the dough. Then press the circles into 2-inch tartlet molds (or lay them over the back side of a mini-muffin tin, and press the sides of the dough down the outsides of the individual molds). Bake the tartlet shells for about 8 minutes, until they are golden brown. Allow the shells to cool completely before you handle or use them.

thai peanut slaw dressing

8	oz	smooth peanut butter
1	T	sesame oil
3	T	brown sugar
1/2	C	granulated sugar
1 1/2	T	Sriracha hot sauce
1	T	soy sauce
1 1/2	C	rice vinegar
4	T	honey
1 1/2	T	fresh ginger root (peeled & minced)
1 1/2	T	garlic (minced)
1/3	C	canned coconut milk
1/2	C	apple cider
1/2	t	ground cumin
1/2	T	kosher salt
1/2	C	vegetable base
1	bunch	fresh cilantro (chopped finely)

In a large bowl, combine all of the ingredients except the cilantro, and whisk them together. Purée the mixture in a blender, in batches, until it is smooth, pouring each batch as you finish it into a covered storage container. Stir the finely-chopped cilantro into the dressing, and use the dressing immediately or store it in the refrigerator.

veal demi-glace

6	lb	veal bones
2	T	olive oil
1	C	carrots (roughly chopped)
1	C	onions (roughly chopped)
1	C	celery (roughly chopped)
1/4	C	garlic cloves (peeled)
1/4	bunch	Italian parsley
1	each	tomato (roughly chopped)
1/2	T	dried thyme
1	each	bay leaves
1	C	red wine
		cold water

Preheat the oven to 350 degrees. Place the veal bones on a sheet pan, and roast them, uncovered, for 2 hours. On high heat, heat the olive oil in a large pot. Add the chopped carrots, onions, and celery, and sauté them for about 3 minutes, stirring them frequently, until they have caramelized. Add the peeled garlic cloves, and sauté the mixture for another 2 minutes, still stirring it often. Add the roasted veal bones to the pot and all the rest of the remaining ingredients, including enough cold water to cover the mixture. Cover the pot with a lid, bring it to a simmer, and then reduce the heat to low. Allow the mixture to simmer on low heat, without boiling, for 6 hours, stirring it occasionally and with the cover still on. Then strain the stock through a fine mesh strainer. Return the strained stock to a large pot on low heat, and bring it to a simmer once again. Allow the stock to simmer for 1 more hour (this time without a lid), still stirring it occasionally and using a ladle to skim off any fat or impurities that collect on the surface. When the stock is finished reducing, it will be clear and thick. Pour it through a fine mesh strainer again. It will yield approximately 2 cups of demi-glace.

whipped cream

2	C	heavy cream (chilled)
1/4	C	granulated sugar
1	t	vanilla extract

Combine the chilled heavy cream, granulated sugar, and vanilla extract in a large bowl, and use an electric mixer to whip them on medium speed for about 5 minutes, until the whipped cream reaches the desired consistency (but taking care not to over-whip it and turn it into butter!). Use the whipped cream immediately, or store it in a covered container in the refrigerator.

Glossary

acetate film
Transparent sheet of thin plastic made of acetate cellulose. Can be cut and shaped to create forms for molding cold foods.

adobo
Mexican sauce made of roasted chile peppers, garlic, and vinegar. Some recipes also include tomatoes, onions, and variety of herbs and spices. Sometimes used as marinade.

ahi tuna (sashimi grade)
Widely-used fish for raw dishes, such as sashimi and sushi. Its firm flesh ranges in color from pink to deep red, and its flavor is mild. More commonly known as "yellowfin tuna."

al dente
Italian term used to describe food cooked through and tender but still slightly resistant to the bite. Used most commonly to describe cooked pasta but can also be used in reference to vegetables, beans, or rice.

ancho chile peppers
Dried form of stout, green poblano peppers. Possesses mild heat and mild flavor.

Arya pistachios
Variety of pistachios originating in Iran and grown exclusively at single ranch in California. Characterized by large, vibrant-green nuts with rich flavor and large, round shells that are similar in appearance to hazelnuts.

Belper Knolle cheese
Hard cow's-milk cheese, with intense, creamy flavor, from small producer in Switzerland. Made in small spheres of 1 to 2 inches that are coated in mixture of Himalayan salt, local garlic, and black pepper and then aged up to 12 months. Usually shaved or grated.

bench knife
Rectangular scraping tool typically made of stainless steel and often with wooden or plastic handle. Used primarily to manipulate and cut dough, as well as to clean dough remnants from work surfaces.

blanching
Cooking method that involves plunging food (e.g., vegetables) into pot of boiling water for specific amount of time before removing it and plunging it immediately into ice water to stop further cooking. Allows for foods to be cooked until just tender, without becoming soft or soggy.

Boursin cheese
Soft, creamy cheese made from cow's milk and available in variety of flavors, with original and most common being blend of garlic and herbs. Texture similar to whipped cream cheese.

braise
Cooking method involving sautéing or searing food and then simmering it slowly in liquid. Sometimes used with vegetables but most often with tougher cuts of meat, to make them tender.

brine
Water-based solution containing salt, sugar, and often other ingredients. Used to soak meat or poultry before cooking, usually for several hours. Results in enhanced flavor in foods and better retention of moisture throughout cooking process.

brulée torch
Small torch for kitchen use, employed to caramelize sugar on top of French dessert, crème brûlée. Most often made with refillable butane fuel source.

brunoise
Technique of dicing vegetables finely and precisely into tiny cubes.

cannele mold
Round, fluted mold in shape of cup and measuring 2 inches in height and 2 inches in diameter. Traditionally made of metal (copper, steel, aluminum) but now also made of heat-proof silicone.

chevre
Any cheese made from goat's milk.

chiffon
Dessert made with beaten egg whites, giving it light, frothy consistency.

chiffonade
Technique of cutting leafy herbs or vegetables into fine strands.

chinois
Cone-shaped sieve made with fine mesh. Used to strain sauces, soups, or any liquid foods.

Chioggia beet
Heirloom variety of beet, with light-red skin and alternating layers of red and white inside that, when cut cross-section, reveal striped rings. Sometimes referred to as "candy cane beet."

chipotle peppers
Smoked, dried form of jalapeño peppers. Possesses medium heat and smoky flavor. Most often available canned and marinated in adobo.

chorizo (Spanish)
Hard, cured Spanish pork sausage made with garlic, salt, and Spanish paprika, which gives it distinctive reddish-orange color.

cipollini onion
Small, flat onion with light-brown skin, white or yellowish flesh, and sweet flavor.

citrus suprême
Wedge of citrus fruit prepared by using knife to remove skin, pith, membranes, and seeds and then separating the segments.

confit
Technique of cooking food slowly and submerged in oil, often as means of preservation. Meat (e.g., duck legs) most often cooked in own rendered fat.

crème anglaise
Rich, pourable custard used as dessert sauce. Made from cream, egg yolk, sugar, and vanilla. Cooked gently to thicken.

crème fraîche
Lightly-sour cream thickened by natural fermentation. Usually made from heavy cream and added buttermilk, sour cream, or yogurt.

crostini
Small slices of bread brushed with oil and toasted, often used as base for canapés.

deglaze
Process of adding small amount of liquid to hot pan that was used to sauté meat or other ingredients. Liquid boils and dissolves browned drippings from bottom of pan, creating flavorful broth that can serve as base for sauces, stocks, or soups.

demi-glace
Rich, glossy brown sauce made by evaporating liquid slowly from brown stock (usually veal or beef).

duxelle
Finely-chopped mixture of mushroom, shallot, garlic, and herbs sautéed in oil or butter and reduced to paste-like consistency.

emulsion
Uniform mixture of two liquids that would ordinarily not mix together, like oil and vinegar, following process and combination of ingredients that allows the particles of one liquid to become small enough to remain suspended within the other.

entremet rings
Heavy-duty stainless steel bands, used for molding and baking various foods.

flan ring mold
Stainless steel, bottomless rings with rolled edges and smooth seams. Used on top of sheet pan lined with parchment paper or non-stick baking mat, most often for making tarts or other pastry shells.

frisée
Member of chicory greens family, with narrow, curly leaves. Also called "curly endive."

ganache
Mixture of melted chocolate and cream. Used as coating or filling when making desserts.

garam masala
Spice mixture used in Indian cooking, containing cumin, black pepper, cardamom, cinnamon, clove, and mace. Sometimes also contains coriander, nutmeg, and turmeric.

gastrique
Syrupy sauce made from caramelized sugar and vinegar and usually infused with other flavors.

guajillo chile peppers
Dried form of thin, red mirasol peppers. Possesses mild-to-medium heat and slightly fruity flavor.

habañero pepper
Variety of chili pepper. One of hottest peppers available commercially.

haricots verts
French term for small, thin green beans.

haute cuisine
Cooking and serving of high-quality food, involving meticulous preparation and careful structure and presentation.

heirloom tomatoes
Non-hybrid varieties of tomatoes available in multitude of rich colors and shapes and derived from seeds passed down through generations.

high-gluten flour
Flour made from hard spring wheat, which has relatively high level of protein. Most often used in artisan breads and other doughs to create additional strength and elasticity.

Idiazabal cheese
Hard cheese made from sheep's milk, with lightly-smoked rind. Produced in Basque and Navarra regions of northern Spain.

instant-read digital thermometer
Small probe thermometer used to measure internal temperature of foods quickly.

julienne
Process of cutting food, usually vegetables, into short, thin strips approximately the size of matchsticks.

mâche
Salad green with small, soft leaves and slightly nutty flavor. Also called "corn salad."

mandoline
Vegetable-slicing utensil consisting of flat frame with adjustable slicing blade.

masa harina
Finely-ground flour made from corn that has been dried, cooked, ground, and dried again. Traditionally used to make tortillas, tamales, and other Mexican dishes.

microplane grater
Sharp style of kitchen grater, commonly used for zesting citrus and grating harder ingredients such as nutmeg or hard cheeses.

mimolette cheese
French cow's milk cheese with bright orange flesh and hard grey rind. Spherical shape makes it similar in appearance to cantaloupe.

mince
Process of cutting or chopping food into very small, often irregularly-shaped pieces.

mirepoix
Combination of chopped vegetables used to provide base of subtle background flavors for stocks, soups, braises, or sauces. Most commonly includes carrots, onions, and celery. Sometimes also includes such ingredients as garlic, leeks, shallots, tomatoes, mushrooms, or parsnips.

nutritional yeast flakes
Ingredient made from deactivated yeast, with nutty, cheesy flavor. Sold with bulk foods in most natural food stores and good source of protein and vitamins.

Oaxacan cuisine
Regional cuisine of southern Mexico. Includes such staples as corn, chile peppers (often in form of various moles), quesillo (white, semi-hard cheese), black beans, and chocolate.

orange blossom water
Aromatic essential water made from fresh flowers of bitter-orange trees. Offers subtle floral and citrus flavors when incorporated in foods.

pan release
Spray form of cooking oil. Applied to pans and other cookware to prevent food from sticking.

panko
Japanese-style white bread crumbs, with large, consistently-sized flakes. Often used as coating for fried foods.

panna cotta
Italian-style custard made with mixture of sweetened, flavored cream and milk that has been simmered, mixed with gelatin, and cooled until set.

Parisian carrots
French heirloom variety of small, sweet carrots characterized by short and round, almost spherical, shape. Also called "Thumbelina carrots."

Pashmak
Persian form of flavored cotton candy, also called "Persian fairy floss." Its long, delicate strands resemble hair or wool.

pasilla chile peppers
Dried form of long, narrow chilaca peppers. Possesses mild-to-medium heat and rich flavor.

pea tendrils
Small, tender leaves and vines of pea plant.

Pecorino Romano cheese
Hard, salty Italian cheese made from sheep's milk.

pepitas
Spanish term for edible seeds of pumpkin or squash.

pesto
General term for sauce made by crushing or blending ingredients along with oil to create paste-like consistency. Most commonly made with basil, garlic, pine nuts, and Parmesan cheese.

poblano pepper
Large, dark-green chili pepper with relatively mild flavor and heat level.

pot de crème
French dessert custard made with egg yolks, cream, sugar, and flavoring. Baked in small cups in water bath until set.

prosciutto
Italian ham cured by salting, drying, and aging. Sliced exceptionally thinly for serving.

ramekin
Small, round dish with straight sides used for baking and serving individual portions of food.

roast
Method of cooking food by exposing it, uncovered, to dry heat. Most often done in oven or over open fire.

roux
Mixture of flour and fat cooked together and used to thicken foods such as sauces and soups. Includes such fats as butter (most commonly-used), olive oil, lard, or bacon fat.

sheet pan extender
Rectangular frame that fits inside sheet pan, creating deeper pan that can be used to bake large cakes or to form other products.

silver-grade gelatin
Grade of sheet (leaf) gelatin with average gelling strength. More readily available and less expensive than other, more powerful grades.

slurry
Mixture of powdered starch (e.g., cornstarch, tapioca starch, arrowroot) and cold water (or other cold liquid) used to thicken sauces and soups. To prevent clumps, starch and cold liquid are combined first, before adding to mixture and bringing to simmer.

sweat
Process of heating foods (usually vegetables) very slowly in covered pan so that they cook in their own juices without searing or caramelizing.

tartare
Variety of dishes made with finely-chopped and seasoned raw meat (usually red meat or fish).

temper
Method of combining hot liquid with cold liquid in small increments so that temperature is stabilized, preventing hot ingredient from cooking cold ingredient. Most often used in reference to mixing beaten eggs or egg yolks with hot liquid.

terrine
Food mixture prepared and allowed to set in container (traditionally, elongated rectangle). Ingredients often arranged in horizontal layers. Usually served in slices, revealing attractive cross-section.

tuile
Thin, crisp, delicate cookie that can be bent and molded into various shapes while warm.

umami
Category of savory taste in food, distinct from saltiness. Emanates from presence of glutamates, with monosodium glutamate (MSG) most apparent source. Aged cheeses, ripe tomatoes, mushrooms, shellfish, and many other meats and vegetables contain naturally-occurring glutamates.

vinaigrette
Salad dressing or sauce made from mixture of oil and acidic liquid, such as vinegar or lemon juice. Often flavored with other ingredients.

xanthan gum/guar gum
Thickening and emulsifying ingredients sold in powdered form. Can be added to many foods to enhance texture or help bind ingredients together. Used often in gluten-free recipes.

yuzu
Small Japanese variety of citrus fruit. Possesses strong, sour flavor, with qualities of grapefruit, mandarin orange, and other citrus fruits. Its juice and zest are used in many applications.

yuzu kosho paste
Japanese condiment made from grinding together chili peppers, yuzu zest, and salt. Available in red and green varieties.

zest (citrus)
Outermost, colored layer of peel of citrus fruit. Can be removed using grater or peeler and is used as flavoring in many recipes.

Sources of Specialty Ingredients & Equipment

At the New Scenic Café, we acquire food and equipment from sources just down the road and across the globe, from an ever-changing and ever-growing list of purveyors. Here, you'll find a list of many of the sellers we use, including their website addresses (if they have websites), phone numbers (including international codes, when appropriate), and a brief listing of the items we purchase from them. We have used many other excellent sources over the years, but these are the suppliers you'll find most helpful for use with this cookbook. (We suggest you take a wander through their websites; you'll find it a visual feast!)

This list will give you the information you need to acquire specialty products, with a focus on some wonderful local suppliers of delicious, handcrafted foods and quality supplies (including suppliers we especially enjoy supporting because they are working to do good things for their communities). Many of these businesses and individuals sell both retail and wholesale, so home cooks can purchase their products directly. A few of them sell only wholesale, but you can still contact them or visit their websites to find convenient resellers. If you happen to live in the northland near us at the New Scenic Café, you will be able to acquire products directly from the local sources listed. Even if you live farther away, though, some of the local vendors ship their products. In any case, we hope you will use those listings as inspiration to seek out local producers in your own area.

Specialty Ingredients:

Alakef Coffee - Duluth, MN
+1 800 438 9228
www.alakef.com
coffee, chocolate-covered espresso beans

Al's Dairy - Two Harbors, MN
+1 218 834 3102
milk, cream, butter, ice cream, eggs

Amarena Fabbri - Bologna, Italy
+39 051 6173111
www.fabbri1905.com
Amarena cherries in syrup

Artisan Specialty Foods - Lyons, IL
+1 800 280 3646
www.artisanspecialty.com
yuzu juice, yuzu kosho paste, specialty foods

AUI Fine Foods - Gaithersburg, MD
+1 800 231 8154
www.auiswiss.com
chocolate, pastry supplies, specialty foods

Bay Produce - Superior, WI
www.challenge-center.org/bay-produce.htm
beefsteak tomatoes

Bent Paddle Brewing Co. - Duluth, MN
+1 218 279 2722
www.bentpaddlebrewing.com
craft beers

Borealis Fermentery - Knife River, MN
+1 218 834 4856
www.borealisfermentery.com
Belgian-style craft beers

Callebaut - Wieze, Belgium
+1 312 496 7300
www.callebaut.com
chocolate

Classic Provisions - Minneapolis, MN
+1 763 544 2025
www.classicprovisions.com
artisan cheese, cured meat, olives, oils, specialty foods

Clover Valley Forest Products - Two Harbors, MN
+1 218 525 4946
maple syrup

Coastal Seafoods - Minneapolis, MN
+1 612 724 7425
www.coastalseafoods.com
fresh fish & seafood

Food Farm - Wrenshall, MN
+1 218 384 4421
foodfarmcsa.wordpress.com
produce

Grassroots Farm - Saginaw, MN
+1 218 341 7481
produce

Great Ciao - Minneapolis, MN
www.greatciao.com
artisan cheese, cured meat, olives, oils, specialty foods

Hafi - Getinge, Sweden
+46 35 550 08
www.hafi.com
cloudberry & lingonberry preserves

King Arthur Flour - Norwich, VT
+1 800 827 6836
www.kingarthurflour.com
all-purpose flour, bread flour, high-gluten flour

Lakewood Berry Farm - Duluth, MN
+1 218 525 5710
www.lakewoodberryfarm.com
black currants, raspberries

Les vergers Boiron - Valence, France
+33 4 75 47 87 00
www.my-vb.com
fruit purées

Muir Glen - Denver, CO
+1 800 832 6345
www.muirglen.com
organic canned-tomato products

New French Bakery - Minneapolis, MN
www.newfrenchbakery.com
artisan breads & rolls

North Farm - Esko, MN
+1 218 878 0434
www.facebook.com/EveNerFarm
potatoes, fiddlehead ferns

Northern Waters Smokehaus - Duluth, MN
+1 218 724 7307
www.northernwaterssmokehaus.com
smoked fish & meats, cured meats

Nueske's - Wittenberg, WI
+1 800 392 2266
www.nueskes.com
applewood-smoked bacon

Pariya - St. Peters, Australia
+61 2 9550 2388
www.pariya.com
Pashmak (fairy floss), Persian delicacies

Patak's - Leigh, England
+1 800 726 3648
www.pataks.com
curry paste, vindaloo paste

Paul's Memorial Orchard - Two Harbors, MN
+1 218 834 2653
apples, carrots, green beans, beets, garlic scapes

Rishi Tea - Milwaukee, WI
+1 414 747 4001
www.rishi-tea.com
organic loose-leaf teas

Roode Food - Herbster, WI
+1 715 774 3831
Sungold tomatoes, heirloom tomatoes,
zucchini, eggplant

Shary's Berries - Two Harbors, MN
+1 218 834 5221
blueberries, raspberries, basil

Sherry Rovig - Duluth, MN
+1 218 343 4909
hand-harvested, wood-parched wild rice

Simple Gifts Syrup & Salmon - Duluth, MN
+1 218 525 5474
www.simplegiftssyrupandsalmon.com
maple syrup, wild Alaskan salmon

Skuna Bay - Vancouver, Canada
www.skunasalmon.com
Vancouver Island craft-raised salmon

Steve Dahl - Knife River, MN
+1 218 525 4679
Lake Superior herring, herring roe, whitefish

The Fish Guys, Inc. - Minneapolis, MN
+1 612 339 7720
www.thefishguysinc.com
fresh fish & seafood

Thousand Hills Cattle Co. - Cannon Falls, MN
+1 507 263 4001
www.thousandhillscattleco.com
grass-fed beef

Wild Acres - Pequot Lakes, MN
+1 218 568 5024
www.wildacresmn.com
duck, pheasant, quail

Specialty Equipment:

Bamboo Imports MN - Bloomington, MN
+1 952 591 1570
www.bambooimportsmn.com
bamboo picks & skewers

Bluebird - Montreal, Canada
+1 800 461 2505
www.bluebird.ca
carbon-steel fry pans

Epicurean Inc. - Duluth, MN
+1 218 740 3500
www.epicureancs.com
cutting boards, cooking utensils,
kitchen accessories

JB Prince - New York, NY
+1 800 473 0577
www.jbprince.com
Masahiro knives, Tamahagane knives,
professional kitchen tools & equipment

Korin - New York, NY
+1 800 626 2173
www.korin.com
Masamoto knives, other Japanese knives

Leelanau Trading Company - Empire, MI
+1 888 509 3188
www.leelanautradingco.com
leather-bound journals

Loll Designs - Duluth, MN
+1 877 740 3387
www.lolldesigns.com
recycled, modern outdoor furniture

Microplane - Russellville, AR
+1 800 555 2767
www.microplane.com
graters, zesters, shavers

Pillivuyt - Excelsior, MN
+1 952 474 4016
www.pillivuytus.com
porcelain dishware

Riedel - Kufstein, Austria
+1 732 346 8960
www.riedel.com
wine glasses

Robot Coupe - Ridgeland, MS
+1 800 824 1646
www.robot-coupe.com/en-usa
professional food processors & mixers

Sitram - St Benoit Du Sault, France
+33 2 54 01 53 00
www.sitram.fr
professional stainless steel cookware

Vitamix - Cleveland, OH
+1 800 848 2649
www.vitamix.com
professional-grade blenders

Then we went
to eat dimer.
The resterront was
cald the synic.

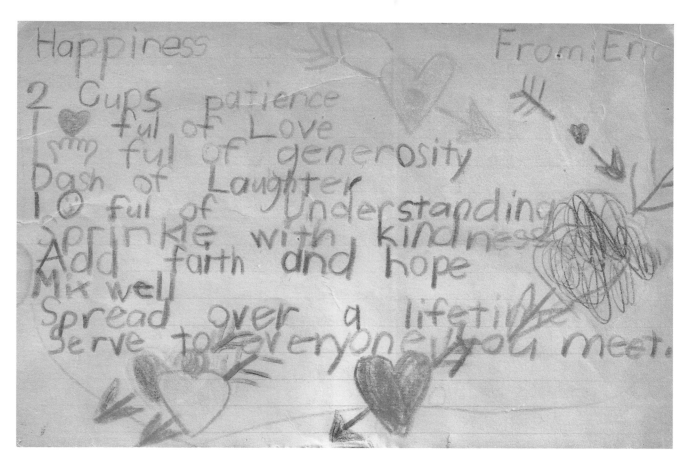

Happiness   From: Eric

2 Cups patience
1 ♥ ful of Love
1 ꟻ ful of generosity
Dash of Laughter
1 ○ ful of Understanding
Sprinkle with kindness
Add faith and hope
Mix well
Spread over a lifetime
Serve to everyone you meet.

Index

Scott Graden

Scott Graden is a chef, artist, innovator, business owner, educator, and friend to the community. In 1999, Scott opened the New Scenic Café, located along the shore of Lake Superior in Duluth, Minnesota, and has been its owner and chef since. Educating has always been at the core of Scott's philosophy, whether teaching his clients and the greater community about quality and food, developing his team of employees, or instructing culinary classes. He has coupled his experience as a business owner with his Master's Degree, to teach business management courses at the college level. Scott's academic work has taken him around the globe, including visits to Zhuhai in the People's Republic of China and Delhi, Agra, and Bangalore in the Republic of India. Scott is the central creative force behind the New Scenic Café's diverse and distinctive food and its captivating atmosphere. He provided the recipes for this cookbook, compiling them—and many others too numerous to fit on these pages—over the lifespan of the New Scenic Café. Scott also did all of the food photography for the cookbook, took many of the other photos contained in the book, and narrated the background and stories that accompany the recipes.

Arlene J. Anderson

Arlene J. Anderson is a business leader, teacher, writer, and inveterate traveler, with a penchant for adventure, music, and great food. Arlene held senior management positions in health care and academic settings throughout the Midwest for 25 years. She lived in Norway for 3 years, where she led international sales for a startup software company and also worked as a musician in Irish pubs. And she served as the faculty for Minnesota-based MBA Capstone Abroad courses, teaching and leading field study in the Republic of India and the People's Republic of China. Arlene also lived in Zhuhai, China, working as a Lecturer for the Business and Management Division of United International College. For this cookbook, Arlene took the lead in shaping Scott Graden's dream of capturing the New Scenic Café experience in book form and bringing it to fruition. Her work included chronicling the stories and history of the New Scenic Café and the narratives behind Scott's recipes, drafting the manuscript, conducting research interviews and focus groups, and managing the project. Arlene has so far dined in 29 countries, but at the top of her list remains the delight of dining along the scenic shores of Lake Superior, at a table in the New Scenic Café.

Eric Sturtz

Eric Sturtz grew up in Neillsville, Wisconsin and got his first taste of professional cooking working at a small café in Snowmass Village, Colorado during summer breaks in high school and college. After earning Bachelor of Science degrees in Mathematics and Spanish from the University of Wisconsin at Madison, his love for that first kitchen job led him to pursue cooking as a full-time career. Eric spent the next 5 years working at several top restaurants in Minneapolis, Minnesota before moving north to Duluth in 2008 and joining the New Scenic Café family as a line cook. Over the next 5 years, he went on to become the Café's sous chef and then general manager. In 2012, Eric and his family moved from Minnesota, but Eric continues to serve a multitude of significant roles for the Café. Eric brought not only his cooking talent to this book; he also did the graphic design and layout, edited photos, and assisted with writing and editing. Eric's experience working side by side with Scott Graden and his understanding of Scott's approach to food was crucial to adapting the recipes in this book for home use and to designing a book that mirrors the charm and atmosphere of the New Scenic Café.

Barb Olsen

Barb Olsen spent her earliest days growing up along the north shore of Lake Superior, where her great-grandparents were early settlers and fishermen, just up the road from where the New Scenic Café stands today. Barb is a writer, reporter, editor, political strategist, educator, and cooking enthusiast. For 13 years, she was the author of the newspaper column, "Out of Order! A Voter's Field Guide to the Duluth City Council," and has worked in television and radio as a reporter and political commentator. She has written for and managed political campaigns, from the city to the national level. And Barb worked as a technical editor and writer for Boeing, Weyerhaeuser, and Microsoft Corporations, including in Microsoft's book-publishing division, Microsoft Press. Barb also taught technical editing for 5 years at the University of Washington in Seattle. She is the mother of two children, Annika and Trevor, on whom she has doggedly tested her many family recipes, recording the family's favorites in her own family cookbook. Barb served as executive editor for this cookbook, as well as technical reviewer and writer. Her work on this book was pivotal in bringing the recipes, stories, and spirit of the New Scenic Café to life.

Gratitude

All the gratitude that is worthy of inclusion in this book would constitute a volume of its own—a work that, despite its length, would undoubtedly still be incomplete. The New Scenic Café has been influenced by every person who has walked through its doors, even by those who frequented the original Scenic Cafe. Over the years and through all the valleys and peaks, the New Scenic Café has truly taken on a life of its own. Many restaurants refer to their staff members as "family," as we do, too. Yet our Café family extends beyond those bounds, to the Scenic's customers, purveyors, tradespeople, friends, relatives, and saucy acquaintances, all of whom are part of our family and deserving of our thanks for their roles in shaping the restaurant as well as this cookbook.

For the team of the four of us who set this book in motion and nudged it lovingly out the door—Scott, Arlene, Eric, and Barb—we thank each other equally. Each one of us did what the others could not, or at least not nearly so well, somehow melding into a congenial blend befitting the tradition and history of the New Scenic Café.

The New Scenic Café Journals

There's nothing like putting our experiences on paper to help us reminisce over the years and review our journey through life. It also allows us to share those experiences with each other and create a community of learning, affection, and understanding.

Ever since the early days of the New Scenic Café, we have delivered a journal to each table at meal's end to give diners a way to connect with us and with each other, capturing on those journal pages people's memories and artwork and thoughtful comments. We have collected an untold number of pages filled with our guest's experiences. They include tales of anniversary dinners, artwork depicting a cherished bloom in the Café's garden or the humorous demand for the return of a favorite menu item, children's accounts of their first taste of a new flavor, and so much more.

On the following pages, you'll find a few of our favorites from the journal collection. We wish we could include them all! But if after you see these you have a hankering for more, stop in for a visit at the New Scenic Café. We'll bring you a cup of coffee and a journal or two, and you can settle in for a tour through our memories.

We came here for our first wedding anniversary + it was fantastic! Now we know what pashmak is!

We boids of a feather love getting together at the Scenic

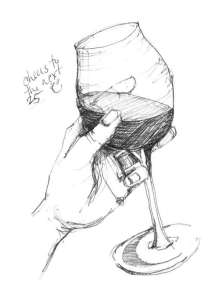

cheers to the next 25

Por segunda ocación, he degustado de un buen alimento, por supuesto con mi esposa Mollie y nuestro bebé Ryan que esta creciéndo muy sanamente... Gracias por la comida, fue muy buena!
From: Chavarrillo, Veracruz, Mexico

Great place. Great food. Great date. Thanks!

She said yes!

Sol   Kristi
...then we ate here.

GOTTA LOVE THE SCENIC CAFE! IT'S DEFINITELY A FALL FAVORITE... MAKE A EFFORT TO GET UP HERE EACH YEAR TO ENJOY THE LEAVES, THE WEATHER AND FIGS. WE WILL KEEP COMING BACK EACH YEAR. FANTASTIC DINNER AND STILL ORDERS OUR FAVORITES BACK IN THE CITIES. CHEERS TO A GREAT NIGHT WITH MY BEAUTIFUL DARLING GIRLFRIEND. HAPPY FALL!

FIGS!

JUST HIKED 33 MILES ON THE SUPERIOR HIKING TRAIL. TIRED & HAPPY. NEW SCENIC CAFE WAS OUR REWARD AND A GREAT WAY TO END A WONDERFUL TRIP!
BECKY & LEAH

BRING BACK THE PISTACHIO-CRUSTED GOAT CHEESE MEDALLIONS ON CRANBERRY RYE BREAD!

KEEP GOATS EMPLOYED!

Tack för utmärkt mat och service - jag kommer gärna tillbaka, jag åt Thuna, perfekt.
Ernst Frens Stockholm-Sweden
↑ Brother Sister
Ja, es hat gut geschmeckt. Ich hatte Hering auf Brot Sehr gut!!! auch die Bedienung.
Mutter ↑ Margot daughter
and Suzy Eastman, Wayzata, MN who brought us here!

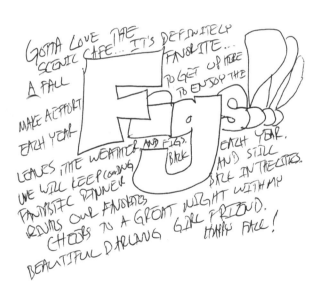

WORTH THE VISIT FROM BRAZIL! THANKS...

Do not go gentle into that dark night before having a wonderful dinner @ Scenic Cafe

Well, let's see here...

Satisfact-O-Meter

OKAY | BETTER | EXCELL...

A+B
from the
TC

Tack för maten!
Vi älskar det.
Randi och Staffan

SVERIGE BREV

We LOVE it here so much... this is
our 2nd meal here in 5 hours! Yummy!
Everything is exquisite! can't wait
to get the cookbook!

Kit Victoria, MN

My dad made
me try wasabi
for the first time!!!
I got paid $2!
My sister just
spit it out.

♡

Danika my sister →

Cordelia

Wonderful food & great atemosphere!
Dan & Francheska (Yes... we are the ones who
made our children eat wasabi ♥)

8/20

MUST COME BACK

♡

Jess & David
- together for
1 year.
- we <3 the
scenic.
JD

SIX SMILEY FACES
NEED WE SAY MORE!??

WHITE BEAR LAKE • FRANCONIA
WOODBURY • MOUNDS VIEW •
THANK YOU.

We love Scenic Cafe We love
that, no matter what we order,
we leave completely pleased.

We love that patrons come
as they are, and the staff
is as good-humored as they
are knowledgable. We love the
view. We love the wine. Obviously.
R & M

---

new
Scenic
café

Directions:
UNSCRABLE THE LETTERS TO HEAR ABOUT
MY FAMILY'S EXPERIENCE!

We ___ ___ ___ ___ ___ our food & desserts.
      O V d T e

The service was very ___ ___ ___ ___ ___ ___ ___ ___ ___
                        e c F i n F F T

My family & I always ___ ___ ___ ___ ___ coming
to this ___ ___ ___ ___ ___!   n o e y J
         F a e c

answers: loved, efficient, enjoy, cafe

♥ Happy Spring ♥

A beautiful spot to view the lake
and fantastic food to share with
good friends! Thank-you!

The chef clearly studies
the Kama-Sutra — he
lasts though all the Courses
          Minneapolis MN
A,C,N (aka The Milky Way)

CAME ALL THE WAY
FROM CHICAGO JUST
FOR LUNCH
WAS GREAT